Lydia B. Marple

INDIA IN THE EYES OF EUROPE

India

IN THE EYES OF EUROPE

The Sixteenth Century

DONALD F. LACH

PHOENIX BOOKS

THE UNIVERSITY OF CHICAGO PRESS

CHICAGO AND LONDON

THE UNIVERSITY OF CHICAGO PRESS, CHICAGO 60637
The University of Chicago Press, Ltd., London W. C. 1

Preface to the Phoenix Edition

Students of Indian history long ago learned how indispensable the European sources are to the reconstruction of the subcontinent's past. Traditionally the writers of India's modern history have depended heavily upon the voluminous and reliable materials prepared by or for the British and French. But the extensive materials in Portuguese, Dutch, Italian, and Latin for the sixteenth and seventeenth centuries have been badly neglected both by general historians and by writers of monographs. This neglect is understandable inasmuch as serious students of Indian history have correctly placed their primary emphasis upon mastering the Sanskrit and Persian sources for the study of the sixteenth century. So it is only recently that a somewhat hesitant attack has begun to be made upon the relevant corpus of literature in the less well known European languages.

To date, most of the references to the early Portuguese sources have been limited to those that have been translated into English or French. For example, the writings of Duarte Barbosa and Tomé Pires which were done into English under the auspices of the Hakluyt Society have been cited repeatedly by historians and other scholars concerned with India in the sixteenth century. But little effective use has so far been made of the extended histories of João de Barros, Fernão Lopes de Castanheda, and Gaspar Correa—seemingly because none of these has so far appeared in a complete and recent translation in one of the major European languages.

In this study an effort has been made to determine by use of the Portuguese and Jesuit sources, as well as the better-known travel accounts, what was known in sixteenth-century Europe about India. These voluminous materials were combed for data which were then organized into comprehensive topical summaries. An effort was made to avoid violating chronological order and the blurring of the developmental character of the revelation of India to the West by treating the sources roughly in the order of their relevance: that is, the Portuguese sources for the period from 1498 to 1540, and the Jesuit materials and the travel accounts for the latter half of the century. The assertions of contemporary writers were checked out, wherever possible, against the best of modern scholarship. But, as is almost always the case, there were many facts mentioned in the sixteenth-century writings for which no later confirmation or direct contradiction could be located.

From these European materials emerge clear pictures of the social practices of Malabar, the decline of the great Hindu empire of Vijayanagar in the south and the rise of Mughul power in the north, and the vitality of international trade at the great ports of Cambay, Goa, and Calcutta. As might be expected, the depiction of India given by the Europeans is generally better on the coastal areas than on the interior, and is far better on the surface aspects of life than on the religion, thought, and history of the Indian people. Even with these limitations, however, it is possible to obtain from these materials a vivid impression of India's exciting variety of social practices, arts, crafts, and beliefs in the sixteenth century.

This book is an exact reproduction of Part III, Chapter VI, from Volume I, of my *Asia in the Making of Europe* (Chicago and London, 1965). This chapter is being published separately in the hope that students of Indian history will find it a useful supplement to the other materials available on the sixteenth century, a period noted for its complexity, turbulence, and persistent importance in the life of the subcontinent. Because this book was originally prepared as a chapter for my larger work, the reader will occasionally find cross references in the text and footnotes which allude to materials not reprinted here. It was thought wise to retain these cross references to give the enterprising student the opportunity to locate easily those items in my original work on which he might like to have further clarification. With regard to the footnotes it should also be observed that a full bibliographical reference is given on the first occasion when a source is cited. Thereafter, when the same source is cited again, a reference to the footnote number of its first mention appears in parentheses after the *op. cit.* or *loc. cit.* This device, it is hoped, will make for easier consultation of the numerous and extended footnotes.

Finally, I wish to thank some of my friends and colleagues for the help they gave me in preparing this work. It owes much to the specialized knowledge of J. A. B. van Buitenen, Milton Singer, and Father Cyriac Pullapilly, a priest of the Malabar Church.

Introduction

Asia's image, as it gradually evolved in Europe during the sixteenth century, retained shadings from the past but became sharper and more definite in its outlines and divisions. The vague geographical terms inherited from the Ptolemaic and medieval traditions (India before and beyond the Ganges, Further India, and Cathay) were gradually replaced in Europe by names similar to those then in use in Asia itself. India, Southeast Asia, Japan, and China were recognized for the first time as being distinct and different parts of Asia, and Europeans came to think of them along roughly the same lines that we do today. And, as Europeans of the sixteenth century came to understand that Asia was not simply of one piece, they also learned that its parts and peoples were as numerous and different from one another as were the various parts and peoples of Europe itself.

By 1600 a literate European might easily have known a good deal about the East from the published writings of merchants, travelers, and missionaries, and from the printed maps of the cartographers. Dimensions of depth and increased realism were added to the European impressions by the regular appearance of Asian merchants, emissaries, and goods in the commercial, administrative, religious, and intellectual centers of Europe. During the course of the century, images of the four parts of Asia and a new and composite picture of Asia as a whole emerged from Europe's great experience in the East, and this new conception became and remained a permanent part of Europe's view of the world.

Contents

Illustrations

India

Most of what Europe in general learned about the East during the first half of the sixteenth century related to the spice trade. In connection with it a number of Indians were taken to Portugal and Priest Joseph of the Malabar church even visited the papacy. While the Portuguese titillated the curious of Europe by sending rich embassies to Rome to announce their successes, the concrete information on India which leaked out was not much more specific or extensive than that which Varthema provided in 1510. The circumnavigation of the world by Elcano, Pigafetta, and their companions awakened Europe to the great breadth of the Pacific Ocean and provided additional details on the East Indies. But of India only very little was added to the store of Europe's information from 1520 to 1550. Even the accounts of the voyages to India, which the Aldine Press of Venice published in 1543 as *Viaggi fatti alla Tana*, were confined to discussions of the conditions of trade on the Malabar Coast.

Before 1550 the European image of India was formed by the traditions inherited from the prediscovery period as modified by the short accounts of the coastal areas and Vijayanagar provided by Varthema and others. Still, certain notions inherited from the past were rectified even on the basis of the scanty information which the Portuguese let escape. It had been learned, though the tradition died slowly, that the Indians, except for the Malabar Christians and the Moors, were not Christians but "heathens." Calicut was reported to be larger than Lisbon, and the people of India, even though "heathen," were recognized to possess a complex civilization. Through the spice trade, it had become general knowledge in Europe that the Moors were powerful in India, especially in the north. By similar means it was learned that the rest of India was divided among a number of rulers who persistently fought among themselves. The early Christian missionaries who settled at Goa and other Portuguese merchant communities had soon let it be known in Europe that extensive religious conquests were about as unlikely as great territorial acquisitions. Europe learned that the Moors, who were waging successful religious war in Africa and Europe, were also making many more conquests, both political and religious, in India than the Portuguese and Franciscans could possibly hope to match. India, it was generally realized, was going to be a hard nut to crack.

The European literature on India actually published during the latter half of the sixteenth century divides into three major categories: the Portuguese commercial reports and the great chronicles of conquest, the Jesuit newsletters and histories, and the *fin de siècle* reports of Italian, English, and Dutch commentators who managed in one way or another to travel and reside in India. The Portuguese materials deal with India down to 1540. The Jesuit newsletters, while recording details on events as they unfold, provide a helpful documentation, which is unfortunately not always continuous, for the period after the Portuguese secular histories break off their narratives. The Jesuit histories combine information from the secular sources with systematic accounts of the mission's progress to give more general coverage for the entire century. The travelogues of the non-Iberian writers which were published at the end of the century deal with India during the period from 1564 to 1591. Since they are unofficial reports which were issued outside of Portuguese and ecclesiastical jurisdiction, they act as something of a check upon the semiofficial Portuguese and Jesuit materials and are much more critical of the Portuguese rule and the Catholic mission.

I

THE PORTUGUESE PROFILE

Practically all the Portuguese works dealing with the discoveries contain information on India.[1] Before 1600, many of them were in print and all of those originally published in Portuguese were translated, in whole or in large part, into other European languages.[2] On the basis of four works (by Pires, Barbosa,

---

[1] For a survey of them see above, pp. 181–200.

[2] A contemporary work of great value by Gaspar Corrêa (1496–1563), *Lendas da India*, seems not to have been published until the nineteenth century (4 vols.; Lisbon, 1858–66). A. Kammerer (*La découverte de la Chine* [Leiden, 1944], p. 5) mentions without citing his source that there might have been an edition of it in twelve volumes published at Lisbon in 1556 which has since disappeared. It seems highly unlikely, however, that practically all references to this work, had it been published in the sixteenth century, would likewise have vanished. It seems more probable that this excellent compendium existed in several manuscript copies in Lisbon and that these circularized to authorized persons only. It is known that shortly after his death his manuscript of 3,500 pages was taken from India to Portugal by Miguel da Gama. For those interested in India's history or the story of Portuguese expansion, Corrêa's work is an indispensable contemporary source. He spent over thirty-five years preparing it, during which time he lived and worked in the East. Corrêa clearly had at his disposal sources of information which were untapped or unknown to Barros and Castanheda. For his biography and a critical evaluation of the literary merits of the *Lendas* see Aubrey F. G. Bell, *Gaspar Corrêa* (Oxford, 1924).

Castanheda, and Barros), supplemented by the others, it is perhaps possible to determine what educated and interested Europeans of the latter half of the century could have known of India through Portuguese sources. To a degree the four authors of these works depend upon one another and upon the manuscript materials of others which probably circulated in Portugal in their day. While these four main accounts exhibit many similarities which enable the careful reader to check one against the other, they are fundamentally quite different and of varying degrees of authority. Pires and Barbosa outline their personal travels and experiences in the East and describe as well the lands, peoples, and products seen. Castanheda and Barros depend heavily at certain points upon the firsthand observations of an earlier generation. But Castanheda's *História* combines the patient research and collation of information gathered by interviewing firsthand observers with personal experience in the field. Barros' history is rich in official materials and humanistic erudition, but it lacks quite naturally much of the individualistic viewpoint and local color which he might have given his story had he had the opportunity to travel in India.

A. GEOGRAPHICAL PLACEMENT AND ADJACENT ISLANDS

A glance at the Ptolemaic map of the world or a study of its descriptions of India within and beyond the Ganges will reveal immediately that its compilers knew little about India south of the Godavari River, that they extended India's boundaries much too far to the east, and that they greatly exaggerated the size of Taprobane (Ceylon).[3] Perusal of Marco Polo brings out the fact that he saw "Seilan" (Ceylon) as "the best island of its size in the whole world" and Malabar as "the best of all the Indias."[4] Particularly important here is Polo's emphatic addition of south India to the European image of the peninsula proper; for even though the Romans had visited the Malabar Coast, no clear idea of its configuration seems to have persisted in medieval Europe. During the fifteenth century, several reports got back to western Europe, as we have seen, which confirmed Polo's generally exalted view of the wealth, trade, and Christianity of south India. Thus, from the Ptolemaic tradition, Europe had at hand before 1500 some geographical data on the Gangetic plain of the north. On the ports and kingdoms of south India there were available the Poloan tradition and the more detailed accounts of the fifteenth-century overland travelers to India. It remains

---

[3] See the maps and texts in S. M. Sastri (ed.), *McCrindle's Ancient India as Described by Ptolemy* (Calcutta, 1927).

[4] H. Yule and H. Cordier (eds.), *The Book of Ser Marco Polo* (New York, 1903), II, 312. Cf. Orta's remark about Ceylon being "the most fruit bearing and best island in the world." (Sir Clements Markham [trans. and ed.], *Garcia da Orta. Colloquies on the Simples and Drugs of India* [London, 1913], p. 135.)

now to see what the Portuguese discoveries did to round out the European conception of India's geography. The early newsletters and private dispatches which circulated in Europe after 1500 dealt mainly with the sea route to India, trade prospects, and the Portuguese triumphs. More extensive, confirmatory detail was relayed to Europe through the *Itinerario* (1510) of the Italian Ludovico di Varthema recounting his experiences in the major cities of maritime India, principally at Calicut, from 1504 to 1506. Varthema also gives greater detail than most of his predecessors about India's eastern coastal regions. But, to the death of King Manuel in 1521, none of the Portuguese accounts of India was allowed to circulate freely. Whatever information did leak out from Lisbon to other parts of Europe was slight. The accounts of India which appear during the generation from 1520 to 1550 are all written by non-Iberians and are mainly significant as vehicles for diffusing the hazy geographical picture that was slowly emerging from the mixture of traditional and recent testimony garnered from the few available materials.

The works of Tomé Pires and Duarte Barbosa, first published by Ramusio in 1550, are organized according to large geographical areas. In writing about India, they deal first of all with the west coast and focus their discussion upon its major cities and ports. On the whole the descriptions of the west coast, especially Malabar, are far superior in detail to the cursory treatment which they give to the cities on India's eastern coast. Barbosa, however, gets inland to Vijayanagar and a few other places of which he gives an eyewitness account. Like Barros and Castanheda, Barbosa dwells at some length on Ceylon and other insular areas. Well aware of the shortcomings of his work as a geographical description, Barbosa frankly acknowledges that it was his intention to write "only a short summary of that which can in truth be ascertained regarding the chief places in India." [5] In the frame of reference of both Pires and Barbosa the "chief places" are clearly those where the Portuguese did business. Castanheda's *História*, organized chronologically in terms of Portugal's conquests, introduces geographical description mainly as incidental or introductory information to the discussion of other topics.

The first effort to produce a systematic and general description of India's geography is published in the *Décadas* of Barros. He starts off by commenting that India proper in the Ptolemaic geographies was considered to encompass only the territory between the Indus and the Ganges, the locale of the old kingdom of "Eli" (Delhi).[6] The Persians, who live adjacent to northern India, call it in Barros' words by "its proper name, Indostan." [7] The whole of India,

---

5 M. L. Dames (trans. and ed.), *The Book of Duarte Barbosa* (London, 1918), I, 177.

6 H. Cidade and M. Múrias (eds.), *Asia de João de Barros* (Lisbon, 1945), I, 153. In the fifteenth century the Delhi sultanate, which had begun establishing its power at the beginning of the thirteenth century, began to disintegrate and collapsed completely by 1526. See for discussion R. C. Majumdar *et al.*, *An Advanced History of India* (rev. ed.; London, 1958), pp. 338–90.

7 Persian for *Hindustan*, or "the country of the Hindus."

the Portuguese chronicler observes, is bounded by the Indus, the Ganges, the Indian Ocean, and the great mountains of the north called "Imaos" by Ptolemy.[8] To Barros the shape of the peninsula resembles a rhombus, an oblique-angled equilateral parallelogram, with its greater length extending in the north-south direction from the foot of the mountains to the tip of Cape Comorin. From north to south the land stretches about 400 leagues (1,600 miles); at its greatest breadth it is not less than 300 leagues (1,200 miles).[9]

Hindustan includes both "idolaters" and Muslims whose customs and rites differ quite markedly. It is divided into many kingdoms: "Maltan" (Multan), Delhi, "Cospetir" (Gajpati or a territory held by Orissa),[10] Bengal, Orissa, "Māndū" (Malwa), "Chitor" (Mewar), and Gujarat (often called Cambay after its great port city).[11] The Deccan "kingdom" to the south is divided among many lords who have the stature of kings,[12] and it is bordered by the kingdom of "Pale."[13] Vijayanagar, lying on the other side of "Pale," is a great kingdom which controls a number of minor kings; and the Malabar Coast is divided into a number of petty states, each of which is ruled by a king or a prince. These states are so bellicose and covetous toward each other that, were it not for natural boundaries, the entire region would fall into the hands of the greediest and most powerful. Great and numerous rivers, mountains, lakes, jungles, and deserts, inhabited by countless and diverse animals make communication difficult and help to frustrate would-be conquerors. Among the most conspicuous of these natural barriers in the south are a number of rivers, not connected with the Indus or the Ganges, which enfold the lands they water in

---

[8] "Mount Imaos (in Sanskrit, *himā*, meaning cold), a name which was at first applied by the Greeks to the Hindu-Kush and the chain of the Himalayas running parallel to the equator, but which was gradually in the course of time transferred to the Bolar range which runs from north to south and intersects them." (S. M. Sastri [ed.], *op. cit.* [n. 3], p. 35.)

[9] In the Portuguese rules of the leagues (cited in Armando Cortesão [trans. and ed.], *The Suma Oriental of Tomé Pires* [London, 1944], II, 299–301) the length of the league naturally varies depending on the point of the compass from which it is calculated. On a straight line from north to south each degree is said to equal 17½ leagues, or slightly under four statute or land miles. Hereafter, we shall use "four" as a round number to simplify calculations, but with the understanding that this will make the distances in miles somewhat greater than the Portuguese actually thought them to be.

[10] This name appeared regularly on maps of the sixteenth and seventeenth century in the area to the west of the Ganges Delta. Scholars were perplexed by it until the mid-nineteenth century when it was ascertained that "Cospetir" was the Bengali genitive of Gajpati. Hence it is now assumed that "Cospetir" was simply another name for Gajpati, and that this territory belonged to the Gajpati rulers of Orissa. See H. Yule and A. C. Burnell, *Hobson-Jobson. A Glossary of Anglo-Indian Colloquial Words and Phrases* (London, 1886), pp. 201–2.

[11] "Māndū," sometimes written "Mandou," was frequently used as the name for Malwa, though it is simply the name of Malwa's capital city. "Chitor," the capital of Mewar, was likewise used as the name for the country as well as the city. While this is not a complete list of the independent states north of the Deccan, it does give the reader a feeling for the divided condition of northern India. For further discussion see below, pp. 418–19

[12] "Five separate Sultanates arose in the Deccan, one after another, on the breakup of the Bahmanī kingdom." (Majumdar *et al., op. cit.* [n. 6], p. 363.)

[13] Appears in central India on the map dated 1561 of Giacomo Gastaldi as reproduced in R. H. Phillimore (comp.), *Historical Records of the Survey of India* (Dehra Dun, 1945), Vol. I, plate xvi. Cf. the account of "Palu" in E. Thornton (comp.), *A Gazetteer of the Territories under the Government of the East-India Company . . .* (London, 1857), p. 749.

their twists and turns as they slowly make their way to the surrounding seas. There are also many inlets of salt water which penetrate the coasts so deeply that ships sail inland via them from one place to another. The most striking of the divisions imposed on India by nature is the chain of internal mountains called Ghats (or Sierras to Barros) which extend as far south as Cape Comorin. Between the Ghats and the Indian Ocean the land is flat and marshy. It is in such a lowland area that Malabar and Calicut are situated.

In Book IX of the first *Década*, Barros describes in detail the maritime regions of the Orient based on the reports funneling into Lisbon from merchants, sailors, and administrators.[14] The whole of this vast region he divides into nine parts, three of which are concerned directly with the coastal regions of India. He starts at the Indus and proceeds to list and comment upon cities, rivers, and other landmarks along the coast of India all the way around the peninsula to the delta of the Ganges and with frequent references to the distances separating one place from the other. Not all of the names he uses are readily indentifiable. It is certainly possible, however, that the majority of his identifications can be verified by anyone willing to expend the necessary time and effort.

On Ceylon, the work of Barros is particularly full,[15] probably because the Portuguese began to have important contacts with that island as early as 1505–6. He locates it across from Cape Comorin, indicates that it has an oval form, and estimates its length as seventy-eight leagues (312 miles) in a north-south direction and its extreme east-west breadth as forty-four leagues (176 miles).[16] He compares Ceylon's position in relation to India with Sicily's relation to Italy, and speculates on whether it was once united to the mainland as the Indians believe. He concludes that there is more reason to believe that Ceylon was once a part of India than that Sicily was once attached to Italy. The name "Ceilam" (Ceylon) leads him into a series of philological and historical speculations, some of which turn out to be egregious errors. After observing that the ancient Europeans called it Taprobane, Barros notes in puzzlement that by native tradition the island was previously called "Ilanare" or "Tranate."[17] The name "Ceilam," he speculates from what he has heard of the island's

[14] Cidade and Múrias (eds.), *op. cit.* (n. 6), I, 351–62.

[15] *Ibid.*, III, 55–61. For ready reference and helpful documentation see D. Ferguson (trans. and ed.) "The History of Ceylon, from the Earliest Times to 1600 A.D., as Related by João de Barros and Diogo do Couto," *Journal of the Royal Asiatic Society, Ceylon Branch*, Vol. XX (1908), No. 60, pp. 29–53.

[16] The actual length and breadth are 270 by 140 miles. Like the ancients, but not so grossly, Barros exaggerates the size of Ceylon. Orta (in Markham [ed.], *op. cit.* [n. 4], p. 135) underestimates the size of Ceylon, for he makes it have a length "thirty leagues by six to eight broad." Barros is much closer.

[17] "Ilanare" probably represents Tamil, "Ilan-nādu," the "country of Ceylon" (Ilan = Silam = Simhalam); "Tranate" may represent Tamil *tiru-nádu*, the "sacred country." See Ferguson (ed.), *loc. cit.* (n. 15), p. 30. Castanheda (in Pedro de Azevedo [ed.], *História do descobrimento e conquista da India pelos Portugueses* [3d ed.; Coimbra, 1928], I, 258) says that the Arabian and Persian Moors called it "Ceilão," while the Indians called it "Hibernāro" meaning "luxuriant land." For further discussion see Dames (ed.), *op. cit.* (n. 5), II, 109, n. 1.

history, dates back to the Chinese "conquest."[18] He clearly believes that the Chinese in the early fifteenth century were masters of the Coromandel coast, part of Malabar, and the entire island of Ceylon. After arguing that the name "Ceilam," the Sinhalese language, and certain Ceylonese peoples were derived from the Chinese, Barros claims that China did for Ceylon what Rome did for Portugal. In this conclusion he appears to go far beyond his evidence and contradicts what we know of these matters from other sources.[19]

Ceylon is described as being lush and fertile, especially its southwestern region. The bulk of its population is located in the rich area around Colombo where cinnamon, elephants, and precious stones are the major items of trade. For all its ancient reputation as an island rich in gold, Barros points out that iron is really the only metal actually mined on Ceylon.[20] The island is well endowed with large palm groves, good water, cinnamon, and sweet oranges. Its elephants, the tamest and most trainable to be found in India, are bred in captivity.[21] Trained elephants are often used to capture their wild relatives, and Castanheda describes in some detail how elephants are hunted.[22] Cattle and buffalo are also bred, and "ghee" (*ghī*, boiled butter used in cookery in India, as oil is in southern Europe, and also in other ways) made from their milk is exported to "many parts."[23] To Barros, who was obviously impressed by the fertility of Ceylon, "it seems as if nature had made of it a watered orchard."[24] But as Barbosa more realistically points out: "Of rice there is but little, they bring the more part of it, hither from Coromendel [Coromandel], and this is their principal diet."[25]

[18] The Chinese sources indicate that the expeditions usually associated with the name of Cheng Ho visited Ceylon, possibly as early as 1406. In the course of a subsequent voyage, the Chinese in 1411 got into a serious conflict with King Algakkōnara, defeated him, took him captive, and carried him back to Peking. A trilingual inscription (in Tamil, Chinese, Persian), evidently prepared in China ahead of time, was also set up at Galle in Ceylon to commemorate the Chinese victory. Later Chinese records include Ceylon among those states sending tribute to the Ming court. See J. J. L. Duyvendak, "The True Dates of the Chinese Maritime Expeditions in the Early Fifteenth Century," *T'oung pao* XXXIV (1939), 367–73. For a brief summary of Duyvendak's conclusions as they relate to Sino-Sinhalese relations see Luciano Petech, "Some Chinese Texts Concerning Ceylon," *The Ceylon Historical Journal*, III (1954), 227. The last tribute mission was sent in 1459 from Ceylon to China. See H. W. Codrington, *A Short History of Ceylon* (London, 1947), p. 91.

[19] Ferguson (ed.), *loc. cit.* (n. 15), p. 33. Actually the name "Ceylon," in one form or another, became common about the thirteenth century, though traces of it can even be found at much earlier dates. See Yule and Burnell, *op. cit.* (n. 10), p. 138. Castanheda in Azevedo (ed.), *op. cit.* (n. 17), I, 261, says that the Sinhalese language is derived from those of Kanara and Malabar. Barbosa (in Dames [ed.], *op. cit.* [n. 5], II, 111) says that it is "drawn partly from Malabar and partly from Coromandel." Barros (in Cidade and Múrias [eds.], *op. cit.* [n. 6], III, 57) fantastically derives Sinhalese from "Chins de Galle." Sinhalese actually has no relation to Malayālam; it is an Indo-Aryan tongue.

[20] This assertion is borne out by Robert Knox, *An Historical Relation of Ceylon* (*1681*), pp. 153–54, reprinted as Vol. VI (1956–57) of the *Ceylon Historical Journal* and edited by S. D. Saparamadu.

[21] Ferguson (ed.), *loc. cit.* (n. 15), p. 35.

[22] Azevedo (ed.), *op. cit.* (n. 17), I, 258–59. Also see Dames (ed.), *op. cit.* (n. 5), II, 113–15. On the training of elephants see Orta's remarks in Markham, *op. cit.* (n. 4), pp. 185–90.

[23] Ferguson (ed.), *loc. cit.* (n. 5), p. 35.

[24] *Ibid.* On the fruits of Ceylon see Duarte Barbosa's account in Dames (ed.), *op. cit.* (n. 5), II, 111; also Orta's remarks in Markham, *op. cit.* (n. 4), pp. 135–36 where he suggests: "Certainly very good profit might be made of the oranges, for they are the best fruit in the world."

[25] Dames (ed.), *op. cit.* (n. 5), II, 111–12. Ceylon still imports most of its rice.

While describing the sea coast as low, marshy, and luxuriant, Barros depicts the mountainous regions of Ceylon as forming a kind of inner oval, concentric with the generally spherical outlines of the island. This hollow oval, which he calls a corral, is flat in the interior and must be entered through passes in the encircling mountains. The mountains are heavily wooded and swift rivers flow down their sides to the sea. About Adam's Peak (elevation 7,352 feet) Barbosa, Barros, and Castanheda write at length. "Three or four principal rivers" [26] rise in this mountain which can be seen from the sea and which is located about forty-five miles east of Colombo. [27] Pilgrims make regular trips from the coast to its conical summit which is revered as a shrine. On their way to the mountain the pilgrims, clad in weeds and animal skins, often have to wade waist-deep through flooded lands and swollen rivers. [28] To climb the mountain's steep sides the pilgrims cling to ladders made of iron chains to pull themselves to its various levels. On the narrow, oblong platform at the top of the peak, there is to be found a rock that rises out of the generally flat surface. In the middle of this table-like rock, it is possible to see a hollow that resembles a man's footprint. This phenomenon is thought by the natives to be the footprint of a holy man who brought the worship of "Deunú" [29] from Delhi to Ceylon. Barros also tells the story of the holy tooth of Buddha, another sacred relic associated with "Deunú," presumably without knowing that it had been destroyed in Goa in about 1561. [30] He also comments on the distant and numerous pilgrimages made to the mountain by "jógues" (Yogis) [31] who are "like men that have left the world and dedicated themselves entirely to God." [32]

Barros reports that Ceylon is divided into nine states, each of which claims to be a kingdom. The most renowned of these kingdoms is that which produces the cinnamon and has Colombo as its chief city. Its king lives in a *Cóta* (Kotte, meaning fortress) [33] which lies nearby the city, though it is set apart from the metropolis' busy commercial life. Barbosa implies that the king's revenues are derived from his monopoly of cinnamon, elephants, and precious stones. [34] To the south of Colombo at the tip of the island is the kingdom of Galle which is bordered on the east by "Iáula" (Yāla) and on the north by "Tanavaca" (Dinavaca). [35] Its king reportedly forbids his vassals to pass on their property from one generation to the other and so discourages enterprise. The easternmost kingdom is "Batecalou" (Batticaloa) and between it and "Cande"

[26] Ferguson (ed.), *loc. cit.* (n. 15), p. 36.
[27] Barros puts it at twenty leagues (80 miles) from the seacoast, obviously an exaggeration. Castanheda and Barbosa simply place it in the middle of the island; a mistake, for it is actually located in southern Ceylon.
[28] Barbosa in Dames (ed.), *op. cit.* (n. 5), II, 118–19.
[29] From Sinhalese, *Diviyamsé.*
[30] Ferguson (ed.), *loc. cit.* (n. 15), p. 36.
[31] From Sanskrit, *yogī.*
[32] Ferguson (ed.), *loc. cit.* (n. 15), p. 37.
[33] Jayawardhana Kōttē, six miles from modern Colombo.
[34] Dames (ed.), *op. cit.* (n. 5), II, 113–17.
[35] For discussion see P. E. Pieris (trans.), *Ribeiros History of Ceilão* (Colombo, 1909), pp. 3–4.

(Kandy) lies another called "Vilacem" (Wellassea). North of Batticaloa along the coast are successively the kingdoms of "Triquinámale" (Trincomalle) and "Jafanapatam" (Jaffna). But Barros, even while listing these kingdoms, warns the reader that their frontiers cannot be defined with accuracy "for they have no other demarcations than the power of each."[36] Actually, the rulers of the Kōttē dynasty of Colombo apparently sought to hold the other states in vassalage.[37]

Castanheda indicates that Ceylon has seven major seaports.[38] Barros, who is always interested in information pertinent to Portugal's expansion, describes in some detail the location and natural defenses of the port of Colombo. All of the people in these towns are heathens except for the Moorish merchants. Priesthood and government among the heathen are but two sides of the same coin.[39] Not only do the kings work closely with the Brahmans; they themselves are superior Brahmans having secular control over the bodies of their subjects and spiritual control over their minds. The common people, while living in abject subjection, are described as being well formed, white, and devoted to good and gentle living. They go naked from the waist up and wear garments of silk and cotton called *patolas* from their hips down. They carry ornaments in their hair and suspend precious stones from their ears. A poor man may sell himself into slavery; the rich are great collectors of gold, silver, and precious stones. Ceylon boasts many talented lapidaries.[40] The Sinhalese are unskilled in war, somewhat effeminate, and apparently ignorant of firearms.[41]

The Maldive Islands, an archipelago lying in the Indian Ocean about four hundred miles southwest of Ceylon, are alleged by Barros to derive their name either from the Malabar term *mal-diva*, meaning chain of islands, or from the name of the island of "Male" (Mahal) where the king (sultan) resides.[42] Ibn Batuta, the great Arabic traveler of the fourteenth century, was the first writer to bring the Maldives to the attention of Europe.[43] The Portuguese first touched upon the Maldives in 1507, but they were acutely aware beforehand of the strategic importance of the islands in the trade of the Indian Ocean. They soon sought, but unsuccessfully, to establish control over them. Barros contends that the islands were organized into groupings called *patana* (towns).[44] Neither

---

[36] Ferguson (ed.), *loc. cit.* (n. 15), p. 37.

[37] For a more recent listing see Codrington, *op. cit.* (n. 18), pp. 98–99.

[38] Castanheda in Azevedo (ed.), *op. cit.* (n. 17), I, 261. Barbosa (in Dames [ed.], *op. cit.* [n. 5], II, 117) says that besides Colombo, "there are also four or five other ports . . . which are under the rule of other Lords, nephews of the King of Ceilam, to whom they owe allegiance; yet at times they rise up against him."

[39] Ferguson (ed.), *loc. cit.* (n. 15), pp. 44–45.

[40] Barbosa in Dames (ed.), *op. cit.* (n. 5), II, 115–16.

[41] Castanheda in Azevedo (ed.), *op. cit.* (n. 5), I, 261; Ferguson (ed.), *loc. cit.* (n. 15), p. 53.

[42] Cidade and Múrias (eds.), *op. cit.* (n. 6), III, 142–46. For further discussion of this name, but surprisingly without reference to Barros, see Yule and Burnell, *op. cit.* (n. 10), pp. 417–18.

[43] On this and other points see M. A. H. Fitzler, "Die Maldiven im 16. und 17. Jahrhundert," *Zeitschrift für Indologie und Iranistik*, X (1935–36), 215–56; and Albert Gray (trans. and ed.), *The Voyage of François Pyrard . . .* (London, 1890), II, Pt. II, 423–508.

[44] S. R. Dalgado, *Glossário Luso-Asiático* (Coimbra, 1919), II, 188.

Barbosa nor Barros seems to have distinguished clearly between the Maldives and the Laccadives (from *Laksha-diva*, meaning 100,000 islands). Barros apparently thought of the two groups as forming a single arc like a diadem extending from the neighborhood of Mount Deli south around India and all the way to Java.[45]

The inhabitants of these islands are described as being short, puny, and malicious, and as possessing their own language.[46] The common people are heathen, but their government is in the hands of the Moors.[47] Silk and cotton garments worn by the upper classes are often woven in the islands, even though the raw materials have to be imported. Their cloths are said to be superior to those then being woven in Bengal and Coromandel. The most important export of the islands is coir, rope made from coconut fibers, used generally in the areas bordering the Indian Ocean for stitching together the Indian and Moorish ships that were made without nails, and for cables and rigging. These ropes, Barros notes, swell and recover their freshness in salt water and so contract and stretch with the movements of the sea.[48] He remains convinced, however, that ships constructed in this manner could never survive in the stormy seas at the Cape of Good Hope. The Maldivians also export fish and cowrie shells,[49] the latter being used for buttons and especially for currency in Bengal and Siam.[50] Most interesting also is Barros' reference to their export of the Coco-de-Mer, the fruit of the *lodvicea sechellarum*, reputed to be an antidote for poison. The virtues of this huge double-coconut were renowned throughout the Orient, and, its reputation being carried to Europe, the Emperor Rudolf II (reigned 1576–1612) tried in vain to buy one that had been brought to Europe by some Dutch merchantmen early in the seventeenth century.[51]

To the north of the Maldives the Portuguese notice that the Laccadive Islands and Anjediva, which they used as stopover places and sources of fresh water, were originally inhabited by Malabar peoples who had become converts to Islam.[52] On the pearl fisheries of the Gulf of Manaar, lying between Ceylon

45 See Pyard in Gray (trans. and ed.), *op. cit.* (n. 43), II, Pt. II, p. 480, n. 2.
46 Perhaps a reference to the dialect *Gabali-Tana*, formerly in general use throughout the island. See W. W. Hunter, *The Imperial Gazetteer of India* (London, 1881), VI, 265.
47 Today the entire population is Muslim. For a more recent discussion of Maldive religion and government see ibid., VI, 264–65. For more details on government see Fitzler, *loc. cit.* (n. 43), pp. 223–24.
48 Cf. Orta in Markham (ed.), *op. cit.* (n. 4), p. 141, on the subject of "coir": "Of it they make the rigging and cordage for all the ships. It is very serviceable for us, for it is very flexible and does not rot in salt water. All the ships are caulked with it, so that it serves as linen, as oakum, and as matting. These qualities make it good merchandise for Portugal, and the space it requires is small, which is the reason for so much being used." For trade in coir see Dames (ed.), *op. cit.* (n. 5), I, 197.
49 For details on cowries in European literature see Dames (ed.), *op. cit.* (n. 5), II, 105, n. 3. Barros also says that in certain years two or three thousand hundredweight of cowrie were carried to Portugal as ballast in the ships.
50 See below, p. 417.
51 See Yule and Burnell, *op. cit.* (n. 10), pp. 176–78. Barros remarks that it is said to be a more efficacious antidote than bezoar stone. Orta questions its powers. See Markham (ed.), *op. cit.* (n. 4), p. 145.
52 For Barros' description of Anjediva see Cidade and Múrias (eds.), *op. cit.* (n. 6), I, 337–38.

and the tip of the Indian peninsula, Castanheda comments at some length.[53] He reports that the people "of Calicare[54] go pearl-diving twice each year,"[55] presumably off the northwest coast of Ceylon. Two to three hundred little boats, each containing about thirty-five men, go out to the oyster banks. The divers work in pairs, one diving with a sink-stone while the other holds tightly to an attached rope. The diver stays under water as long as possible collecting oysters for his basket. The largest pearls are saved for the king.[56] Castanheda also brings out clearly the fact that the yield from the oyster beds of Ceylon varied greatly and that decline in production was a worry in his day.[57] Orta compares these pearls with those which come from the fisheries of the Strait of Ormuz, Borneo, and China.[58]

B. MALABAR

In turning to the mainland of India, we shall commence with the Malabar Coast where the Portuguese obtained their earliest footholds. Even though the Romans traded there, this southwestern coast of the subcontinent was not clearly delineated in the European maps or narratives of the prediscovery era. From the eighth century down to the advent of the Portuguese the foreign trade of Malabar and the Indian Ocean was in the hands of the Arabs. Only occasional travelers, like Cosmas Indicopleustes and Marco Polo,[59] published notices of Malabar and its place in the trade of the Indian Ocean. All the Portuguese accounts printed in the sixteenth century are exceedingly full on Malabar, but none of them excels in detail or accuracy the first one to be published—that of Duarte Barbosa.

A Portuguese official in India from about 1500 to 1516 or 1517, Barbosa was secretary of the Portuguese factory in the Malabar port of Cannanore for a number of years. Here he reputedly mastered the local language "so well, that he spoke it better than the natives of the country." [60] It is probably because of his long residence in Malabar, his official position, his acute powers of observation,

---

[53] Azevedo (ed.), *op. cit.* (n. 17), I, 259–60. Cf. the even more vivid accounts in Marco Polo (in Yule and Cordier [eds.], *op. cit.* [n. 4], II, 331–32; 337) and Orta (in Markham [ed.], *op. cit.* [n. 4], pp. 297–300).

[54] This place I have not been able to identify.

[55] Normally today they go but once each year, beginning in the second week of March. Polo has them also going in September, so perhaps Castanheda is correct. See Yule and Cordier (eds.), *op. cit.* (n. 4), II, 337.

[56] Once Ceylon was taken over by Portugal, we know that the pearl fishery was operated as a royal monopoly. See Codrington, *op. cit.* (n. 18), p. 125.

[57] Cf. for an account of the cyclical character of the production of the Ceylon reefs, G. F. Kunz and C. H. Stevenson, *The Book of Pearl* (New York, 1908), pp. 103–4.

[58] Markham (ed.), *op. cit.* (n. 4), pp. 296–98.

[59] On Malabar as described in foreign sources of the prediscovery era see W. Logan, *Malabar* (Madras, 1951), I, 245–94.

[60] In the opinion of Gaspar Corrêa as quoted in Dames (ed.), *op. cit.* (n. 5), I, xxxvi.

and his linguistic ability that Barbosa was able to write a description of Malabar customs which still is regarded as an authoritative source. When supplemented by the details given by the other Portuguese authors, we can readily see that there was available in sixteenth-century Europe a substantial amount of reliable information on Malabar. Of the other Portuguese authors, only Pires, Castanheda and Orta wrote about Malabar from personal experience, and both Castanheda and Barros seem at times to be heavily indebted to Barbosa for their descriptive material.

The "land of Malabar"[61] (the natives prefer the name Kerala) extends, according to the Portuguese, from Cambola on the Chandragiri River, or from Mount Deli, to the tip of Cape Comorin.[62] On the north, Malabar is bordered by the Hindu kingdom of Vijayanagar. Castanheda relates the native tradition which asserts that the marshy lowlands of the coast were once covered entirely by the sea and that the mountains of the interior were connected by a land-bridge to the Maldives (meaning the Laccadives presumably).[63] These mountains are so high that they prevent the winds of the Indian Ocean from penetrating into the interior.[64] Barros notes that it is possible to travel inland by water from one place to the other along the coast via the maze of waterways.[65] Aside from such general statements, the Portuguese have very few remarks to make on topography.

The southernmost of the Malabar Kingdoms, Quilon, is called "Coilam" or "Coulan" by the Portuguese,[66] an area which in modern terms corresponds closely to the state of Travancore. In ancient times, Malabar was ruled from Quilon by a single ruler. The last of the line to govern the Malabar peoples from this port city and early center of the pepper trade was Chērumān Perumāl,[67] who died more than six hundred years before the Portuguese arrived in Malabar. It was during his reign that the Moors reportedly first began to trade on a large scale in India. The proselytizing Muslims soon converted the *Perumāl* (emperor) to the law of the Prophet, and convinced him to abandon his territories and to

---

[61] Malabar, meaning "hill country," was probably derived by the Arabs from the ordinary Dravidian *mala* (hill) with the addition of the Arabic *bar* (country). See Logan, *op. cit.* (n. 59), I, 1.

[62] This makes the Malabar Coast about 400 miles in length, or just about the same as the north-south extension of Portugal. Pires estimates it as having a coastline of 110 to 120 leagues and as extending into the interior from 5 to 15 leagues (or 20 to 60 miles). See Cortesão (ed.), *op. cit.* (n. 9), I, 66–67.

[63] Azevedo (ed.), *op. cit.* (n. 17), I, 34.

[64] Pires in Cortesão (ed.), *op. cit.* (n. 9), I, 66.

[65] Cidade and Múrias (eds.), *op. cit.* (n. 6), I, 372. Barros uses the Arabic word *leziras*. This may be *jaza'ir*, a term in vulgar Arabic which was used to denote the rivers. See notes under the adjectival form *jazirigy* in R. Dozy, *Supplément aux dictionnaires arabes* (2 vols.; Leyden, 1881). On the rivers, backwaters, and canals of the coast as arteries of traffic see Logan, *op. cit.* (n. 59), I, 8–17.

[66] For alternative identifications see Dames (ed.), *op. cit.* (n. 5), II, 3, n. 2.

[67] Barbosa writes "Cirimay Pirençal"; Castanheda makes it "Sarrana-perima"; and Barros gives it as "Sarama Pereimal." In all cases they are certainly referring to Chērumān, the last king of the Perumāl epoch (to about A.D. 826). For traditional history see accounts in Logan, *op. cit.* (n. 59), I, chap. iii; and P. K. S. Raja, *Medieval Kerala* (Chidambaram, 1953), chap. i. Barros (in Cidade and Múrias [eds.] *op. cit.* [n. 6], I, 370–72) asserts on the basis of certain Indian writings "interpreted for us" that Chērumān's reign ended precisely 612 years before the Portuguese first arrived in India.

leave in one of their ships for Mecca.[68] Before departing on his pilgrimage, Chērumān partitioned his lands among his kinsmen[69] leaving for himself only the uninhabited coastal strip on which Calicut, his embarkation point, was later to be built. This slight territory and the emblems of his authority, the sword and "a golden lamp,"[70] he finally bequeathed to one of his favorite nephews and enjoined the other nobles, excepting the kings of Cannanore and Quilon, to regard and obey his appointee as their new sovereign. It was also from the date of his departure that the Malabars began to reckon their calendar.[71]

The division of Chērumān left three independent kingdoms in Malabar: "Coulam" (Quilon), according to Barros the seat of the Brahman faith, "Kolathiri" (Cannanore), and Calicut.[72] The Zamorin, as the heir of the *Perumāl*, was to have the exclusive right of coining money, a traditional recognition of Calicut's importance in foreign trade. With the help of the Moors the Zamorin was gradually to make himself the supreme secular ruler in Malabar;[73] over religious affairs the king of Quilon, called the *cobritim* (or pontiff) by Barros,[74] was to assume control; apparently the king of Cannanore was not to possess jurisdiction over anything outside of his own boundaries. Besides these three rulers, Barbosa notes that other great nobles "wish to be called kings" but cannot be considered so since they neither coin money nor "roof houses with tiles."[75] Most of the Portuguese stress the fact that the Zamorin's strength lay in his close association with the Muslim merchants.

In describing the individual kingdoms and towns of Malabar, Pires, Barbosa, and Barros start in the north, proceed southward along the coast, and rarely

---

68 On the debated question of Chērumān's conversion and subsequent pilgrimage to Mecca see Raja, *op. cit.* (n. 67), pp. 6–8.

69 "All available Malayālam sources agree that there was a *bhuvibhaga*, or partition of the Empire by the last Perumāl, before his abdication." (*Ibid.*, p. 8.) Also see Logan, *op. cit.* (n. 59), I, 243, and Dames (ed.), *op. cit.* (n. 5), II, 4–5, n. 1.

70 The sword was still preserved in the Zamorin's palace in Calicut early in the twentieth century, and was seen there by Mr. J. A. Thorne who was then in charge of the Zamorin's estates. No trace of the "golden lamp" seems to be left. See Dames (ed.), *op. cit.* (n. 5), II, 3–4, n. 3. Castanheda (Azevedo [ed.], *op. cit.* [n. 17], I, 34) calls it a "tocha mourisca" or "Moorish lamp."

71 Castanheda in Azevedo (ed.), *op. cit.* (n. 17), I, 34.

72 Barros (in Cidade and Múrias [eds.], *op. cit.* [n. 6], I, 370–71) also points out, unlike the others, that the Arabs "according to what we hear" already had a settlement at Calicut before the abdication of the Perumāl.

73 "Zamorin" is equated with "emperor" by Castanheda and Barros. Ordinarily it has been defined as literally meaning "sea-lord." Thorne gives an alternative analysis in Dames, *op. cit.* (n. 5), II, 260–61.

74 In this designation Barros disagrees with Barbosa (*ibid.*, II, 6), who states that the ruler of Cannanore was called "Cobertorim" and the ruler of Quilon the "Benetady." Perhaps Barros is here repeating a tradition of the St. Thomas Christians which claims that the founding of Quilon in A.D. 825 was the work of Christian immigrants who then made it into their metropolitan see.

75 Dames (ed.), *op. cit.* (n. 5), II, 6. In Thorne's note he observes it has traditionally been the prerogative of Malabar rulers "to forbid roofing with tiles instead of thatch without permission." The right to grant such permission is a symbol of superior status.

refer to places or events in the interior.[76] The northernmost territory is the kingdom of Cannanore: it borders Vijayanagar and has "Coticolam" (Kottakulam) as its northernmost outpost. This fortress is commanded by the "Warden of the Marches," a nephew of the king of Cannanore, and is situated north of the "Miraporam" (Nileshwaram) River. In the estuary of this river there is a center of trade ruled over by another of the king's nephews, who was apparently restive under Cannanore's suzerainty. Farther south, close to the foot of Mount Deli, lies the prosperous old town of "Maravel" (Madayi or Pazhayangadi) which is a center of trade and fishing. A short distance farther to the south is the fortress town of "Balaerpartam" (Vallerepattanam) located on the river of the same name where the ruler of Cannanore makes his permanent residence. Inland a few miles is the town of "Taliparam" (Taliparamba) which is an entrepôt in the trade between Malabar and Vijayanagar.

The city of Cannanore itself is described as an international trading center which deals in goods of all sorts from the other great port cities surrounding the eastern rim of the Arabian Sea. Had the Portuguese not taken over the city, Pires believes that it would have fallen to Mohammed Ali and the Moors.[77] But since 1504, the Portuguese had a fortress, trading station, and colony there made up of Portuguese and their Christianized wives and families.[78] Castanheda, who apparently visited Cannanore, writes:

This is a large city with a fine bay, the houses being built of earth, and covered with flat stones or slates. . . . It abounds in fish, flesh, and fruits, but has to import rice from other places. The king or rajah is a bramin . . . but is not so rich as the Zamorin, or even as the rajah of Coulan [Quilon].[79]

To the south of the city of Cannanore, Barbosa identifies two rich and powerful Moorish towns, "Cragnate" (Eddakād) and "Tremopatam" (Dharmadam?), as the last places "which the King of Cananor hold against Calecut."[80] Inland and upriver from these two Moorish strongholds is the landlocked trading center called "Quategatam" (Kottayam?) whose inhabitants deal with the merchants of Vijayanagar and are traditional enemies of Cannanore.[81] Though Barbosa spent a number of years in Cannanore, he has very little to say about life there.

---

[76] Barros (in Cidade and Múrias [eds.], *op. cit.* [n. 6], I, 356–57) treats the west coast of India from Cambay to Cape Comorin as a single area which is divided naturally into subareas by the rivers which empty into the Arabian sea. Pires (in Cortesão [ed.], *op. cit.* [n. 9], I, 73–75) and Barbosa give long lists of the seaport towns and their rulers. In the discussion which follows we shall mainly follow Barbosa.

[77] Cortesão (ed.), *op. cit.* (n. 9), I, 77.

[78] Barbosa in Dames (ed.), *op. cit.* (n. 5), II, 81. Beginning in 1504, the Portuguese won the support of Cannanore in their fight against the Zamorin of Calicut and thereafter began to build up a colony there. For a description of the reception given to the Portuguese in 1504, see Castanheda's account as translated in Richard Eden (trans.), *The First Booke of the Historie of the Discoveries and Conquest of the East Indies by the Portingals* (London, 1582) as reprinted in Robert Kerr (ed.), *A General History and Collection of Voyages and Travels* (London, 1824), II, 493–94.

[79] Eden (trans.), *op. cit.* (n. 78), II, 425. Cf. P. K. Raja, *op. cit.* (n. 67), p. 61 on the higher social status of the *Kolattiri* (king of Cannanore).

[80] Dames (ed.), *op. cit.* (n. 5), II, 82.

[81] Pires in Cortesão (ed.), *op. cit.* (n. 9), I, 77.

Aside from mentioning that Cannanore produces a number of spices, the only other items that he feels inclined to discuss are the crocodiles and cobras of the country.[82]

The territory of Cannanore is described as being separated from Calicut by Moorish towns on both sides of the Anjarakandi and Tellicherry rivers. Just south of the rivers are the three Moorish commercial towns belonging to northern Calicut called "Tiramunigate" (Tiruyangad), "Manjaim" (Mayyazhi or Mahe) and "Chamobai" (Chombāla). Inland from these thriving seaports the land is heavily populated with Nāyars "who give obedience to no king," and are "divided between two lords who rule them."[83] The jurisdiction of the Zamorin of Calicut begins at the south bank of the "Pedirpatam" (Kotta) River. Between the border and the city of Calicut itself, Barbosa mentions three coastal towns: "Tircore" (Trikkodi), "Pandanare" (Pantalāyini), and "Capucate" (Kappata). Seven or eight miles south lies the Zamorin's capital, but Barbosa merely mentions it at this juncture since most of what he has to say later about Malabar in general is based upon conditions prevailing in Calicut. Along the river which runs south of the capital stands the town of "Chiliate" (Chāliyam) "where dwell many Moors, natives of the land who are merchants."[84] Barbosa then lists several other trading and fishing villages situated between Calicut and the important port of "Pananee" (Pounani) from which the Zamorin "draws a great revenue in dues."[85]

Further to the south is the river called the "Chatua" (Chittuvayi) down which comes the "greater part of the pepper"[86] grown in the area. Still further south is "another river which forms the frontier area with the Kingdom of Cochim [Cochin], on the hither bank of which is a place called 'Crangalor' [Cranganore]."[87] In this border territory live some of the native Christians of St. Thomas, and Barbosa understands that other members of this sect "dwell from here as far as *Charamandel* [Coromandel]."[88] The Malabar Christians, who are judged to be very devout, have two churches in Cranganore, one dedicated to St. Thomas and the other to Our Lady. Castanheda reports in summary what the Portuguese were told in detail by a native priest of the traditional history of the St. Thomas Christians, of their community at Cranganore, and of their religious practices.[89] Once having reached the southern extremity of the

---

[82] *Ibid.*, p. 83. Like any modern visitor, Castanheda was impressed by the crocodiles, reptiles, and bats of the area (in Eden [trans.], *op. cit.* [n.78], II, 425). Also see Pires in Cortesão (ed.), *op. cit.* (n. 9), I, 72–73. On the failure of the Portuguese to remark on the scenic beauty of this area see J. Gerson da Cunha, "The Portuguese in South Kanara," *Journal of the Bombay Branch of the Royal Asiatic Society,* XIX (1895–97), 251.

[83] Dames (ed.), *op. cit.* (n. 5), II, 85. The Nāyars are the warrior caste of Malabar.

[84] *Ibid.*, p. 87.

[85] *Ibid.*, p. 88.

[86] *Ibid.*

[87] *Ibid.*

[88] *Ibid.*, p. 89. Pires (in Cortesão [ed.], *op. cit.* [n. 9], I, 73) says that the Malabar Christians "live in the district from Chittuvaye to Quilon."

[89] See Eden (trans.), *op. cit.* (n. 78), II, 422–23. Cf. G. Schurhammer (trans. and ed.), "Three Letters of Mar Jacob Bishop of Malabar, 1503-1550," *Gregorianum,* XIV (1933), 62–86.

Zamorin's dominions, Barbosa comments at length on the palm tree and its multiple uses. The products of the palm are so abundant in Malabar that they are exported in dried or preserved form to Cambay and distant Dacca.[90] Pires observes that Malabar imports most of its rice and he discusses where it comes from and how it gets to the southwest coast of India from Coromandel and Kanara.[91]

Cochin, which owed its independence in the sixteenth century to Portuguese support of its ruler, is described as the land where pepper and other valuable spices grow in abundance. Castanheda, who visited the Portuguese colony there, writes that Cochin is located

... on a river [actually an inlet] close to the sea, and is almost an island, so that it is very strong and difficult of access, having a large and safe harbour. The land in its neighborhood is low and intersected by branches of the river into many islands. The city itself is built much after the same manner with Calicut. . . .[92]

Both Barbosa and Castanheda are well aware of the fact that the "king" of Cochin is generally regarded in Malabar as a vassal of the Zamorin. They acknowledge that traditionally he did not possess the coveted rights of coining his own money or of roofing his palace with tiles. They also recognize that the Zamorin possesses rights of investiture over the rājās of Cochin, that tribute and military support are owed to Calicut, and that the vassal must always be of the same faith as the suzerain. The Portuguese (since 1503) possess a fine fortress at Cochin, and "every day" refugee Christians of St. Thomas from "Coilam [Quilon] and other places" seek sanctuary with the Europeans.[93] The Portuguese themselves, in addition to their merchandising at Cochin, use their outpost for the repairing and building of ships, "both galley and caravels in as great perfection as on the Lisbon strand."[94]

In a disputed border region separating Quilon from Cochin, Barbosa locates the small town of "Porqua" (Porakád). Living under their own ruler, Porakád's inhabitants survive on fishing and piracy. In their forays against becalmed vessels, they use light rowboats called *caturs* to surround and attack their victims. South of Porakád is the first port belonging to Quilon, the trading town of "Cale Coilam" (Kayankullam) "whither come numbers of Moors, Heathens, and Christians of the doctrine of the Blessed Saint Thomas and many of them also dwell in the inland country."[95] Immediately to the south lies the "very great city" of Quilon where trade is carried on with merchants from Ceylon and other marts as far east as Malacca. At one time, Pires contends, the foremost king of Ceylon paid annual tribute to Quilon.[96] Apparently, however, traders

90 Dames (ed.), *op. cit.* (n. 5), II, 92.
91 Cortesão (ed.), *op. cit.* (n. 9), I, 76–77.
92 Eden (trans.), *op. cit.* (n. 78), II, 419.
93 Barbosa in Dames (ed.), *op. cit.* (n. 5), II, 93.
94 *Ibid.*
95 *Ibid.*, pp. 96–97.
96 Cortesão (ed.), *op. cit.* (n. 9), I, 80.

from the north did not ordinarily come to Quilon, since Barbosa remarks that they "trade not with Cambaya [Gujarat]."[97] Of Quilon Castanheda writes:

Coulan is twelve leagues [48 miles] from Cochin, and twenty-four [96 miles] from Cape Comorin. Before the building of Calicut, Coulan was the principal city of Malabar, and the port of greatest trade on that coast. Its buildings, more especially the temples and shrines of their idols are larger and more splendid than those of Cochin.[98]

Near Quilon on a small peninsula is a great church reputedly built by St. Thomas for his Indian converts. Barbosa comments extensively on the traditions surrounding St. Thomas' part in constructing this church.[99] In the Ramusio version, Barbosa gives 7,000 households as the number of St. Thomas Christians scattered over Malabar, both on the coast and inland.[100] All of the Portuguese authors agree that the ruler of Quilon is both rich and powerful militarily, but Castanheda observes that "the men are mostly of a low stature" and that the king's palace guard consists of three hundred female archers.[101] South of the city of Quilon is the area called "Tiramgoto" (Tiruvankodu) by Barbosa and "Travancor" by Barros. Apparently it was a semi-independent state, and it was, of course, the area from which the former province of Travancore received its name. While Cape Comorin "ends the land of Malabar," the territory of Quilon is said by Barbosa to extend further eastward to "a city named Cael [Palayaka-yal]," where the rāja usually resides.[102]

Most of what the Portuguese writers have to report on the customs and political organization of Malabar is based upon the situation prevailing in Calicut. Often they generalize on the practices of Calicut and apply them to the whole of Malabar, though this is not to say that they are unconscious of variations from place to place. The kings of Malabar, Barbosa observes, are of one caste and custom,[103] with little difference between them.[104] They worship idols

---

[97] Dames (ed.), *op. cit.* (n. 5), II, 97.   [98] Eden (trans.), *op. cit.* (n. 78), II, 467.

[99] "This ancient church is now no more, and the encroaching sea has covered even its site . . ." See Rao Bahadur L. K. Anatakrishna Ayyar, *Anthropology of the Syrian Christians* (Ernakulam, 1926), p. 14.

[100] Dames (ed.), *op. cit.*, II, 100, n. 1. Pires (in Cortesão [ed.], *op. cit.* [n. 9], I, 73) estimates their numbers at fifteen thousand of whom some two thousand are "men of repute," the rest being poor artisans.

[101] Eden (trans.), *op. cit.* (n. 78), II, 467.

[102] Dames (ed.), *op. cit.* (n. 5), II, 102, 124. Also see below, pp. 408–9.

[103] The English word "caste" is derived from Portuguese *casta*, a word meaning "family," "stock," "kind," "strain," "clan," "tribe," or "race." The English words "caste" and "chaste" have the same Latin root, *castus*, which originally meant "pure." The early Portuguese writers, confronted by a social situation for which they had no precedent in their own experience or even a descriptive word, quickly begin to apply this Latin term to the various subdivisions which they observed in Indian society. They do not, however, use the term "caste" exclusively with reference to Hindu groups. Barros talks about the "caste of Moors" and others assert that the St. Thomas Christians belong to the general "caste of Christians." It was the Dutch (their word is *kaste*) and the English who seem to have taken the Portuguese *casta* for a technical social term. For further discussion see A. L. Basham, *The Wonder That Was India* (London, 1954), pp. 148–51. In what follows we use the word "caste" in its ordinary English sense as a one-word description of the approximately three thousand subdivisions within Hindu society.

[104] Dames (ed.), *op. cit.* (n. 5), II, 6–7. See especially Thorne's notes on the basic similarity in customs prevailing in the Kshatriya and Sāmantan families. Most of the ruling families claim to be Sāmantan.

and they are classified as heathens by the Portuguese. In color the ruling families of Malabar are thought of as being "tawny," or brown, or "almost white," and with some being "blacker than others." [105] Generally they go about naked above the waist, but at times they wear jackets called *bajus* [106] made of cotton, silk, or rich brocades which are open in the front and come down to the middle of the thigh. The lower parts of their bodies they clothe in silk or cotton garments. [107] They tie their hair into a knot on the tops of their heads and sometimes "wear small hoods like Gallego caps." [108] They shave their beards with razors leaving short mustaches in the Turkish mode. From their ear lobes hang precious stones, and over their garments they wear broad belts decorated with jewels. Across their chests, shoulders, and foreheads they streak themselves with ashes which they put on in three stripes "according to the manner of their caste." [109]

The Portuguese, especially Barbosa, appear to have made a special study of the establishment and customs of the Zamorin. His palace is "only constructed of earth," but it is considered to be an extensive and "handsome structure." [110] On state occasions the Zamorin sits on a high platform "plastered daily with cow dung" on which "they place a very white stool" and "a coarse cloth of sheep's wool dyed black." [111] The sword mentioned earlier as part of the traditional regalia is also brought out on ceremonial occasions at which times it never leaves the Zamorin's side. Barros and Castanheda dwell at length on the richness of the Zamorin's garb and his wealth in gold, jewels, and pearls. In describing the reception of Da Gama at a special durbar, Castanheda writes that the Zamorin

lay on a sofa covered with a cloth of white silk and gold, and a rich canopy over his head. On his head he had a cap or mitre adorned with precious stones and pearls, and had jewels of the same kind in his ears. He wore a jacket of fine cotton cloth, having buttons

---

The Zamorin is a Sāmantan who is generally considered to be of Erōde background. The customs of all the royal families approximate those of the Nāyar caste. See Pires (in Cortesāo [ed.], *op. cit.* [n. 9], I, 67). But Castanheda (in Azevedo [ed.], *op. cit.* [n. 17], I, 36) categorizes the Zamorin as a Brahman. K. M. Panikkar (*Malabar and the Portuguese* [Bombay, 1929] p. 11), who is himself of the Nāyar caste, states flatly that the Zamorins "belong to the Nair caste."

[105] Barbosa in Dames (ed.), *op. cit.* (n. 5), II, 7.

[106] Castanheda in Azevedo (ed.), *op. cit.* (n. 17), I, 36. A modern Portuguese dictionary defines *bajú* as a "kind of shift used by Indian ladies." Dames (ed.), *op. cit.* (n. 5), II, 7, n. 3 notes that "coats" were no longer worn at the beginning of the twentieth century. Yule and Burnell (eds.), *op. cit.* (n. 10), refer to the "badjoe" or "bajoo" as a Malay jacket and derive the term from Malay, *baju*. Cf. Dutch *baadje* meaning jacket.

[107] For an example of his dress see the photograph of Mānavikrama Rājā, Zamorin of Calicut from 1912 to 1915, in the frontispiece to Dames, *op. cit.* (n. 5), II.

[108] *Ibid.*, p. 8. Apparently the hoods were not worn any longer in Thorne's time.

[109] *Ibid.* In reality these streaks of ashes indicate the religious affiliation rather than the caste of the wearer.

[110] Castanheda's remarks as given in Eden (trans.), *op. cit.* (n. 78), II, 365.

[111] Dames (ed.), *op. cit.* (n. 5), II, 9. This black cloth, "as large as an Alentejo cloak," called *kavimpadam* was, along with the white cloth called *vella*, part of the ceremonial apparatus still in use by the Zamorins of the twentieth century.

of large pearls and the button-holes wrought with gold thread. About his middle he had a piece of white calico, which came only down to his knees, and both his fingers and toes were adorned with many gold rings set with fine stones; his arms and legs were covered with many golden bracelets.[112]

Impressed as the Portuguese are with the wealth and display of the Malabar kings, they are even more fascinated by their peculiar system of marriage, inheritance, and succession. These "kings" (or *tamburāns*), including the Zamorin, never marry or found families in the European sense of these terms. They reportedly take as a mate "a woman of good family, of Nayre [Nāyar] descent, and beautiful for their delight."[113] The Zamorin, for example, who ordinarily resides just outside of Calicut, erects a house near his own palace for the private use of his "wife." She also has her own allowance and staff of servants, so that she may live "quite independently and well supplied."[114] If the king desires it, he may always replace her with another woman taken from the same caste. The children of such alliances are treated exceedingly well when they are young, but upon reaching maturity the Zamorin's sons "receive no more honour than comes to them from their mother's rank."[115] While the "king" often gives special presents to his sons, they remain only slightly better off than other Nāyars. They may not inherit their father's property or succeed to his kingdom. To many Europeans of the sixteenth century such a peculiar scheme of inheritance seemed almost to run contrary to nature.

The "kings" of Malabar are succeeded by their brothers, or, failing these, the throne passes to the sons of their sisters.[116] Under this matrilineal system of descent, the royal sisters never marry in the Western sense. Ordinarily the *tamburāttis* (royal ladies) take their mates from among the *Nambūtiri*, a Brahman group native to Malabar. The tamburāttis always remain in their own residences (*kovilagams*) and receive periodic visits from their mates. To Castanheda this was a rather shocking practice, for he sees the tamburāttis as "free and dissolute in their manners, choosing paramours as they please."[117] In such a system the ruler really has no certainty respecting the identity of his father—a state of affairs which the Europeans could hardly conceive of in terms of their own patrilineal background. But perhaps Barbosa reflects the attitude of the Nāyar when he asserts that they consider that the sons of their sisters "are their true sons, for they know who is their mother. . . ."[118] And, in summarizing the effects of this system, Barbosa points out that "the Kings of Malabar are always

---

[112] As translated in Eden (trans.), *op. cit.* (n. 78), II, 365. A similar description may be found by Barros in Cidade and Múrias (eds.), *op. cit.* (n. 6), I, 158.

[113] Barbosa in Dames (ed.), *op. cit.* (n. 5), II, 10.

[114] *Ibid.*

[115] *Ibid.* See also Pires in Cortesão (ed.), *op. cit.* (n. 9), I, 70.

[116] Cf. Albuquerque who asserts that "the sons of Malabar kings do not inherit; instead the kingship usually devolves on the sons of their sisters, who are usually the mistresses of Brahmins." See Walter de Gray Birch (trans.), *Affonso de Albuquerque. Commentaries* (4 vols.; London, 1875–84), II, 71.

[117] As translated in Eden (trans.), *op. cit.* (n. 78), II, 351.

[118] Dames (ed.), *op. cit.* (n. 5), II, 10.

old." [119] He might also have added that this means that their reigns are uniformly short and usually limited in constructive effectiveness.

In considering the role of the tamburāttis, the Portuguese observe that the nieces and sisters of the rulers have their independent residences and revenues. When such a girl reaches puberty, custom requires that a young noble from outside the kingdom be called in to deflower her. He is sent money and gifts before making the journey and upon his arrival he is feted "as if it were a wedding." [120] After remaining with her for several days, he hangs a small golden jewel (*tāli*) around her neck as a token of her maturity. This ceremony being performed, the young noble returns to his own land and "thereafter she may dispose of herself according to her own desires." [121] In a word, she may then enter into more permanent relationships with men of her own kingdom who are Nambūtiri Brahmans in caste.

The Portuguese have a number of arresting and puzzling comments to make on the crucial problem of succession. Barbosa contends that if the ruler dies without heirs a council is convened to elect a successor from among the surviving relatives of the king; or, failing relatives, any "suitable" person may be chosen. [122] Castanheda asserts that it is traditional for the Zamorins to die in a temple, and that custom ordains that all Zamorins must serve the gods of this temple before death. [123] Each Zamorin therefore retires from his secular office with the death of his predecessor. In retiring from civil office to take up his religious duties the Zamorin has no choice. As an example of this procedure, Castanheda later in his account cites the events of 1504 when the Zamorin was defeated by Portuguese arms. [124] Crestfallen and despairing, the Zamorin took up religious seclusion in a *turcol* (temple). [125] There, in the company of his Brahman advisers, he was forced to spend the rest of his days in an effort to propitiate the gods. Simultaneously he yielded the government of the state to his brother. From what we know from other sources about succession practices in Calicut, it appears that Castanheda's generalization about forced retirement to the temple before death is quite incorrect. None of the other sources bears him out in his contentions about the succession. [126]

Funeral rites and mourning ceremonies also attract the attention of the

---

[119] *Ibid.*, p. 11.

[120] *Ibid.*, p. 12.

[121] *Ibid.* Cf. account of Castanheda (Eden [trans.], *op. cit.* [n. 78], II, 351).

[122] Dames (ed.), *op. cit.* (n. 5), II, 11. For a much more detailed discussion of practices followed in Malabar on determining the succession in the absence of a legitimate heir see the *Historia do Malavar* prepared around 1615 by the Portuguese Jesuit, Diogo Gonçalves, as published by Josef Wicki as No. 20 of the *Missionswissenschaftliche Abhandlungen und Texte* (Münster, 1955), pp. 14–15.

[123] Azevedo (ed.), *op. cit.* (n. 17), I, 36; for English translation see Eden (trans.), *op. cit.* (n. 78), II, 350.

[124] Azevedo (ed.), *op. cit.* (n. 17), I, 183–84; Eden (trans.), *op. cit.* (n. 78), II, 489–90.

[125] Used by Castanheda as a synonym for "pagode," this is probably a Portuguese rendition of Malayālam, *tiru-koyil* (temple). See Yule and Burnell, *op. cit.* (n. 10), p. 713.

[126] There was a tradition, however, which persisted until 1743 that the Zamorin deposed himself as suzerain of Malabar at the festival of *Mahamakham* (big sacrifice) which was presumably held every twelve years. See Logan, *op. cit.* (n. 59), I, 163–65 and Raja, *op. cit.* (n. 67), pp. 28–31.

Portuguese as they deal with the rulers of Malabar.[127] On the death of a king his kinsmen, officials, and retainers assemble in an open field to observe the cremation of the body. Once the ashes are buried the mourners shave their bodies completely, "saving only their eyelashes and eyebrows," and, after cleaning their teeth, refrain from chewing betel and eating meat or fish for thirteen days. From the estate of the deceased ruler alms are distributed to fishermen, and many of the poor as well as the Brahmans are fed at his expense. In this period of official mourning, the successor of the dead Zamorin performs no official acts and is not formally installed "lest there should be someone to oppose him." The state is meanwhile governed by a regent appointed from the Nāyar nobility. At the end of the thirteen days, the new Zamorin is sworn into office before the assembled notables. In this ceremony he swears to preserve and enforce the laws, to pay the outstanding debts left by his predecessor, and to strive to regain what former rulers had lost.

While taking this oath, having his sword in his left hand, he holds in his right hand a burning candle,[128] on which is a gold ring which he touches with his finger. After this they throw some grains of rice over him, using many other ceremonies, and numerous prayers, and then they worship the sun three times. When all the *Caymales*,[129] or lords of noble birth, taking hold of the candle, take an oath to be true and faithful subjects to the new king.

While all others are released from restrictions after this investiture ceremony, the new Zamorin continues his personal mourning (the *diksha*) for a whole year.

At the end of the Zamorin's official year of mourning another ceremony (the *tirūmāsam*) takes place.[130] The heir apparent (*erālpād*), the other kinsmen, and the nobles of the realm congregate to "confirm the prince [erālpād] as heir, and the others after him, each in their degrees."[131] Once the succession has been determined, the Zamorin makes his own appointments to office. He confirms in their appointments some of those who had served his predecessor; others he removes completely and replaces them with men of his own choice. The assembly then disperses and the erālpād withdraws to "lands set apart for him, and he may come no more to Calicut as long as the King lives."[132] The departure of the heir apparent and his pilgrimage to the headquarters of the

---

[127] Dames (ed.), *op. cit.* (n. 5), II, 12–13, and Castanheda in Azevedo (ed.), *op. cit.* (n. 17), I, 36–37.

[128] Quotation from the sixteenth-century English translation of Castanheda in Eden (trans.), *op. cit.* (n. 78), II, 352. Almost identical to the description by Barbosa as translated in Dames (ed.), *op. cit.* (n. 5), II, 13. In the original Portuguese Castanheda (Azevedo [ed.], *op. cit.* [n. 17], I, 37) refers to a *candea acesa* which the sixteenth-century English translator renders as a "burning candle"; the translator of Barbosa renders the same words as a "lighted oil lamp." Both translations of the Portuguese are possible, but it is likely that a lamp is meant.

[129] Malayalam, *kaimal*, meaning a Nāyar chief. See Yule and Burnell, *op. cit.* (n. 10), p. 770. For details see Dames (ed.), *op. cit.* (n. 5), II, 13–14, n. 3.

[130] Cf. Thorne's eyewitness account of this ceremony in 1916 in Dames (ed.), *op. cit.* (n. 5), II, 16, n. 1.

[131] *Ibid.*, p. 16.

[132] *Ibid.*

erālpād is performed with great ceremony and according to rites prescribed by tradition.[133] In connection with his description of court ceremonies at Calicut, Barbosa incidentally gives a few details on the functioning of the central authority. The regent (*mangāt achan*), who traditionally acts in place of the Zamorin during the thirteen days of general mourning, is described as having "all the laws of the Kingdom"[134] in his possession and as holding complete control over the treasury. Upon coming into power the new Zamorin makes his own political appointments. At his court he maintains a large number of secretaries who write down on palm leaves "everything connected with the King's Exchequer" and with the "justice and governance of the realm."[135] The Zamorin employs a "thousand women" of "good caste" as "sweepers of his palace,"[136] each one being a specialist in her particular job. Aside from pages and other attendants, the court of Calicut is guarded by large contingents of Nāyars who accompany the ruler whenever he goes abroad. Over the city of Calicut the Zamorin appoints a governor from the Nāyar caste who is called "Talixe"[137] and who is responsible for maintaining order and meting out justice. In administering justice, the governor is responsible to the Zamorin. Outside the city itself, the Zamorin appoints a chief justice who is called *contante carnaxies* and who has his deputies in every town.[138] Calicut obviously is outfitted with a customs office, and Castanheda comments that the Zamorin is able because of the huge revenues flowing into his coffers "to raise a force of thirty thousand men in a single day, and could even bring a hundred thousand men into the field, completely equipt for war in three days."[139] Even while allowing for conventional exaggeration in the use of figures, one gets the impression that the Zamorin's efficiency in bringing an army into existence was startling to the Portuguese.

On the administration of justice, Barbosa gives many details. He is well aware of the fact that the castes themselves take the responsibility for the misdeeds of their members, and he points out that the methods of trial and punishment differ depending on the caste of the offender or on his status as native or foreigner. Persons of the lower castes, if they confess to or are caught in the act of committing a theft, are executed summarily by beheading or impalement of the body on short stakes (*kazhu*).[140] Moors are treated in a similar fashion, except that they are executed by thrusts of a sword. If a thief so executed has stolen goods from a private person, the owner forfeits his goods to the state, presumably in payment for its execution of justice. When the thief is not apprehended, even though

---

[133] Cf. on these ceremonies and others connected with the succession the accounts of the installation rites of 1909 by the Zamorin of Calicut himself in *ibid.*, pp. 249–55.
[134] *Ibid.*, p. 14.
[135] *Ibid.*, p. 18.
[136] *Ibid.*, p. 19.
[137] *Kozhikkot Talachannavar*, or the Calicut Talachan. See *ibid.*, p. 27, n. 1.
[138] Identification uncertain. *Contante* is possibly a Portuguese word meaning roughly "to give account." See *ibid.*, p. 32, n. 2; also cf. Castanheda in Azevedo (ed.), *op. cit.* (n. 17), I, 37.
[139] Eden (trans.), *op. cit.* (n. 78), II, 350.
[140] Dames (ed.), *op. cit.* (n. 5), II, 27, n. 2.

the stolen goods are recovered, the authorities retain the property in question for a specified period of days, and, if the thief is not caught in the interim, all the goods less one-fourth are returned to their owner. Should an accused thief deny being guilty, they imprison him for nine or ten days under very harsh conditions. Should he still refuse to confess, the accuser is asked whether he wants the accused to be released or tried. If the decision is for trial, the accused is ritually prepared for trial by ordeal. If he is a native, he is required to testify to his innocence and then plunge the first two fingers of his right hand into a pot of boiling oil. Should his fingers be burnt, the accused is tortured to force a confession of what he has done with the stolen goods. Whether he confesses or not, he is still executed. Should the accused's fingers not be burnt, he is released and the accuser is either executed, fined, or banished. Moors are subjected to the same trials, except that their ordeal is to lick a red-hot axe with their tongues. The procedures and punishments for theft are likewise followed in cases where the individual is accused of murder, cow-killing, attacks on Brahmans or Nāyars, or of having relations with a Brahman's wife. In no case, however, is a woman ever executed by the law (she may be by her caste); if guilty, she is either fined or banished. Vagrants (all of those who have no parents, master, or employment, whether they be men or women) are wards of the state and are sold at low prices to any willing purchaser. Such an account at once raises the question whether Barbosa was not describing some modes of trial and punishment drawn from his European background which he then transposed to India and incorporated in his account to make it seem more complete and authoritative. Misgivings are not warranted, however, for Barbosa's report agrees very closely with accounts of justice in Malabar written by British official and unofficial observers in the eighteenth century.[141]

The status of the Nāyars under the law is quite different from the lower castes. No matter what crime he commits, the Nāyar is never imprisoned or fettered. If a complaint is made against a Nāyar, he is summoned to appear before the governor. Should he fail to appear, the governor issues a warrant which prescribes death for the offending Nāyar at the hands of three or four appointed Nāyars. After being hunted down, the offending Nāyar is slain by his fellows, the warrant is placed upon his breast, and his body lies exposed until it is devoured by "the fowls of the air and the jackals."[142] If the accused Nāyar responds to the summons, he is confronted by the complainant in the governor's presence and each is called upon "to say all that he knows regarding the other."[143] If the accused denies the charge, the litigants are given eight days in which "to establish clearly what each one has said."[144] Should each hold to his original position then at the end of eight days a trial by ordeal in boiling oil is decreed as for the lower castes.

[141] See Thorne's note in *ibid*.

[142] *Ibid*., p. 31. Some additional references by Castanheda to the Nāyar's status under the law may also be found in Azevedo (ed.), *op. cit.* (n. 17), I, 39–40.

[143] Barbosa in Dames (ed.), *op. cit.* (n. 5), II, 31.   [144] *Ibid*.

Barbosa and the other Portuguese writers are particularly intrigued by the caste system of Malabar and go to considerable pains to understand and explain certain of its aspects. None of the Portuguese is very clear on the precise relationship of the ruling families to the Brahmans. Barbosa (and who could expect a European to think otherwise) evidently thought that the ruling families, not the Brahmans, form the highest caste. Pires claims that the "best" of the Brahmans are the *Kshatriyas* and that in rank they are followed by the *Pattars* and the *Nambūtiris*.[145] Barros[146] makes the king of Quilon the leader of the Brahmans, and Castanheda[147] declares outright that the Zamorin is of the Brahman caste. All of them agree that the Brahmans are a learned and priestly caste who "all speak the same tongue"[148] and serve as courtly functionaries. Albuquerque declares that they have a "scientific language [Sanskrit] which is like our Latin."[149] The only way to be a Brahman is through being born into a Brahman's family. In Malabar, since most Brahmans were and are Nambūtiris, the descriptions of the Portuguese, who make no such distinction themselves, refer to the practices of the Nambūtiri group.[150]

The male children in a Nambūtiri family are ritually invested when seven years of age with a strip of untanned skin which they wear over the shoulder. In other Brahman groups it is customary to bestow a thread rather than a skin upon the novice who is entering the stage of life called *brahmāchāryam*. For the next seven years of his training period the young Nambūtiri must wear his strap and refrain from eating betel. The novitiate being over, the leather strip is ceremoniously removed and the Nambūtiri is invested with a three-stranded cord of twenty-seven threads as a symbol of his having attained full status as a Brahman. "Thereafter, he may eat betel, but not flesh or fish,"[151] his diet consisting of rice, milk, butter and fruit.[152] In a Nambūtiri family only the eldest son marries and he marries "only once in our manner,"[153] and he is looked upon as the successor to an entailed estate.[154] His younger brothers officially remain unmarried. Though they form alliances (*sambandhams*) with Nāyar women, "they may not sleep with any woman older than themselves."[155]

---

[145] Pires in Cortesão (ed.), *op. cit.* (n. 9), I, 68.

[146] Cidade and Múrias (eds.), *op. cit.* (n. 6), I, 371.

[147] Azevedo (ed.), *op. cit.* (n. 17), I, 36.

[148] Barbosa in Dames (ed.), *op. cit.* (n. 5), II, 33.

[149] Birch (trans.), *op. cit.* (n. 116), II, 78.

[150] Also known as the Kerala or Malayāla Brahmans, this group was the dominant priestly and aristocratic group in Malabar from ancient times. For a detailed exposition of their customs see L. K. Anatha Krishna Iyer, *The Cochin Tribes and Castes* (Madras, 1912), II, 170–288. There is also a sizable group of Tamil Brahmans, who are looked upon as being foreign in contrast to the native Nambūtiris.

[151] Barbosa in Dames (ed.), *op. cit.* (n. 5), II, 34.

[152] Albuquerque in Birch (trans.), *op. cit.* (n. 116), II, 78. For more details on diet see Iyer, *op. cit.* (n. 150), II, 284.

[153] Barbosa in Dames (ed.), *op. cit.* (n. 5), II, 34, n. 3.

[154] Family property is called *Brahmāswum* and every member of the family has an equal claim; in practice, however, the eldest son succeeds to the father's estate and the others receive maintenance from him. See Iyer, *op. cit.* (n. 150), II, 214.

[155] Dames (ed.), *op. cit.* (n. 5), II, 35.

The eldest son keeps his wife under close surveillance; when the eldest son dies his wife never remarries. Should a wife be unfaithful to her husband, she is put to death by poison.

The Brahmans are universally revered among the natives. They live apart from others "in their own houses and cities," [156] and act as clergy in the numerous temples. Their houses of worship have three principal portals which "face the west." [157] Over the central portal of the temple in which Vasco da Gama was received there hung seven small bells.[158] On the outside of the temple, in front of the main portal, there stands a stone (*maṇḍapa*) as tall as a man with three steps leading up to it.[159] The interior of the temple houses a tower-like chapel (*srī-kōyil*) which contains the "idol" and which none may enter except the officiating Brahmans. These priests wear a "kind of petticoat of cotton" that covers them from the waist to the knees, calico patches in their armpits, and nothing on their legs, feet, and heads.[160] Twice each day the Brahmans, after performing ceremonial ablutions, take the "idol" out of the chapel and carry it around the outside of the temple (always remaining within the surrounding enclosure) in a great procession. They also wash the stone three times each day and place upon it twice each day a ritual offering of boiled rice for the crows. In the interior of the temple which Vasco da Gama visited were "many images painted on the walls" possessing "monstrous teeth" and having "as many as four arms." To Castanheda such paintings appeared "ugly," but he nevertheless comments admiringly on the temple as an edifice of "splendid workmanship." [161]

In their religious practices, the Malabars are judged to be superstitious, given to soothsaying, and prone to believe in lucky and unlucky days. They are often visited by the devil, and they believe that people are moved to behave in extraordinary ways by the gods of the temple who enter into them. Their deities are the sun, moon, stars, fire, cows, and whatever they first meet on going out in the morning. The Brahmans look upon "three" as a sacred number and they believe in a god who has three persons.[162] This god is "Bermabesma Maceru" and he is believed "to have been since the beginning of the world." [163] Of Christ they have no knowledge, but, according to Garcia da Orta, they believe in the transmigration of souls.[164]

Barbosa also notes a number of other features about the Brahmans' life. Under law they are never subject to the death penalty and ordinarily receive

---

[156] *Ibid.*
[157] See *ibid.*, pp. 35–36, n. 3. Incorrect. Actually the principal portals face the East.
[158] Castanheda in Azevedo (ed.), *op. cit.* (n. 17), I, 44.
[159] This stone platform could be used only by Brahmans; see Dames (ed.), *op. cit.* (n. 5), II, 36, n. 1.
[160] Castanheda in Azevedo (ed.), *op. cit.* (n. 17), I, 44.
[161] In Eden (trans.), *op. cit.* (n. 78), II, 363.
[162] *Ibid.*, p. 355.
[163] Sanskrit: *Brahma, Vishnu, and Maheśvara*, the three gods who are combined to make the *Trimūrti*, the triune god of Hinduism. See Dames (ed.), *op. cit.* (n. 5), II, 37, n. 1. See also Pires in Cortesão (ed.), *op. cit.* (n. 9), I, 66.
[164] Markham (ed.), *op. cit.* (n. 4), p. 291.

India

for their wrongdoings only a "mild chastisement" from their superiors.[165]
After bathing, they always paint certain marks on their foreheads with ashes.
They cremate their dead. When a husband learns that his wife is pregnant, he
cleans his teeth, abstains from betel and food, and does not trim his beard until
she is delivered.[166] The Brahmans serve their rulers in everything except war.
They are cooks in the royal court, couriers, and emissaries to foreign lands.
Even in times of war, they travel about freely and "none does them any ill."[167]
They are learned in religion, possess many books on religious subjects, "believe
and respect many truths,"[168] and have powers of excommunication and
absolution.[169] For their learning and piety, they are held in the highest esteem
by everyone, even the kings.

The Nāyars,[170] or warrior caste, particularly attracts the attention of the
Portuguese writers, for it was the dominant caste of Malabar and the one which
possessed social customs most foreign to Europeans. Barbosa, whose account of
the Nāyars is still considered to be the most accurate Western narrative of his
day, states categorically that the *fidalgos* (nobles) of this caste "have no other
duty than to serve in war."[171] Pires believes that there must be 150,000 Nāyars
in Malabar.[172] Armed at all times with swords, bows, or spears, the Nāyars act
in periods of peace as guards for the king and other great lords. As retainers of
the aristocracy, they serve their lords loyally and live at the lord's expense.
Neither the king nor any other lord can create a Nāyar, since descent is the only
entry to this soldierly aristocracy. Upon becoming seven years of age, young
Nāyars begin to receive instruction in physical training, fencing, and the use
of arms. The teachers, called "panicals" (*pannikars*),[173] are highly esteemed
by people of all ages, and in the rainy season each year they give refresher
courses in fencing which are compulsory for the mature Nāyar throughout his
life.

Once sufficiently prepared at the school (*kalari*) in the arts of war, the fledgling
soldier presents himself for investiture as a Nāyar. In Cannanore the ceremony
is performed by the king; in Calicut by the youth's teacher with the approbation

[165] *Ibid.*, p. 37.
[166] Though nothing is said of this particular practice, for details on pregnancy rites among certain
of the Nambūtiris see Iyer, *op. cit.* (n. 150), II, 199–201.
[167] Barbosa in Dames (ed.), *op. cit.* (n. 5), II, 37.
[168] *Ibid.*
[169] Pires in Cortesão (ed.), *op. cit.* (n. 9), I, 68.
[170] The name Nāyar is possibly the same as the Malayālam word *Nagar*, "serpent men." See
K. M. Panikkar, "Some Aspects of Nāyar Life," *Journal of the Royal Anthropological Institute*, XLVIII
(1918), 289–91, appendix, n. 1. Also see Dames (ed.), *op. cit.* (n. 5), II, 38, n. 1, who concludes that
none of the derivations so far propounded can be considered satisfactory.
[171] Dames (ed.), *op. cit.* (n. 5), II, 38. Panikkar (*loc. cit.* [n. 170], p. 256) comments that this kind of
observation is "unscientific and unreliable." He feels that a historical reconstruction "is possible only
after a thorough and searching study of Nāyar literature."
[172] Cortesão (ed.), *op. cit.* (n. 9), I, 67.
[173] For further details on military training see E. K. Gough-Aberle, "Changing Kinship Usages in
the Setting of Political and Economic Change among the Nayars of Malabar," *Journal of the Royal
Anthropological Society*, LXXXII (1952), 76.

of the king. The ceremony of investiture in Cannanore is naturally the more elaborate of the two. Here the youth who wants to receive initiation as a soldier presents himself at the king's palace at an appointed time in the company of his soldier-kinsmen. Upon being ushered into the royal presence, the youth makes a gift in coins to the king. He is then asked if he will uphold the laws and customs of his caste. When an affirmative answer is given by the applicant and his kinsmen, the king commands the youth to gird himself with a sword. The royal hand is then placed on the initiate's head, the king utters a prayer in a low voice, and then embraces the young man while commanding him to "Protect cows and Brahmans." [174] This ceremony being finished, the youth is asked to declare his name and lineage before the assemblage; this information is then entered into the king's register so that he may henceforward be on the royal payroll. The rites of initiation followed in Calicut are essentially the same, except that the teacher acts in the place of the king.

Among the Europeans the Nāyars are held in high esteem as warriors. Though they are mercenaries, they abide by their oath to die for their lords. Should a master be killed, his Nāyars relentlessly search out the slayer without regard for their own lives. The private person who hires Nāyars as bodyguards may even be able to escape the king's wrath, so great is their prestige and influence with the crown. In war they never give up until they are all slain. Certainly, the Portuguese do not look in this case, as they do in so many others, upon the Indians as being weak, effeminate, and unwarlike. Through bitter experience the Portuguese, from Vasco da Gama onward, had every practical reason for respecting the military prowess of the Nāyars.[175]

The marriage customs and the matrilineal kinship system of this soldierly caste engage the attention of all the Portuguese writers. They contend that the Nāyars are not permitted to marry, rear families, or control property because such duties might interfere with their devotion to the military life.[176] The Nāyars live in their own villages in seclusion from other groups and possess their own palm trees and water tanks. Since they never "marry" in the Western sense of the word, the children never know their own fathers and a father never has a son. Three or four Nāyars customarily cohabit with the same woman at certain specified times which all members of the group (*taravad*) have agreed upon.[177] All members of the taravad stem from the same caste (or subcaste) and both sexes are forbidden on pain of death to cohabit with persons of a

---

[174] Barbosa (Dames [ed.], *op. cit.* [n. 5], II, 46) gives the king's words in transliteration as "Paje Gubramarca"; Barros (in Cidade and Múrias [eds.], *op. cit.* [n. 6], I, 375), who seems to follow Barbosa in other matters, writes this admonition: "*Paguego bramenta bisquera*." For an effort to analyze these words see Dames (ed.), *op. cit.* (n. 5), II, 46, n. 2. Castanheda (in Azevedo [ed.], *op. cit.* [n. 17], I, 38) tells much the same story, evidently based on Barbosa, but does not attempt to give a transliteration of these words.

[175] Even as late as World War I, the Nāyars joined the Indian army in large numbers. See Dames (ed.), *op. cit.* (n. 5), II, 38, n. 2.

[176] Cf. Gough-Aberle, *loc. cit.* (n. 173), LXXXII (1952), 77, for a recent and a similar opinion.

[177] Based on Castanheda in Azevedo (ed.), *op. cit.* (n. 17), I, 37–38.

lower caste. Nāyar women are free to accept Brahmans as lovers. A kinsman or friend is invited by the mother to perform the ceremony of tying the *tāli* of each twelve-year-old daughter. Thereafter a young Nāyar is chosen to initiate the girl into sexual relations so that she will be "fit for association with men," [178] and will be ready to establish her own taravad.

In such a system all relationship and inheritance is necessarily based on the mother. The property of a male passes on to his brothers and to the sons of their sisters, all of whom must be born of the same mother. Even though all Nāyars receive stipends from the king, "some of them possess also estates on which they live and support their sisters for whom they have great regard." [179] To their older sisters the Nāyars show great respect and affection. Their relations with younger sisters are very distant, for they never enter the same room with them, or touch them, or even speak to them. With their brothers and other relatives the Nāyars are exceedingly respectful and courteous.

On the death of a Nāyar, his body is burned within his own compound and the ashes are cast into running water. [180] He is mourned for a stipulated period by his mother and other kinsmen. [181] The nephew, or whoever is his heir, mourns for a full year. [182] During the year of obligatory mourning, the heir does his own cooking, bathes before eating, and ceremoniously changes his clothes. He feeds crows from his own food and gives alms to the poor and the Brahmans. The Nāyars believe that "with the proper signs a man who has died may be born again of another woman." [183] They worship the sun, moon, the lamp, and cows, and are great believers in omens, tabus, and unlucky and lucky days. If a cat crosses the path of a person bent on business, he does not do it. On going out of doors, if they see a crow carrying a stick they turn back. When a person is departing, he postpones his leaving if someone in the party sneezes. The Nāyars, it is evident to Barbosa, "believe in ghosts of many kinds." [184]

The Nāyars are depicted as being even more afraid of staining their nobility by association with lower castes than are the Brahmans. They will neither touch nor eat and drink with lesser people. In walking along the road they order lower-caste people to get out of their way. Should such a person be foolhardy enough to refuse to give way, the Nāyar "may kill him without punish-

---

[178] Barbosa in Dames (ed.), *op. cit.* (n. 5), II, 42; for an account of more recent practices see Pannikar, *loc. cit.* (n. 170), pp. 268–69. On what is considered normal sexual posture in Malabar see Pires in Cortesão (ed.), *op. cit.* (n. 9), I, 69.

[179] Barbosa in Dames (ed.), *op. cit.* (n. 5), II, 53.

[180] In recent times "only the eldest members [of the Nāyar caste] are burnt; others are buried." (Panikkar, *loc. cit.* [n. 170], p. 275).

[181] Panikkar (*ibid.*, p. 276) gives the period as fourteen days.

[182] He also takes a vow (*diksha*) to lead a pure and pious life (*ibid.*).

[183] Barbosa in Dames (ed.), *op. cit.* (n. 5), II, 55.

[184] *Ibid.* Cf. this statement with Panikkar, *loc. cit.* (n. 170), p. 278. ". . . it is nothing short of marvelous to see the Nayars, who have, it must be remembered, assimilated a very great deal of the material and intellectual culture of their neighbors . . . still maintain with undiminished vigour their spirit-worship, black-magic, and demoniacal ceremonies. . . ."

ment."[185] Even if a low-caste man touches a Nāyar woman by accident, he will be killed by her kinsmen.[186] In the towns lower-caste individuals walk close to the walls to avoid touching and thereby polluting a Nāyar. Business transactions between Nāyars and the lower castes are conducted through intermediaries to avoid pollution. When a Nāyar is unavoidably polluted, he cleanses himself by bathing and changing his clothes before entering his dwelling. Ordinarily, the Nāyar women strictly avoid going into the towns. In all matters relating to pollution by lower castes the Nāyars are judged by Barbosa to be "great sticklers."[187] It is only when they go off to war that the Nāyars are relieved from worry about performing purification rites.

In their role as warriors the Nāyars are kept on the king's list throughout their lives. The mothers and nephews of Nāyars slain in battle are given a royal pension. In case a Nāyar is wounded, he continues to receive his regular stipend as well as medical care. When the Nāyar is on active duty, he receives his wages at the end of each day. Should the king fail or be unable to pay the customary stipends, the aggrieved Nāyars join together in warning the delinquent king that they will take service under another master. If he does not immediately pay them one-third of their back wages and give them a definite promise of payment for the remainder, they take employment elsewhere. Their departure constitutes an injury to the king's reputation, presumably both with his own subjects and his fellow rulers.

While the Nāyars are praised for their unswerving devotion to duty, Barbosa[188] and Castanheda[189] both observe that they seem able to bring personal and popular grievances to the attention of the crown in their role as protectors of the people. Apparently under the pressure of injustice, a Nāyar sometimes acts as if possessed. Uttering terrible threats, he appears before the king with a naked sword in his hand. While slashing himself, as a vivid demonstration of his sincerity, he asserts: "I am such and such a god, and I have come to tell you such and such a thing." Should the king doubt his words, the Nāyar keeps on shouting and slashing until the king takes heed of his complaint. Apparently, as in later times, the Nāyars were the only group who could remonstrate with the king and still expect to receive a hearing and to see justice done.[190]

On the other castes of Malabar, Barbosa is the only Portuguese writer who attempts any systematic description of them. Pires gives a partial list of the lower castes, and adds a few details not included in Barbosa's more detailed description.[191] Barros, who notes that he will talk about the castes in more detail in

[185] Dames (ed.), *op. cit.* (n. 5), II, 49.

[186] Cf. account of Pires in Cortesão (ed.), *op. cit.* (n. 9), I, 71.

[187] Dames (ed.), *op. cit.* (n. 5), II, 50. For the importance of ritual purity and pollution in caste-ranking see E. K. Gough-Aberle, "Criteria of Caste Ranking in South India," *Man in India*, XXXIX (1959), 115.

[188] Dames (ed.), *op. cit.* (n. 5), II, 55.

[189] Azevedo (ed.), *op. cit.* (n. 17), I, 39.

[190] On the Nāyars as political leaders see Logan, *op. cit.* (n. 59), I, 132–33.

[191] For a comparison of the two lists see Cortesão (ed.), *op. cit.* (n. 9), I, 72, n. 1.

his *Geografia* (which has never been found), observes only that the farmer is distinct from the fisherman and the weaver is different from the carpenter in a variety of ways.[192] None of the writers clearly makes the distinction commonly talked about now between the castes of the "Right-hand" (agricultural groups) and the "Left-hand" (artisan groups).

Barbosa places the "Biabares"[193] (*Vyābāri*), a caste of native merchants, just below the Nāyars, for they are "of such established lineage that the Nayres may touch them."[194] Dealers in goods of every kind, both inland and at the seaports, they are described as being an ancient and wealthy caste. Their wealth is not only in trade, but also "in land inherited from of old."[195] Like the Nāyars, they are never executed by legal process, but by members of their own group. Unlike the Nāyars, they have but one wife and her sons are their heirs. Upon death the members of this caste are cremated. The wives, even when they are widowed at a young age, never remarry; the husbands may remarry after the death of a wife.

The "Cuicavem" (probably potters, called *Kusavan*) are said to be related to but separate from the Nāyars.[196] The members of this subcaste, whose sons may adopt no other occupation, make pottery and roofing bricks. They have their own religious practices, gods, and temples. Their marital customs are the same as the Nāyars', and presumably their inheritance and related practices follow the same general pattern as those of the Nāyars. Another non-military subcaste is the "Mainatos" (*Mainattu*) "whose occupation is to wash clothes for the Kings, Bramenes and Nayres."[197] In addition to washing clothes they also run a linen supply service which daily furnishes the higher castes with clean clothes for a regular monthly fee. Finally, among the Nāyar-related groups there are the "Caletis" (*Chaliyans*), a caste of weavers of low social and economic status.[198] Many of them are the sons of Nāyars, and like their fathers they carry arms and act as soldiers. Although he does not say so specifically, Barbosa is apparently aware of the fact that Nāyars can associate with these subcastes without being polluted.

There are, according to Barbosa, eleven polluting castes. The purest of these is the "Tuias" (*Tiyans*) who cultivate and harvest the palm groves and make toddy, quarry for stone, and sometimes fight in the wars. The majority of them work as serfs on the lands of the Nāyars. They worship their own gods, live apart, and strictly avoid all contact with castes lower than their own. As with the Nāyars, their brothers and nephews are their heirs because "their women openly earn their living with their bodies."[199] The "Manens" (*Mamans*), a caste of

---

[192] Cidade and Múrias (eds.), *op. cit.* (n. 6), I, 372.
[193] Dames (ed.), *op. cit.* (n. 5), II, 56, n. 1.
[194] *Ibid.*, p. 57.   [195] *Ibid.*, p. 56.
[196] Cf. *ibid.*, p. 57, n. 1 which quotes the *Malabar Gazetteer* (p. 120) as listing the *Kusavan* as "non-military classes ranking as *Nayars*." Pires (in Cortesão [ed.], *op. cit.* [n. 9], I, 71) remarks that "there are also Nayars who sell oil and fish, and many are craftsmen."
[197] Dames (ed.), *op. cit.* (n. 5), II, 58.
[198] *Ibid.*, p. 59, n. 1.   [199] *Ibid.*, p. 60.

washermen who serve the polluted castes, are omitted from Ramusio's version of Barbosa's account, but Pires mentions them in the list which Ramusio did publish.[200] The "Canaquas" (*Kaniyans*), a polluted caste still lower on Barbosa's scale, monopolize the manufacture of bucklers and umbrellas and have astrology and fortune telling as important sidelines. The artisans he groups together (castes of the Left-hand?) as "Ageres" (*Asari*), and notes that there are subcastes of masons, carpenters, smiths, metalworkers, and goldsmiths. These groups have their own gods, their own systems of apprenticing sons in their father's trade, and a patrilineal kinship organization. The "Mogeres" (*Mogers*), most of whom "gain their living on the sea," [201] are very few in number and of foreign origin. In addition to fishing and sailing, they work as carriers "of all things belonging to the Royal State" [202] and act as slaves to the Nāyars. They live in their own villages, possess no recognizable "marriage law," and bequeath their properties to their nephews rather than their sons. The "Monquers" (*Mukkuvans*), "who have no other work than fishing," [203] are considered to be expert seamen, rude fellows, and shameless thieves. Though their women "sleep with anyone soever," [204] they marry and pass on their goods to their sons. Some of them are rich landowners who seem to run the danger of having their properties confiscated by the king "whensoever he wills." [205] Still, as a caste they enjoy the privilege of not paying tax on fresh fish, although on dried fish they are required to pay a duty of 4 per cent.

Barbosa seems to descend to a lower level in his caste hierarchy (castes of the Right-hand?) when he talks of the "Betunes" (*Vettuvans*). These poverty-stricken people make salt, grow rice, and live in houses "standing by themselves in the fields." [206] An even ruder people are the "Pāneens" (*Pānans*) "who are great sorcerers and live by no other means." [207] Barbosa describes at some length the ceremonies which they follow when they are called in to help diagnose and prescribe for a sick king. They live in the hinterlands and hills, entirely apart from other people. Being good hunters and mountaineers, they live on game and wild fowl. And, at this point, Barbosa inserts a short description of the "Revoleens," a term which possibly denotes the *Eravallens*, a primitive jungle tribe.[208] Clad only in filthy rags, these poor people carry firewood and grass to the towns. While all of these low-caste people are untouchables, the group most feared by the Nāyars is the "Poleas" (*Pulayans*). These primitive people, who live in "secret lurking places" [209] or mean huts, cultivate rice with

[200] Cortesão (ed.), *op. cit.* (n. 9), I, 72.
[201] Dames (ed.), *op. cit.* (n. 5), II, 64.
[202] *Ibid.*
[203] *Ibid.*
[204] *Ibid.*, p. 65.
[205] *Ibid.*
[206] *Ibid.*
[207] *Ibid.*, p. 66.
[208] For a discussion of this identification see *ibid.*, p. 67, n. 1.
[209] *Ibid.*, p. 68.

buffalos and oxen. This "evil race"[210] will try at certain months of the year to take revenge upon their masters by intentionally polluting Nāyar women. The most degenerate of the lowest castes is the "Pareans" (*Parayans*) who "dwell in the most desert places"[211] and eat cow's flesh. Even though some of them are lettered men, they are thought to be so base that the sight of them will pollute the beholder.[212]

In all, Barbosa identifies eighteen upper and lower castes indigenous to Malabar with "each one separate and unable to touch others or marry with them."[213] He also identifies four immigrant castes as dwelling in Malabar. The first foreign caste on his list is the "Chatis" (*Chettys*),[214] a merchant group. The majority of the "Chatis" are rich merchants who deal in precious stones, pearls, and corals. They dress differently from the natives and possess "spacious houses in their own appointed streets."[215] They speak "a tongue [Konkani] which differs from that of Malabar [Malayālam] as it is with the Castilians and Portuguese."[216] They live outside the local law and maintain peace and order among themselves, apparently to the king's satisfaction. They have their own gods, temples, marital and burial customs, and dietary habits. Evidently they live in peace with the other foreign merchant colony whom Barbosa calls the "Guzarates" (*Gujarati banyā*), and he correctly identifies them as natives of Cambay. These Gujarati merchants dwell in great houses on their own streets "as the Jews are wont to dwell in our land."[217] The rulers of the Malabar cities look upon the Gujarati with favor because of the revenues they pay into the treasury in the form of duties.

Both Barbosa and Barros give considerable attention to the Moors of Malabar. They are described as being of two kinds: those who are natives and those of foreign origin. The mestizo group called "Malpueres" (*Moplahs*)[218] intermarry with low-caste natives. They speak Malayālam and dress like the natives except for little round caps that they wear on their heads as emblems of distinction.[219] Making their living by trade, the indigenous Moors are scattered throughout Malabar, especially in the cities, and constitute about 20 per cent of the total

210 *Ibid.*, p. 69.

211 *Ibid.*

212 Pires in Cortesão (ed.), *op. cit.* (n. 9), I, 72.

213 Dames (ed.), *op. cit.* (n. 5), II, 70. He actually lists only seventeen separate castes, but clearly considers that the kings form a separate caste. Though not exhaustive, Barbosa's listing "includes nearly all the castes of importance which still exist in Malabar." (*Ibid.*, n. 2.)

214 Barros (in Cidade and Múrias [eds.], *op. cit.* [n.6], I, 372–73) calls them *chatins* and reports: "These are men who have a genius for trade and are so sharp in their dealings that our people, whenever they desire to blame or praise a man for his subtlety and skill in bargaining, they say 'He is a *chatim*,' and they use the word *chatinar* for 'to haggle'—these words now being very commonly adopted by us." The modern Portuguese dictionary defines a *chatim* as a "crooked merchant" and *chatinar* as meaning "to deal crookedly."

215 Dames (ed.), *op. cit.* (n. 5), II, 72.

216 *Ibid.*, p. 73.

217 *Ibid.*

218 This is the name used by Barbosa (*ibid.*, p. 75); Barros (in Cidade and Múrias [eds.], *op. cit.* [n. 6], I, 373) refers to these mestizo Moors as "naiteás."

219 They still wear these marks of identification. See Dames (ed.), *op. cit.* (n. 5), II, 74, n. 1.

population. They have a great number of mosques and generally follow the teachings of Mohammed.[220] Barbosa contends that they were so numerous and their influence so great that the advent of the Portuguese was the only thing which prevented Malabar from becoming a Moorish state.

The danger of a Muslim conquest was apparently made even more possible by the presence in Calicut and other Malabar towns of sizable communities of foreign Moors. Arabs, Persians, Gujaratis, Khorasanis, and Daquanis[221] who congregated there with their wives and families were all called "Pardesis" (*Paradēśī* or foreigners). Virtually in control of Malabar's overseas trade, the foreign Moors, like their indigenous co-religionists, enjoy a preferred position because of the substantial revenues that they bring to the towns of Malabar. They are ruled over by their own governor who acts independently except for giving "an account of certain matters to the King"[222] and administers justice according to Muslim precepts. In their keeled ships built without nails the Moors sail for the West with each favorable monsoon. The returns from their spice trade are enough to make most of them wealthy and to attract a constant stream of newcomers to Malabar. The king, ever mindful of the great returns to to be derived from trade and customs, co-operates to the utmost with the foreign traders. As soon as a new merchant arrives at a port city, he is assigned a Nāyar to protect and serve him, a Chetty clerk to keep his records, and a broker to arrange his purchases and sales. This commercial relationship between Malabars and Muslims remains thriving and mutually beneficial until the arrival of the Portuguese in India. "Now," Barbosa laconically comments about the Muslim traders, "there are, it may almost be said, none, and these that are [here] do not live independently."[223]

C. THE HINDU EMPIRE OF VIJAYANAGAR

In about 1346, a century and a half before the Portuguese arrived in India, the Hindus of the Deccan rallied to form a political and military confederation to halt the Muslim onslaught from the north. By 1400, Bukka I had consolidated Vijayanagar's control over the southern half of the peninsula and Hindu civilization hereafter seemed relatively secure in the south. Great ports like Goa, Chaul, and Dabhul were also brought under Vijayanagar's jurisdiction and Ceylon soon became a tributary state. But the northern frontiers of this last citadel of Hindu civilization, especially those fronting on the Bahmani kingdom

---

[220] They are generally Sunnites. Logan, *op. cit.* (n. 59), I, 199.

[221] Probably merchants from Dhaka (often written Dacca) in eastern Bengal, a great center of muslin weaving.

[222] Dames (ed.), *op. cit.* (n. 5), II, 76.

[223] *Ibid.*, p. 78.

in the Deccan, subsequently came under constant pressure from the Muslims as well as from non-Muslim Orissa. The rulers of Vijayanagar thereafter found that they had to be eternally vigilant to prevent their vassals in the border region from revolting and trying to aggrandize themselves by joining forces with the enemy. Still, despite the problem of the unstable northern frontier, the kingdom of Vijayanagar flourished in the fifteenth century, and the city of Vijayanagar rapidly became the economic and cultural center of south India.

The earlier European accounts, those of Conti, Nikitin, and Varthema, describe the wealth and power of Vijayanagar in colorful language if not always in great detail. In 1510, Varthema extravagantly hails the city itself as "a second paradise." [224] Pires, writing between 1512 and 1518, reports that Vijayanagar, reputed to be the largest state in India, was not as extensive as it once had been. [225] This was so because of Muslim expansion in the Deccan and the severance of Goa from Vijayanagar's control.

Viceroy d'Almeida first learned of Vijayanagar in 1505 from a native, and thereafter began to think that Portugal might have more to gain in India by trade than by conquest. [226] Albuquerque in his war against Calicut invited the co-operation of Vijayanagar, and the Franciscan friar, Luis do Salvador, was sent there in 1510 as his emissary. Later in 1510, after Albuquerque captured Goa for the second time, a mission was sent from Vijayanagar to establish friendly relations with the Portuguese and to bring to Albuquerque the written recommendations of Friar Luis. [227] Soon a treaty was concluded with Vijayanagar for the continuation of the traditional horse trade that the Hindu state depended upon so heavily for its military activities. Relations were generally good thereafter for a long time between the Hindus and Christians who were united, if for no other reason, by their common hostility to the Moors. [228]

For the re-creation of sixteenth-century Vijayanagar, the Portuguese sources are of critical importance. Pires makes a number of general comments on it based perhaps on reports which he heard from others in the marts of India. Of special significance is the account of Barbosa written around 1518; Barbosa probably visited Vijayanagar just a few years after Albuquerque's second conquest of Goa in 1510. Shortly after 1520, the Portuguese merchant, Domingo Paes, wrote a lengthy description of Vijayanagar as it was in his day. For the next fifteen years there are extant no Portuguese sources on the Hindu empire. The next important document was prepared around 1535 by Fernão Nuniz, who wrote a chronicle of Vijayanagar based on information which he acquired during three years of residence there (*ca.* 1532–35). It appears that Garcia da Orta, the physician and herbalist of Goa, might have visited Vijayanagar in 1534

[224] J. W. Jones (trans.), and G. P. Badger (ed.), *The Travels of Lodovico di Varthema* . . . ("Hakluyt Society Publications," Old Series, Vol. XXXII [London, 1863]), p. 126.

[225] Cortesão (ed.), *op. cit.* (n. 9), I, 64.

[226] Robert Sewell, *A Forgotten Empire (Vijayanagar)* (London, 1900), p. 117.

[227] Albuquerque in Birch (trans.), *op. cit.* (n. 116), III, 35–38. Friar Luis was shortly thereafter slain "by the hand of a Turk." (*Ibid.*, p. 38.)

[228] Frederick C. Danvers, *The Portuguese in India* (London, 1894), I, 301.

while Nuniz was still there.[229] And it was in these same years (*ca.* 1528–38) that Castanheda was in India. Whether or not he ever visited Vijayanagar is not clear, but it is certain that Castanheda inquired about the Hindu capital from merchants who had been there.[230] Finally, it was around 1537 that the accounts of Paes and Nuniz were dispatched to Portugal, probably addressed to Barros.[231]

Though Barros had these accounts at his disposal while working on the *Décadas*, he evidently made little use of them.[232] Paes provided a good description of Vijayanagar and Nuniz a detailed chronicle, but Barros' references to the Hindu state are relatively few and generally incidental to the development of his larger narrative. Certainly, it may be true that the Paes and Nuniz accounts were circulated in Europe as manuscripts. But, so far as I know, they were not used extensively by later authors, though Castanheda may have derived information from them. The only accounts of Vijayanagar published around mid-century were those by Pires, Barbosa (both in Ramusio's collection) and Castanheda. And, in the case of Castanheda, he repeats almost verbatim several of the eyewitness stories told by Barbosa, though it must not be concluded from these borrowings that Castanheda's account is completely dependent upon the earlier observers. In Orta's *Colloquies* there are a few additional references to Vijayanagar which substantiate and amplify the basic accounts.

The European writers, beginning with Varthema, refer to the empire of Vijayanagar as the "kingdom of Narsinga."[233] The capital city of the empire is called "Bisinegar" as an approximation of Vijayanagar,[234] then the leading metropolis of Kanara. According to Castanheda,[235] Vijayanagara, the largest state in the "second India is bordered on the east by the state of *Deli*,"[236] on the west by the Indian Ocean and Malabar, on the north by the Deccan "kingdom," and on the south by the "kingdom" of "Doria" (Orissa).[237] Barbosa describes the country as being "high and rugged," and "very hard to cross" if one is tempted to leave the seacoast for the interior. On the western side the terrain is so difficult to climb "that it is like mounting to the sky, and so rough . . . that men can only pass through it by certain places and passes." This is, in Barbosa's view, the reason why the coastal Malabars succeeded in maintaining

---

[229] Sewell, *op. cit.* (n. 226), p. 115, n. 2.

[230] Cf. Azevedo (ed.), *op. cit.* (n. 17), I, 246.

[231] Sewell, *op. cit.* (n. 226), p. vi.

[232] His scanty comments are devoted mainly to warfare; see Cidade and Múrias (eds.), *op. cit.* (n. 6), III, 189–93.

[233] Or "Narsyngna," "Narasinha," and "Narsin." This name was apparently derived from the name of the ruler, Vira Narasihma, who was in power until 1509. Varthema probably visited there at the end of 1504. (Sir Richard Carnac Temple [ed.], *The Itinerary of Ludovico di Varthema of Bologna* [London, 1928], p. xxv.)

[234] Also "Bisnegar" or "Bijanagher." Conti, around 1420, refers to it as "Bizenegalia" and Nikitin in 1474 as "Bicheneger." See Yule and Burnell, *op. cit.* (n. 10), p. 73. On the various names under which the city was known to the people of south India see B. A. Saletore, *Social and Political Life in the Vijayanagara Empire* (A.D. 1346–A.D. 1646) (Madras, 1934), I, 112–13.

[235] Azevedo (ed.), *op. cit.* (n. 17), I, 242.

[236] The Delhi sultanate.

[237] Castanheda is certainly misplacing Orissa which is roughly east-northeast of Vijayanagar.

their independence of Vijayanagar. But beyond the mountains on the eastern side of the peninsula, the land is reported to be "flat and level," [238] and presumably no barrier to the spread of Vijayanagar's rule.

Vijayanagar is divided into five "provinces." The first of these political divisions is called "Talinate" [239] and it extends along the west coast from "Cintacora" [240] on the border of the Deccan in the north to the beginning of Malabar in the south, a distance of about fifty leagues (200 miles). For this coastal territory Castanheda gives a list of eleven towns all of which are said to be large and good ports. [241] Barbosa in his separate treatment of these towns indicates clearly that they enjoyed a high degree of political independence. [242] The second province, which borders on the "kingdom" of Deccan and is in the interior, is called "Teãrragei." [243] A third province, also in the interior, is named "Canarâ," and herein is located the capital city of Vijayanagar. "Choramandel" is the fourth province and it extends along the coast for almost a hundred leagues (400 miles) from the southern border of "Coulão" (Quilon) northward to the mountains called the "Udigirmele" [244] which divides "Narsinga" from "Doria." The fifth province is in the interior and is given the name of "Telingue." [245] Except for Castanheda's confusion over the location of "Doria" (Orissa), his account of the extent of Vijayanagar corresponds well with what is known from other sources. [246] His political divisions of the empire appear to be approximately correct, even if unavoidably vague. [247] Pires and Barbosa, unlike Castanheda, pay attention to the language divisions as well, and Barbosa asserts that each province has its own language; [248] in Coromandel, for instance, he knows that the prevailing tongue is Tamil. [249] Pires reports that the ruler of

[238] Dames (ed.), *op. cit.* (n. 5), I, 198–99.

[239] Talinate = Tólinate = Tulu-nãda = North and South Kanara. *Ibid.*, p. 183 n.

[240] The name of this fortress town has disappeared from modern maps, though it is shown on European maps of the sixteenth and seventeenth centuries. Evidently it was situated at the southern extremity of the mainland territory of Goa north of the Liga (now the Kalinadi) River. See note in *ibid.*, p. 171.

[241] These towns in his order are: "Ancolâ," "Manjavarrão," "Bracelos," "Mangalor," "Vdelbarrão," "Caramate," "Bacanor," "Banaverrão," "Baticalo," "Honor," and "Mergen." Similar lists, though not identical ones, are given by Barros (in Cidade and Múrias [eds.], *op. cit.* [n. 6], I, 357) and Barbosa (in Dames [ed.], *op. cit.* [n. 5], I, 182–97). For identification of many of these towns with modern places see *ibid.*

[242] Dames (ed.), *op. cit.* (n. 5), I, 182–87.

[243] Corresponds with the territory called "Danseam Rayen" by Barbosa and may perhaps be identified with modern Bankapur (*ibid.*, p. 183 n.).

[244] The Udayagiri chain south of the Krishna River (*ibid.*, II, 130 n.).

[245] Probably Telingãna, the area in which Telegu is spoken. This designation agrees with that mentioned in Barbosa except that the latter gives it a coastal outlet (see *ibid.*, II, 236).

[246] Under Krishna Dēva Rāyya (reigned 1509–29) the jurisdiction of Vijayanagar extended to all of India south of the Krishna River, except for the Malabar states. For further detail see T. V. Mahalingham, *Administration and Social Life under Vijayanagar* (Madras, 1940), pp. 174–77.

[247] The provinces, known as *rájyas*, had their boundaries changed from time to time to suit administrative requirements. See K. A. N. Sastri, *A History of South India from Prehistoric Times to the Fall of Vijayanagar* (2d ed.; Madras, 1958), p. 298.

[248] Dames (ed.), *op. cit.* (n. 5), I, 183.

[249] *Ibid.*, p. 184.

Vijayanagar speaks Kanarese, and that many other languages are also spoken at his court.[250]

Every one of these provinces is well supplied with rice, meat, fish, fruits, and the game of forest and field. Each is luxuriantly provided with gardens, groves, springs, and rivers.[251] The mountains are covered with forests which shelter wild boars, deer, elephants, ounces, leopards, tigers, bears, and—"certain ash-coloured animals like camels," which are "so swift that no man may kill them"[252]—antelopes. The farmers grow rice and other grains and breed goats, cows, and sheep. Oxen and asses are used as beasts of burden and for plowing. Barbosa notices rice cultivation, both by wet and dry methods, on a fertile plain near "Baticala" (modern Bhatkal). He also indicates that in plowing flooded fields the seeds are sown by a drill contained in the plowshare. After pointing out that the Indians obtain two crops a year, he gives the names of the various grades of rice produced and asserts that "each of these differs from the rest in price."[253]

In the seacoast towns of "Tolinate province" there is "traffic in goods of divers kinds."[254] Coarse, black rice grown in the valley of the "Mergen" (Gangawali) River is traded for coconut and palm products brought in from other places. At Bhatkal and other Kanara ports white rice, powdered sugar, and iron are bought by the merchants of Ormuz and Malabar to exchange for horses and pearls, and for palm products, respectively. Spices, ivory, and copper, used inland for coinage, are all traded in these coastal ports. The rice is husked, cleaned, and packed in uniformly sized bales of its own straw for shipment abroad. Although black rice is cheaper, Barbosa esteems it as being "better and more wholesome than the white."[255]

All of these, and many other more precious items, can be found in the great markets of the capital city "because all the merchants of the world are able to go there safely to buy and sell."[256] To encourage the traders, particularly those who deal in horses, the "king of Narsinga" makes it his business to see that they pass duty-free through his territories from the seaports to the capital.[257] This does not mean, however, that they are exempted from duties at the ports, quite the contrary being true. Finally, the merchants of any faith may trade freely in the city "without suffering any annoyance and without inquiry."[258]

---

[250] Cortesão (ed.), *op. cit.* (n. 9), I, 69.

[251] General description of Castanheda in Azevedo (ed.), *op. cit.* (n. 17), I, 242.

[252] Barbosa in Dames (ed.), *op. cit.* (n. 5), I, 199.

[253] *Ibid.*, p. 192.

[254] *Ibid.*, p. 184.

[255] *Ibid.*, p. 195 and n. 1.

[256] Castanheda in Azevedo (ed.), *op. cit.* (n. 17), I, 245. He also lists many of the commodities available in the capital, including among them the "velvet taffetas of Mecca" and "the camphor of Borneo."

[257] *Ibid.* This fact is not mentioned, so far as I know, in any other contemporary Western source. Nor is it noticed in G. S. Dixit, "Economic Conditions in the Time of Krishnadevaraya," in the *Vijayanagara Sexcentenary Commemoration Volume* (Dhaswar, 1936), pp. 220–24.

[258] Barbosa in Dames (ed.), *op. cit.* (n. 5), I, 202.

The diamonds, precious stones, and jewelry of Vijayanagar are commented upon in some detail by all the Portuguese writers. In Kanara, and also in the Deccan, diamonds of enormous size and great value are mined and brought to be marketed in the capital.[259] Orta describes the mining of diamonds as an industry from which the ruler of Vijayanagar obtains great revenue.[260] Guards are placed at the mines to supervise the work and to make certain that the largest diamonds get safely to the royal court. All diamonds weighing 30 *mangelims* or more belong to the king, and some, according to Castanheda, reach 200 *mangelims* in size.[261] The ruler of Vijayanagar entrusts his huge diamonds to skilled lapidaries and apparently manages to market the cut and polished stones at a vast profit to himself. Other semi-precious stones such as amethysts and sapphires are found in the streams and rivers of the mountainous areas.[262] Any precious stones or jewels not native to the country, such as pearls, are readily imported.[263] These, along with imported coral, gold, and copper, are made up into all sorts of jewelry and other ornamental baubles. Even some of their umbrellas, which "are so made as to open and shut," [264] are inlaid with precious stones and covered with fine silk ornamented by gold tassels. So skilled are the lapidaries and jewelers that they fabricate a wide variety of false stones to meet the great demand for rings, earrings, nose jewels, and ornamental pieces like coral branches.[265] To put it mildly, the Portuguese were impressed by the great quantity of precious stones and fine jewelry available in Vijayanagar and never seem to tire of describing how jewels are used for personal adornment by both sexes.

The city of Vijayanagar as the entrepôt, administrative center, and royal residence occupies the center of the stage in all accounts of the empire. Situated forty leagues (160 miles) inland, the city stands in the midst of a "very level plain" between two great mountain ranges.[266] On one side of the city runs a great river (the Tungabhadrā) and in its outskirts stand low hills covered with mammoth boulders. The city itself, except for the river fort, is encircled with

---

[259] *Ibid.* Castanheda in Azevedo (ed.), *op. cit.* (n. 17), I, 242; Orta in Markham (ed.), *op. cit.* (n. 4), p. 345. The diamond mine of Kanara was probably at Vijrakurur, north of the Krishna and about twenty miles southwest of Gooty (Dixit, *loc. cit.* [n. 257], p. 218), or in the neighborhood of Kamul, south of the Krishna (Dames [ed.], *op. cit.* [n. 5], I, 227 n). For further confirmatory detail see Sewell, *op. cit.* (n. 226), appendix A, pp. 399–401, who says that "in their way they were the richest in the world." These mines were subsequently referred to as the fabulous Golconda centers of diamond production.

[260] Markham (ed.), *op. cit.* (n. 4), p. 235.

[261] Azevedo (ed.), *op. cit.* (n. 17), I, 246. *Mangelim*, equivalent more or less to a carat, is derived from the Telegu, *mañjāli*, or Tamil, *mañjādi*. See Dalgado, *op. cit.* (n. 44), II, 29–30. Orta himself claims to have seen a diamond weighing 140 *mangelims* and to have heard from a trustworthy informant that "he saw one in Bisnaguer the size of a small hen's egg." (Markham [ed.], *op. cit.* [n. 4], p. 437.)

[262] Barbosa in Dames (ed.), *op. cit.* (n. 5), I, 200.

[263] *Ibid.*, p. 227.

[264] *Ibid.*, p. 207.

[265] See the part of Barbosa which appears in Ramusio, but not in the extant manuscripts, as translated in *ibid.*, II, 221–22.

[266] *Ibid.*, I, 201. Castanheda (Azevedo [ed], *op. cit.* [n. 17], I, 244) places it sixty leagues (240 miles) from the coast.

strong ramparts.[267] Within the walls the city is divided into streets that funnel into great squares. The royal palaces are numerous, well built, and enclosed by courtyards. The great lords of the city likewise live in fine stone palaces and travel about the city in elegant litters. The houses of the common people are thatched, "but nonetheless are very well built and arranged according to occupations, in long streets with many open places." [268] The people of the capital are numerous beyond counting and the streets overflow with the multitude of them.[269]

In this city the "king," called "Rayen" (*rāyya* or *rājā*), [270] has his residences and he stays in them unless at war. Dwelling in great luxury, the "king" leaves the administration of the realm in the hands of his provincial governors. But should his governors or lords prove to be unworthy of trust, the royal vengeance is swift and terrible. Barbosa and Castanheda describe graphically how the rājā severely punishes those nobles who deserve it without respect to their rank, connections, or wealth.[271] Indeed, some of the nobles so disciplined are reputed to "possess more land than some kings in Europe." [272] The "king's" justice is meted out in a public hall where he holds regular audiences; his will is respected as being final and absolute.[273] Nevertheless, justice is administered with great equity "not only by the rulers, but by the people." [274]

On occasion disputes are settled by the sword. Castanheda writes: "There are many duels over women whom they love in which many men lose their lives."[275] Duels are also fought between officials who are at odds over administrative problems. Such disputants receive permission to fight a duel from the king, who assigns them a field of battle, seconds, and judges. Should they be men of position, the king himself may go to watch the duel. The combatants fight naked, except for turbans on their heads, with daggers, swords, and shields. Such combats are usually over quickly, and the king awards to the victor a golden chain (*berid*) [276] to wear on his right arm as a symbol of his valor. Custom

---

[267] In Castanheda's account the capital is described as having the shape of a half-moon. On this point and its symbolic significance see Saletore, *op. cit.* (n. 234), I, 121.

[268] Barbosa in Dames (ed.), *op. cit.* (n. 5), I, 202.

[269] *Ibid.* Pires (in Cortesão [ed.], *op. cit.* [n. 9], I, 64) estimates that the population is 20,000, though he apparently never actually visited the city himself. It is estimated by modern scholars that the city had a population of 500,000 in the first half of the sixteenth century. See Dixit, *loc cit.* (n. 257), p. 215.

[270] This term used by Barbosa in Dames (ed.), *op. cit.* (n. 5), I, 201; the "king" in his day was Krishna Dēva Rāyya.

[271] Castanheda in Azevedo (ed.), *op. cit.* (n. 17), I, 246; and Barbosa in Dames (ed.), *op. cit.* (n. 5), I, 208-09.

[272] Castanheda in Azevedo (ed.), *op. cit.* (n. 217), I, 246.

[273] *Ibid.* For a more balanced view of the king's role in administration and justice see Mahalingham, *op. cit.* (n. 246), pp. 9-26.

[274] Barbosa in Dames (ed.), *op. cit.* (n. 5), I, 202.

[275] Azevedo (ed.), *op. cit.* (n. 17), I, 243; for other confirmatory literature see Saletore, *op. cit.* (n. 234), II, 416-19, and Barbosa's similar account of dueling at Bhatkal in Dames (ed.), *op. cit.* (n. 5), I, 190-91.

[276] Sanskrit: *biruda*—a device or insignia of superiority or excellence in the form of an arm-bracelet or chain. See Dalgado, *op. cit.* (n. 44), I, 119.

ordains that he who possesses the golden chain must accept further challenges in order to keep it. In addition to helping settle disputes, dueling is described as a source of amusement and sport.

The Portuguese particularly delight in recounting how elegantly the rulers live, Castanheda asserting that they are waited upon with greater splendor than the "kings" of Malabar.[277] Barbosa insists that "the King and the country-people marry almost in our way, and have a marriage-law," though they may marry as many wives as they can maintain. Castanheda alleges that the "king" does not marry, though he keeps more than three hundred concubines.[278] Both agree that there are many serving women in the palace who are the daughters of the leading families in the realm. These women do all the work of the household, sing and play for the king's amusement, and are well maintained at his expense.[279] Every afternoon they bathe in the numerous tanks within the palace enclosure, and on this occasion the "king" chooses the most appealing of them for his pleasure. The women of the seraglio vie with each other for the "king's" favor so intensely "that some kill others and some poison themselves"[280] when they are scorned or passed over. The first son born to any of the "king's" wives or mistresses is regarded as the heir.[281] On other data regarding succession both Barbosa and Castanheda are silent.

The wealth of Vijayanagar "is the greatest known to the whole world."[282] This is true, in part, because each king is responsible for adding to it and must not touch the accumulated treasure of his predecessors.[283] Among the most prized of the royal possessions are the elephants and horses, the king usually possessing more than 900 elephants and 20,000 horses.[284] Special kitchens are maintained by the "king" to prepare the food for his prized horses and elephants. Nobody is permitted to own horses for personal use. Those held by the crown are parceled out to the great lords for care and maintenance, "and they must continually give accounts of them."[285] Each knight is furnished with a horse, a groom, a serving maid, a monthly allowance, and daily supplies for the horse and groom. Horses, though well taken care of, generally do not thrive or survive very long in south India, and hence are highly valued and very expensive to buy.

The people of Vijayanagar are of tawny color and wear their black hair long and straight. "The men are of good height," Barbosa comments, "and with facial features like our own."[286] Both sexes are well formed and handsome,

277 Azevedo (ed.), *op. cit.* (n. 17), I, 245.

278 *Ibid.* For further details and discussion see Saletore, *op. cit.* (n. 234), II, 174–76.

279 Cf. Pires (in Cortesão [ed.], *op. cit.* [n. 9], I, 65), who alleges that the rājā has one thousand girl entertainers and four or five thousand male performers.

280 Barbosa in Dames (ed.), *op. cit.* (n. 5), I, 208.

281 *Ibid.* It appears that the heir apparent (*yuvarājā*) was not always the eldest son. For this and related matters see Mahalingham, *op. cit.* (n. 246), pp. 11–14.

282 Castanheda in Azevedo (ed.), *op. cit.* (n. 17), I, 246.   283 *Ibid.*

284 Barbosa in Dames (ed.), *op. cit.* (n. 5), I, 210.

285 *Ibid.*

286 *Ibid.*, p. 205.

the women being especially attractive.[287] The men wear girdle-like clothes, with short white shirts which are open in front and pulled down between the thighs. On their feet they wear sandals and on their heads turbans or caps. Some boast garments thrown over their shoulders like capes, and many wear rings and earrings set with precious stones and pearls.[288] The women wear white or colored wrappers of thin cotton or silk which are five yards long. These *saris* (though Barbosa does not use this word) they tie around themselves in such a way that only one arm and shoulder remain uncovered.[289] On their feet they wear embroidered shoes, keep their heads uncovered, dress their hair gathered in a knot at the top, and adorn it with flowers. In their noses and ears they wear precious stones, around their necks they hang necklaces of gold, jewels, and coral beads, and on their arms they fit costly bracelets. Lavish costumes are so common that Barbosa is led to conclude that "the more part of this people is very wealthy."[290]

Like their ruler, the majority of the people of Vijayanagar are "heathens." Most of these "idolaters" worship a god (Vishnu or Shiva) whom they hold to be "lord of everything."[291] They also believe in demons, witchcraft, and sorcery, and are tolerant of the beliefs of others. They celebrate the "Sabbath" on the sixth day, and they believe that the evil are punished and that the good go to their glory.[292] Throughout the kingdom there are many temples (*pagodes*) dedicated to their gods which receive heavy contributions from the "king" and the rest of the faithful. Great festivals are held at these temples to which people make pilgrimages from afar. As an example of their superstition, Castanheda tells the story of a ruler who when ill promised to give his weight in gold to the temple. When, after weighing himself, he gave the clothes which he wore to the priest of the temple, the latter fell dead while dressing in them.[293] Such stories they believe in, as well as in bad omens and the predictions of sorcerers. From such remarks it was clearly not possible for European readers to understand much about Hinduism and the practices associated with it.

Each of Vijayanagar's political divisions includes a substantial number of towns and cities. In the seacoast towns the Moors are especially prominent and numerous; in the interior the cities are peopled almost entirely by the "gentiles."[294] These "gentiles" are divided into three distinct classes:[295] (1) royalty, aristocracy, and soldiery; (2) Brahmans; and (3) a priestly-merchant group called "Baneanes" (*Banyā*) by Castanheda.[296] Such divisions do not correspond

[287] Castanheda in Azevedo (ed.), *op. cit.* (n. 17), I, 243.
[288] Barbosa in Dames (ed.), *op. cit.* (n. 5), I, 205.
[289] *Ibid.*, p. 207.
[290] *Ibid.*, p. 208.
[291] Castanheda in Azevedo (ed.), *op. cit.* (n. 17), I, 242.
[292] *Ibid.*, p. 243.
[293] *Ibid.*, pp. 246–47.
[294] *Ibid.*, p. 242.
[295] Barbosa in Dames (ed.), *op. cit.* (n. 5), I, 212.
[296] Azevedo (ed.), *op. cit.* (n. 17), I, 242. For discussion of "Baneanes" see below, pp. 378–79. For comments on this class division see Saletore, *op. cit.* (n. 234), II, 28–29.

to the caste system, but are probably the classes which seemed individually most distinct to observers from Europe. The members of this first class are distinguished by their polygamy, filial inheritance customs, and the practice of *sati*. Both Barros and Castanheda discourse on sati at length and in a similar vein. The Brahmans, "who are priests and rulers of their houses of worship," [297] are distinguished by their adherence to monogamy, to dietary regulations which forbid their eating anything "subject to death," [298] and to full exemption from the death penalty. As a mark of distinction, the Brahmans wear three linen threads over their shoulders. Some Brahmans live from alms, others have estates of their own, and others reside in the numerous and sumptuous temples which exist everywhere. These pagodes often have good revenues from land which are supplemented by earnings from temple prostitutes. Little girls are educated in the temples "for similar work after they come of age." The Brahmans are alleged never to work "except to feed well" [299] on a diet consisting of honey, butter, rice, sugar, pulse, and milk.

The "Baneanes" (*Banyā*),[300] who are described as similar to the Brahmans, are highly respected and looked upon as holy men. As their mark of distinction, the members of this third group wear around their necks a little cloth bag suspended from twisted cords which contains an egg-shaped stone called a *tambarane* that they believe is their god.[301] Possession of this sacred stone insures their safety wherever they go, and for this reason they are often entrusted with transporting merchandise and money and with carrying on trade in distant parts. In their dietary habits they are vegetarians; in their marital customs they are monogamous. Upon the death of a husband, the wife is buried alive.[302] Barbosa also describes, perhaps for the first time, the hook-swinging ceremony: a sacrifice which a young maiden of the class who is about to be married makes in blood to the god who has helped her win the husband of her choice.[303] He

---

[297] Barbosa in Dames (ed.), *op. cit.* (n. 5), I, 217.

[298] *Ibid.* This also sets them apart from the members of the first class who eat all meats excepting beef.

[299] *Ibid.*

[300] The descriptions of this group by Barbosa and Castanheda are very similar; in fact, I suspect that Castanheda "borrowed" his account from Barbosa. The greatest difference comes in Castanheda's designation of them as "Baneanes," for Barbosa does not use this term in this particular portion of his book. Ordinarily, the term "Baneanes," as used by the Portuguese writers, refers to the merchants of Gujarat (see Dalgado, *op. cit.* [n. 44], I, 93–95): on other occasions it is used to apply to merchants working in the Dravidian areas. But Damião de Góis in his chronicle published in 1566, perhaps following Castanheda, refers to the "Baneanes" of "Narsinga" (*ibid.*, p. 94) as a distinct class of Vijayanagar.

[301] Barbosa in Dames (ed.), *op. cit.* (n. 5), I, 218. In this connection *tambarane* probably refers to the linga, or phallic symbol, thought to be "Siva himself," which is often worn by members of the Lingāyat sect. For the derivation and use of the word *tambarane* see Dalgado, *op. cit.* (n. 44), II, 346–47.

[302] On this custom of the Lingāyats see Edgar Thurston, *Castes and Tribes of Southern India* (7 vols.; Madras, 1909), IV, 236–91. Barbosa (in Dames [ed.], *op. cit.* [n. 5], I, 22) gives a truncated but interesting description of this ceremony.

[303] See account and notes in Dames (ed.), *op. cit.* (n. 5), I, 220–22. For a modern description see E. Thurston, *Ethnographic Notes on South India* (Madras, 1906), pp. 487–501.

also describes a ceremony in which young girls who dedicate their maidenhood to the gods are deflowered.[304] From such descriptions of cultural traits it would seem that Castanheda's designation of this class as "Baneanes" was correct only in the sense that this was a merchant group; actually the ceremonies described seem more typical of the *Lingāyats*, the phallic worshippers of Shiva, who still live in the environs of the ruins of Vijayanagar.

The rulers of Vijayanagar "are always at war with their neighboring rulers," Castanheda reports, and so they constantly have at hand "great multitudes of men, on foot as well as on horseback, to whom they pay wages."[305] In strength this permanent army is estimated to number more than 100,000 by the most conservative of the foreign observers,[306] and all agree, no matter what figures they give, that this is an immense military establishment that the rulers of Vijayanagar regularly maintain. Fighting men of all classes and nationalities, even Muslims, are attracted to serve in the army of Vijayanagar by steady pay, good treatment, and regular work. The system of enlistment particularly attracts the attention of the Portuguese writers, for a prospective soldier apparently gets on the royal payroll only after submitting to a thorough examination.[307] The recruit, especially if a foreigner, is required to appear before four secretaries who examine his nude body to observe its physical condition and to note any distinguishing marks. They also record his name, age, color, height, creed, place of origin, and the names of his parents. Once he has satisfied these requirements, the recruit's name is entered on the royal payroll at a salary that may range from three to fifteen *pardāos* of gold, presumably depending upon the type of post to which he has been assigned. After entering the service of Vijayanagar, the foreign recruit is forbidden to leave the country but is permitted to live according to his own faith and customs. Should he leave the jurisdiction of Vijayanagar without permission, and then be captured, he may expect to be "very evilly entreated."[308] In addition to fighting men, the rulers of Vijayanagar keep on their regular payroll a large number[309] of unmarried courtesans who are allotted to the various fighting groups. For, Barbosa reports, the ruler "says that war cannot be waged where there are no women."[310] Naturally, many of these women are also attached to the royal camp whenever the king goes on a campaign. The courtesans are also credited with attracting many foreign soldiers to take service with Vijayanagar.

[304] In Dames (ed.), *op. cit.* (n. 5), I, 222–23; evidently this was also a ceremony connected with the phallic worship of the Lingāyats.

[305] In Azevedo (ed.), *op. cit.* (n. 17), I, 247. Barbosa qualifies this assertion somewhat by noting that they are "oftentimes" at war with the rulers of the Deccan and Orissa (Dames [ed.], *op. cit.* [n. 5], I, 223–24).

[306] For comparative figures see Saletore, *op. cit.* (n. 234), I, 414–19.

[307] The details are given by Castanheda in Azevedo (ed.), *op. cit.* (n. 17), I, 247.

[308] Barbosa in Dames (ed.), *op. cit.* (n. 5), I, 212.

[309] Four to six thousand are the numbers usually mentioned.

[310] Dames (ed.), *op. cit.* (n. 5), I, 212. Castanheda asserts that these women were paid at a high rate and that with their support an army would fight six times better than without them (Azevedo [ed.], *op. cit.* [n. 17], I, 248).

The rājā rarely goes to war himself but when he does it is apparently a great spectacle and a tortuous effort. He leaves the capital accompanied by a colorful retinue and sets up camp on an open plain. Then he lets it be known throughout his realm that he will depart for the battlefield on a particular date. All the people are required at the appointed time to leave the capital with all their possessions, except for those who remain behind to guard the palaces, fortresses, and temples. Once the evacuation is complete, it is ordered that all the thatched houses of the common folk be burned[311] so that the levies will have no desire left to return home, and will fight better to protect and provide for their families. Once this horde is assembled, the camp is razed, a day's short march ensues, and then a "great town of straw"[312] is again hastily thrown up on a new camping site. Such camps are constructed with streets and open spaces, and while on the march the mass army lives in temporary quarters for three-day periods. Each time they leave the camp it is burned behind them as the motley array slowly progresses toward the battlefield.

The Portuguese give no table of organization for the army of Vijayanagar, but it is possible to conclude from their rambling accounts that the Hindus have infantry and cavalry units, a special corps of armored elephants, and all sorts of provisioning units and entertainment personnel. In this connection Castanheda remarks that whenever "they add a thousand [soldiers] to an army, two thousand [servitors] must also be recruited."[313] The camp followers are unarmed, and the serving men have no defensive armor except shields. The cavalrymen are outfitted with great padded tunics, heavy leather jackets, and helmets; they are armed with Moorish poniards, lances, and javelins. While the horse brigades are obviously numerous and well equipped, the flower of the Vijayanagar army is the terrifying elephant corps. These colossal beasts when prepared for war are covered with copper trimmings and their trunks are similarly protected. On their tusks are fastened great two-edged swords with which they kill many of the enemy by rampaging through their ranks. Wooden towers are strapped to the backs of the leading elephants from which as many as eight archers launch their arrows against the enemy. The vast army of Vijayanagar led by war elephants is, in Castanheda's words, "a very beautiful sight to behold."[314] But, despite the strength of Vijayanagar's arms, its ruler recognizes the might of Portugal and sends emissaries to deal with the viceroy stationed at Cannanore.[315]

---

[311] This may have been an interpolation by the copyist who acquired Barbosa's account for Ramusio (Dames [ed.], *op. cit.* [n. 5], I, 225, n. 1). Nevertheless, it was published in Europe and a similar account of the razing of the capital is given by Castanheda (in Azevedo [ed.], *op. cit.* [n. 17], I, 248).

[312] Barbosa in Dames (ed.), *op. cit.* (n.5), I, 227; for a word picture of a Hindu camp see Saletore, *op. cit.* (n. 234), I, 450–57.

[313] Azevedo (ed.), *op. cit.* (n. 17), I, 247.

[314] *Ibid.*

[315] *Ibid.*, p. 248.

D. THE DECCAN STATES AND GOA

Once the Portuguese became active in the affairs of south India, the Muslim states to the north, in alliance with their coreligionists from Egypt, Turkey, and Persia, prepared a counteroffensive to drive the Europeans out. The Muslim headquarters for a southern push against the Portuguese footholds were the ports of the Deccan and Gujarat, great centers in the Arabic trade with India. Even before the Portuguese arrived in India, the strategic control of Goa, one of these Deccan ports, was hotly contested by the Hindu rulers of Vijayanagar and the Muslim rulers of the Deccan. This island fortress, which is described by Pires as being "as strong as Rhodes,"[316] was taken by the Muslims in 1470 and they held it until Albuquerque in 1510 brought it under the sway of Portugal. Although it was Albuquerque's hope that the taking of Goa would keep "India in repose and quiet,"[317] the Portuguese quickly learned that the Bahmani rulers of the Deccan,[318] divided though they were among themselves, would nonetheless continue to be a source of trouble.

The Deccan (meaning "the south") in its broadest sense is often used to designate all of India south of the Vindhyan hills.[319] The Portuguese writers of the sixteenth century, however, consistently use the word "Decão" or "Daqué" with reference to the Muslim states which, though their jurisdiction varied greatly from time to time, generally extended inland from Chaul in the north to the Tungabhadrā River in the south. Though the earliest Portuguese travelers refer to these territories, their remarks are generally limited to the coastal towns and to matters of trade. Orta is the only one who speaks of the Deccan kingdoms from extensive personal experience. Castanheda writes of them from limited direct exposure and the reports of others. Barros, in Portugal, who gives the most connected and intelligible historical account, bases his narrative to a large extent on a "Deccan chronicle" which he had in his possession. He used this source rather than others because it conforms "much better in its chronology to the general Persian chronicle" which he refers to repeatedly as the "Tarigh" (*Ta'rīkh*) or "History." Clearly, Barros had before him, when he wrote, the translations of several Muslim histories, and this was almost a century before Ferishta (also known as Mohammed Kasim) wrote his basic Persian account of the rise of Muslim power in India.[320]

---

[316] Cortesão (ed.), *op. cit.* (n. 9), I, 58.

[317] Birch (trans.), *op. cit.* (n. 116), III, 259.

[318] For an excellent recent study of these rulers based on most of the available Muslim sources see H. K. Sherwani, *The Bahmanis of the Deccan* (Hyderbad-Deccan, 1953). Consult also for the general picture N. Venkataramanya, *The Early Muslim Expansion in South India* (Madras, 1942).

[319] For a discussion of the nomenclature and extent of the Deccan see H. Raychaudhuri, "Geography of the Deccan," in G. Yazdani (ed.), *The Early History of the Deccan* (London, 1960), pp. 3–4.

[320] Another basic Persian source written in about 1630 is Alî Bin 'Assîz-Ullâh Ṭabâṭabâ, *Burhân-i Ma-âṣir (History of the Bāhmanī Dynasty)*. Translated in an epitomized version by J. S. King in *Indian Antiquary*, XXVIII (1899), 119–38, 141–55, 180–92, 209–19, 235–47, 277–92, 305–23; XXIX (1900), 4–8. Where the two Persian accounts differ on dates, numismatic evidence seems to support Ṭabâṭabâ. For a general survey of the Muslim sources of Deccan history see Sherwani, *op. cit.* (n. 318), pp. 424–37.

Barros reports that in the year 707 of the Muslim calendar, or A.D. 1300,[321] the Sultan of Delhi, "Xá Nasaradim,"[322] began a campaign to conquer the Hindu states of south India. He descended upon the Hindu state of "Canarâ" (Kanara) which then extended from north of Chaul inland and southward to Cape Comorin, being bounded in the west by numerous petty kingdoms and on the east by Orissa. After pillaging and looting, "Xá Nasaradim" returned to Delhi and left in charge of his conquests in Kanara his captain named "Habede-Xá."[323] The latter, who had only a handful of men at his disposal to maintain control over the large and hostile Hindu population, was forced gradually to pull back toward the north. Finally, he consolidated his position and recruited troops from the Hindu converts to Islam, the Christians[324] and from people of varied backgrounds. He held this motley army together by paying the soldiers well, and was subsequently able over a period of twenty years to become powerful enough to found his own dynasty and to win recognition of his preponderance in the Deccan from the court at Delhi.[325]

With the death of the founder of the Bahmani dynasty, Barros reports that his son, "Mamudi-Xá"[326] (Mohammed I, 1358–75), was confirmed in his inheritance by the Sultan of Delhi[327] upon agreeing to pay more tribute than had his father. After meeting the exactions of Delhi for several years, he became sufficiently powerful in his own right to cancel further payments and to refuse to dispatch troops to aid the Delhi ruler in the war then being waged against Persia. Fearing that his recalcitrance would bring reprisals once the war was over, the Deccan ruler allied himself with the Muslim lord of Gujarat. But fortune favored Mohammed I for the Sultan of Delhi died in the war and a difficult period ensued for the northern sultanate. Taking advantage of this situation, Mohammed I declared his independence of Delhi and exalted himself Sultan of "Canarâ," renaming it the "Decão." And this name, it is said, was given to the new kingdom to represent the many different peoples inhabiting it, for in the local language *deçani* means *mestiços*.[328]

Being aged, weary of war, and fearful over the future of his dynasty,

---

[321] The Deccan chronicler, whom Barros uses, gives dates which are exactly twenty years earlier than those listed in the "established chronology" in the Appendix of Sherwani, *op. cit.* (n. 318), pp. 438–44. I have not been able to identify Barros' source, though it is clear that a number of chronicles were then available.

[322] Sultan Julāl-ud-Din. Orta puts this event "about three hundred years ago," or more than a century before it happened (Markham [ed.], *op. cit.* [n. 4], p. 69).

[323] Probably Hasan, who proclaimed himself Sultan of the Deccan in 1347 under the title Alā-ud-Dīn Bāhman Shah.

[324] The presence of "Franks" (presumably European Christians) in the armies of the Deccan is noted in Sherwani, *op. cit.* (n. 318), pp. 81–82. They, along with the Turks, probably brought gunpowder and cannon into the Deccan wars.

[325] Barros in Cidade and Múrias (eds.), *op. cit.* (n. 6), II, 193–94. On this twenty-year period from 1327 to 1347 see Sherwani, *op. cit.* (n. 318), 20–25.

[326] Mohammed I is traditionally known as the organizer of the kingdom.

[327] Probably Firoz Tughlug.

[328] As in a number of other cases, Barros (in Cidade and Múrias [eds.], *op. cit.* [n. 6], II, 195) seems to be wrong in this etymology. See Yule and Burnell, *op. cit.* (n. 10), p. 233.

Mohammed I decentralized his state by dividing its administration among eighteen[329] of his captains and appointing one of them captain-general to watch over the rest. Each captain was charged with defending his own district and with providing from local taxation for the payment of a stipulated number of infantry and cavalry. In an effort to keep these captains from becoming too independent, they were not raised to the nobility and were forbidden to marry except with their own slaves. The captains were also obliged to establish a residence in the capital city of Bīdar[330] in which they were required to live a certain number of months each year. When they were not there personally, their residences were to be occupied by a son or near relative who would perform in their stead the required daily rituals of vassalage.[331]

Barros then describes at some length the ceremonies and reverences ("salema" or *salaams*) which the vassals are required to make before the Sultan, and of how the supplicant is invested with a "Cabaia"[332] as a reward for his loyalty and services. On festival occasions the captains are not permitted to send substitutes, but have to present themselves personally before the ruler, the only excuse being serious illness or involvement in war. Failure to appear in normal times is considered tantamount to rebellion. Apparently, the Portuguese historian is not greatly impressed with this device for maintaining loyalty, because he goes on to remark that it was not long after Mohammed's time that the disintegration of the Deccan state began. With this observation he concludes his brief historical sketch and undertakes to describe the political condition of the Deccan when the Portuguese arrived in India.

Castanheda, who sees the Deccan primarily from the viewpoint of a European resident of Goa, presents a very sketchy and disconnected account of its history during the period of its "last three kings."[333] He himself was in India (1528–38) during the waning years of the Bahmani dynasty at the time when Kalimer ul-lāh ruled (1526–38) the Deccan. Of this king's two predecessors, whose jurisdictions were confined to the environs of Bīdar, Castanheda condemns the first one, possibly Ahmud IV, as "a man greatly given to all the vices of sensuality"[334] and completely incapable of governing. The next king, possibly Alā-ud-dīn Shah (reigned 1520–23), is a quite different type; he devotes himself to good living and to an effort to recover what his intemperate predecessors had lost. Believing his own people to be too unreliable and enervated, he sent to

---

[329] He certainly founded the provincial structure of government which prevailed almost to the end of the Bahmani dynasty (*ca.* 1538), but nowhere else can I find mention of this number. For more details see Sherwani, *op. cit.* (n. 318), p. 80.

[330] At this period the capital was actually at Gulbarga. It was not moved to Bīdar until 1422.

[331] Barros in Cidade and Múrias (eds.), *op. cit.* (n. 6), II, 195. On Mohammed's durbars, held daily except for Fridays, see Sherwani, *op. cit.* (n. 318), pp. 77–78.

[332] Barros (in Cidade and Múrias [eds.], *op. cit.* [n. 6], II, 195–96) describes this tunic of brocade, silk, or muslin in some detail, and rightly mentions that it was generally used by all the Moors "in those parts." For additional discussion see Yule and Burnell, *op. cit.* (n. 10), pp. 105–06, and Dalgado, *op. cit.* (n. 44), I, 158–59.

[333] Azevedo (ed.), *op. cit.* (n. 17), I, 286.

[334] *Ibid.* Cf. similar description in Sherwani, *op. cit.* (n. 318), pp. 414–15.

Arabia for mercenaries to help him regain his power.[335] The last king of the Deccan reverted to a life of intemperance and sloth, and as a consequence he was unable to control his nominal feudatories or even retain Bīdar to pass on to his son.

The divided condition of the Deccan kingdom in the sixteenth century is commented on by the Portuguese at some length. Barros notes that of the eighteen provinces created by Mohammed I in the fourteenth century a number of the stronger had taken over the weaker. Castanheda contends that twelve kingdoms had emerged from the original provinces and Barros lists six of them. Both agree that the ruler of Goa, the "Sabaio"[336] or "Cabai," was the most powerful of the Deccan rulers before Albuquerque captured Goa. The other great lords of the Deccan are entitled, according to Barros, "Nizamaluco,"[337] "Madremaluco,"[338] "Melique Verido,"[339] "Cogi Mocadao,"[340] and "Cotamaluco."[341] Orta, who gives the greatest detail on these Deccan rulers, insists that all of them are foreigners, presumably from western Muslim countries, except for his friend, the "Nizamaluco," who is said to be a native of the Deccan.[342] The "Sabaio" and the "Nizamaluco" possess between them the territory along the seacoast and inland to the Ghats.[343] All of the other provinces are in the "Ballagate," a term used by the Portuguese to mean the Ghat highlands.

On the basis of the Portuguese accounts it is impossible to learn much about the territorial holdings of the Deccan rulers. Barbosa, who describes a number of the port cities, contents himself by saying that their possessions "extend far inland,"[344] and Pires notes that there are twenty principal inland towns.[345] Castanheda describes the Deccan as one of the greatest states of India with a coastline of seventy leagues (280 miles) which borders on the north with Cambay (Gujarat) and which extends into the interior to the frontiers of Vijayanagar

[335] Cf. with the recruitment of Abyssinian slaves during the fifteenth century in Bengal. See below, p. 416.

[336] Probably the popular title of Yūsuf 'Ādil Khan whose capital was at Bijapur. Barros (in Cidade and Múrias [eds.], *op. cit.* [n. 6], II, 197) says that this title was derived from his native place, Sava, in Persia. For additional comment see Dames (ed.), *op. cit.* (n. 5), I, 172–73, n. 1; Markham (ed.), *op. cit.* (n. 4), pp. 73–74; and Cortesão (ed.), *op. cit.* (n. 9), I, 50.

[337] Popular title (Nizamu 'l-Mulk or "The Regulator of the State") for Burhan Nizam Shah whose capital was at Ahmadnagar. Orta (Markham [ed.], *op. cit.* [n. 4], p. 7) describes him as "being well read in his own literature" and as patronizing Turkish and Persian doctors at his court.

[338] A popular title (correctly rendered as Imad 'l-Mulk) which probably refers in this instance to Fath-Ullah 'Imad Shah whose capital was at Berar.

[339] Popular title of the princes who established themselves at Bīdar around the end of the fifteenth century.

[340] Possibly the same as Orta's "Mohadum Coja" (Markham [ed.], *op. cit.* [n. 4], p. 71) who held a number of important places in Sholapur.

[341] Popular title (correctly rendered as Kutb-ub-Mulk or the "Pole Star of the State") for the rulers of the Golconda dynasty.

[342] Markham (ed.), *op. cit.* (n. 4), p. 71.

[343] *Ibid.*, pp. 70–71.

[344] Dames (ed.), *op. cit.* (n. 5), I, 158.

[345] Of these, the largest in numbers of inhabitants are Bīdar, Bijapur, Sholapur, Raichur, Sagar, Kulbarga, and two unidentifiable places. See Cortesão (ed.), *op. cit.* (n. 9), I, 49.

and Orissa. None of the Portuguese seems to know that in 1472 Bahmani supremacy extended across the peninsula from sea to sea and included a large part of Orissa within its dominion. Orta tries to describe the holdings of a few of the rulers as they were in his day, but his remarks are very indefinite. Barros lists the names of the inland cities left to the "Sabaio" after Albuquerque's conquest of Goa, but leaves further discussion of them to his *Geografia*, which he mentions so often in the *Décadas*.

The most concrete information, as might be expected, relates to the coastal towns. Beginning in the north, the Portuguese comment in some detail on Chaul, a bustling entrepôt of the sixteenth century which exists today mainly as a memory.[346] Located at the estuary of the Kondulika River (about thirty miles south of modern Bombay), Chaul is described as lying "more than two leagues [8 miles] inside the bar."[347] It was in this roadstead that a Portuguese fleet was surprised and defeated in 1508 by an Egyptian–Gujarati contingent. Shortly thereafter the Viceroy d'Almeida proceeded northward with a fleet reinforced by new arrivals from Portugal to wipe out the Muslim fleet and its naval bases which threatened the Portuguese footholds in Malabar and the trade with India. After the Portuguese destroyed Dabhul, and defeated the Muslim fleet at Diu, the ruler of Ahmadnagar, whose only port was Chaul, was intimidated enough to agree to pay tribute to the Portuguese for the port's "defense." In 1510 a Portuguese factor arrived in Chaul, and over the following fifteen years the Portuguese built a factory and a fortress at the city as they gradually made it one of their principal trading centers north of Goa.

In 1504, before the advent of the Portuguese, Varthema visited Chaul. His narrative corresponds well to that of Barbosa, who visited Chaul after the Portuguese already had a factor in residence there. Located on "a beautiful river," Chaul is described by Varthema as being "more warm than cold."[348] The city is "extremely well-walled"[349] and its houses are roofed with thatch. Its tawny-colored inhabitants are warlike, but the ruler does not have fighting men at his disposal though he does possess artillery. Horses, cows, and oxen are in good supply, and the country round about "abounds in everything excepting grapes, nuts and chestnuts."[350] The city is populated entirely by Moors and gentiles who speak "a language which seems to be like that of the Guzerats."[351] Chaul has a "Moorish governor" who is subject to a king who is "himself a vassal of the King of Daquem [Deccan] and who accounts to him for his revenues and collects them."[352]

---

[346] Actually it now appears on maps as the village of Revadanda. For its history and decline see J. Gerson da Cunha, *Notes on the History and Antiquities of Chaul and Bassein* (Bombay, 1876). Also see Dames (ed.), *op. cit.* (n. 5), I, 159, n. 1.
[347] Barros in Cidade and Múrias (eds.), *op. cit.* (n. 6), II, 81.
[348] Temple (ed.), *op. cit.* (n. 233), p. 47.
[349] *Ibid.*
[350] *Ibid.*
[351] Castanheda in Azevedo (ed.), *op. cit.* (n. 17), I, 289.
[352] Barbosa in Dames (ed.), *op. cit.* (n. 5), I, 162.

The Portuguese bring out clearly that before they arrived at Chaul ships from Ormuz, Cambay, and Malabar traded there regularly with each other and the merchants of the Deccan. The great trading months were from December through March, and the Portuguese were evidently not long in fitting themselves into this international commercial pattern. Spices and drugs from the south were brought in by Malabar vessels to be exchanged for the grains, cotton cloths, muslins, and calicoes produced in the Deccan. Copper in quantity was also purchased by the Deccan merchants to be used in minting and in the manufacture of cooking utensils. Even after the appearance of the Portuguese, merchants from the interior bring their oxen trains loaded with goods to the outskirts of the city just as the foreign vessels continue to moor themselves along the waterfront each year at the trading season. The city itself in the trading months "is like a fair,"[353] and the taxes on this trade are very slight.[354] The Portuguese purchase at these markets many of the commodities essential to the supplying and outfitting of their fleets. A similar trade is carried on at Danda (Danda Rajpur), another Deccan town located at the mouth of a river just to the south of Chaul and also subject to Ahmadnagar.[355] But even in Pires' time it is possible to see that Chaul and other Deccan ports are beginning to decline.

Dabhul, at the time when D'Almeida sacked it in 1509, is described as being "one of the most populous and magnificent maritime cities"[356] in the East. Varthema, who visited Dabhul in 1504, likens it to Chaul in the customs obtaining there.[357] Barbosa, who probably arrived in Dabhul a few years after the Portuguese sacked the town, reports that it "is now peopled and as prosperous as before, and wealthy."[358] Located on the north bank of the estuary of the Vashishti River, Dabhul in this period is within the territory of the "Sabaio" who maintains a garrison there. Barros describes at length the fortifications of the city and the successful Portuguese attack upon them. Ships from Mecca, Aden, Ormuz, as well as from Gujarat and Malabar, regularly trade at Dabhul. The merchants from the interior bring to the port grains, copper, quicksilver, and vermilion dye.[359] The "Sabaio" of Goa is said to receive great revenues from the customs imposed on this trade.

Some of the merchants of Dabhul, "as well Moors as Heathen,"[360] are very wealthy. These men of substance live in noble houses and sumptuous edifices which are the best to be found in the region.[361] Beautiful villages and mosques line both sides of the river behind Dabhul. The surrounding countryside is

[353] *Ibid.*
[354] Castanheda in Azevedo (ed.), *op. cit.* (n. 17), I, 289.
[355] Barbosa in Dames (ed.), *op. cit.* (n. 5), I, 163; Castanheda in Azevedo (ed.), *op. cit.* (n. 17), II, 284–85; Pires in Cortesão (ed.), *op. cit.* (n. 9), I, 51.
[356] Barros in Cidade and Múrias, *op. cit.* (n. 6), II, 117.
[357] Temple (ed.), *op. cit.* (n. 233), p. 48.
[358] Dames (ed.), *op. cit.* (n. 5), I, 166.
[359] *Ibid.*, p. 165.
[360] *Ibid.*
[361] Barros in Cidade and Múrias, *op. cit.* (n. 6), II, 117.

"well-tilled, rich and fertile, with good ploughing and breeding of cattle."[362] The Portuguese, however, perhaps because they had raided the city and had formed an alliance with the rival port of Chaul, were generally on bad terms with Dabhul; as a result trade was systematically funneled into Goa and Diu, and Dabhul began rapidly to decline. Still, enough trade continued for Orta to be able to enjoy eating in his home in Goa the watermelons of Dabhul.[363]

The Europeans also comment on other smaller port towns of the Deccan, but in no case do they discuss at length the customs and beliefs prevailing in the Konkani country. The people are said to be industrious tillers and excellent soldiers.[364] Castanheda reports that the Deccanese "do not have as many idolatries and superstitions as the Malabars and are much more genteel in living."[365] Beautiful of face and well formed in their bodies, these people wear tunics of white cotton and elaborate headdresses. Although they eat all meats excepting beef, they drink no wine. The Brahmans are especially strict about their dietary habits and their religious beliefs and ceremonies. Castanheda then goes on to discuss at some length the beliefs of the Brahmans in "a single god," in numerous devils who must be propitiated, in transmigration of souls, and in paradise and hell. He clearly thinks that their beliefs resemble Christian teachings, for he alleges that "they have hints of the birth of our lord and his sufferings," venerate the picture of Our Lady, and on festival occasions wash themselves as "a kind of baptismal rite."[366] His analysis of such matters illustrates graphically how difficult it was for a Christian European of limited background and experience to comprehend alien religious practices, even though he observed them at first hand and over a fairly long period of time.

It is only when they consider Goa that we begin to get substantial accounts from the Portuguese sources. This is true primarily because Goa became Portugal's leading port in India and because it was soon elevated to be the administrative and episcopal center for the entire eastern empire. In Malabar the Portuguese held their position by force and by the policy of playing off the local rulers against each other. Their factories at Cannanore and Cochin enjoyed extraterritorial privileges, but even the most co-operative of the Malabar rulers continued to maintain the trappings and some of the substance of sovereignty. In 1510, Albuquerque, after having once been ejected from the city, managed to wrest Goa permanently away from its Muslim ruler. Thereafter the Portuguese took possession of their first real colony in Asia and were confronted for the first time with the task of ruling in India.

Under their mastery the defensive works of the island of Goa, constructed to withstand attacks from the land, were repaired and reinforced. The Portuguese then had the Goans construct some public buildings, a factory, a hospital, and a

[362] Barbosa in Dames (ed.), *op. cit.* (n. 5), I, 166.
[363] Markham (ed.), *op. cit.* (n. 4), p. 304.
[364] Pires in Cortesão (ed.), *op. cit.* (n. 9), I, 48.
[365] Azevedo (ed.), *op. cit.* (n. 17), I, 287.
[366] *Ibid.*, p. 288.

church. The political organization of the colony also went ahead swiftly as Albuquerque sought to develop Goa into Portugal's imperial anchor post on the west coast of India. Initially, the people of Goa seemed to prefer the Portuguese to the Muslim overlords whom the Europeans replaced. This was probably so because the financial exactions of the Portuguese were less and their attitude towards native customs and religion far more tolerant. The only native practice immediately outlawed was *sati*.[367]

Goa played host for varying periods of time to many European writers on India. Varthema touched there when the island was still ruled over by the Muslims. Pires, who visited Goa shortly after its conquest by the Portuguese, calls it "the key to the First and Second India." [368] Barbosa, who wrote shortly before 1518, evidently had only a relatively limited experience in Goa. He writes, in any case, much less about Goa than about Malabar and Gujarat. Castanheda, it seems, was based for most of a decade (1529–38) in Goa and its environs. The physician and apothecary Orta spent more than a generation (1534–ca. 1570) there tending the Portuguese viceroys and other officials. The scene of his *Colloquies* is laid in Goa, where he had his own house and a garden in which he grew medical herbs. Since Goa was a great crossroads of eastern trade, the Portuguese resident in the "Golden City" had splendid opportunities to become acquainted with traders and travelers from elsewhere in India and from the East Indies and the Far East. These itinerants provided the Portuguese with more than a little of their information on Asia. Camoëns, who visited with Orta in Goa in about 1561,[369] wrote in *The Lusiads*:

Goa will be taken from the infidel, and will come in time to be queen of all the East, raised to a pinnacle by the triumphs of the conquerors; from which proud eminence they will keep the idolatrous heathen, and all such as may be tempted to wage war against your beloved people, severely in check.[370]

While outfitting his fleet at Cannanore between the first and second conquests of Goa, Albuquerque wrote in 1510 to King Manuel explaining that possession of this strategic territory was in his opinion essential to the maintenance of the Portuguese position in India and a possible springboard for conquest of the Deccan.[371] Pires concurs in this estimate of Goa's importance and adds that the Muslim rulers of the Deccan and Gujarat have "a bad neighbor in Goa." [372] He describes it as a civilized trading center and "the coolest place in India." [373] Its port and trading facilities have the greatest possibilities for development. News of the conquest of Goa was relayed to Rome by the Portuguese

[367] Albuquerque in Birch (ed.), *op. cit.* (n. 116), II, 94.
[368] Cortesão (ed.), *op. cit.* (n. 9), I, 54.
[369] The great poet wrote a sonnet in honor of the Viceroy, Dom Francisco Coutinho, which was first published at Goa in Orta's *Colloquies* of 1563. For the text see Conde de Ficalho (ed.), *Coloquios dos simples e drogas da India* (2 vols.; Lisbon, 189–95), I, 7–9.
[370] From the modern prose translation of William C. Atkinson (London, 1952), p. 65.
[371] Birch (trans.), *op. cit.* (n. 116), III, 258–63.
[372] Cortesão (ed.), *op. cit.* (n. 9), I, 57.
[373] *Ibid.*

embassy of 1514 to the Vatican; details about the development of Goa as a colony of Portugal were not generally circulated in Europe until after mid-century.

Although Ramusio in his first volume published Pires' and Barbosa's accounts,[374] their narratives of Goa are slight and unsystematic by comparison to the descriptions of the Portuguese chroniclers. Castanheda, Barros, and Albuquerque give similar accounts of Goa's geography, history, and development under the Portuguese. These, supplemented by occasional asides from Orta's *Colloquies* and by incidental references from the other sources were sufficient to give an interested student of the mid-sixteenth century an accurate notion of what the Portuguese were doing in Goa.

The name "Goa," though it may have been used before 1510, begins to be common only after the Portuguese conquest.[375] The natives of the region, the Kanarese, call the island "Ticuari." This means "thirty villages,"[376] the number of units into which the island was divided for administrative purposes when the Portuguese arrived there. "Ticuari," or the island of Goa, is "surrounded on every side with lagoons of salt water and islands."[377] Looked at from the sea side, there are two great bays, north and south of the island, into which flow two rivers: the "Pangim"[378] (now called the Mandavi) and the river of Old Goa (now called the Juari). The bays are joined together by a streamlet that separates the island from the mainland and which is fed by the numerous waters that descend from the "Gate" (Ghats) to the sea. The lofty and extensive Ghat range "hangs over Goa and the sea like an awning."[379] The eastern side of the island, where attacks from the mainland must come, is serviced by two main fords at the villages of "Benestari" (Banastarim) and "Gondali" (Gandaulim).[380] It is said that the crocodiles make crossings at Gandaulim exceedingly dangerous, and that in times of stress the Goans throw condemned criminals and prisoners of war to the hungry reptiles to keep them congregated at the ford. Goa was also protected on its land side by towers and bulwarks mounted by artillery. The length of the island measured from Banastarim in the east to the cape is three leagues (12 miles); its width from north to south is one league (4 miles).[381]

---

[374] G. B. Ramusio, *Delle navigationi et viaggi* (Venice, 1550), I, 320 r & v on Goa.

[375] See discussion in Dames, *op. cit.* (n. 5), I, 170, n. 2. Both Castanheda and Barros note that this is what "we call it."

[376] Cidade and Múrias (eds.), *op. cit.* (n. 6), II, 189. Cf. the note in Yule and Burnell (eds.), *op. cit.* (n. 10), p. 290, in which an unnamed author writing around 1520 is quoted as saying that on the island of "Tissoury" there are 31 *aldeas* (villages). In modern transliteration it is Tisvadi (see José N. da Fonseca, *An Historical and Archaeological Sketch of the City of Goa* [Bombay, 1878], p. 111). For a list of the villages and towns see Barros in Cidade and Múrias (eds.), *op. cit.* (n. 6), II, 198.

[377] Albuquerque in Birch (trans.), *op. cit.* (n. 116), II, 92.

[378] The name used by Castanheda; Barros appears not to know it.

[379] Albuquerque in Birch (trans.), *op. cit.* (n. 116), II, 95.

[380] Barros lists five fording places between the islands and the mainland: "Pangi," "Daugi," "Gondali," "Benestari," "Agaci." See Cidade and Múrias (eds.), *op. cit.* (n. 6), II, 198–99.

[381] *Ibid.* p. 189; Fonseca, *op. cit.* (n. 376), p. 111 gives these measurements as nine and three miles respectively.

India

One of the few general descriptions of the island of Goa available early in the sixteenth century was written by Castanheda:

The greater part of this island is encircled with rocky cliffs and mires: the land itself is very beautiful and luxuriant with numerous and tall groves of palm trees that give much wine, oil, vinegar, and jaggery,[382] that almost tastes like sugar. It also has areca palms that give areca with which betel is eaten.[383] All this makes them much money, and now many Portuguese have large incomes from it. They have also many gardens in which they grow numerous and very singular fruits of the earth, and have many and very healthful waters. They produce much rice and other vegetables which are different from ours and all good to eat. They have a large amount of sesame from which they make a very good oil which spares our own, and it is in such abundance that they make it in presses as we do ours. They produce much livestock, cows and oxen, many pigs and hens, and much good fish, as well as numerous other foods of land and sea. There is a large population of gentiles whom they call canarins [*Kanarese*], including brahmins and other learned doctors, who possess numerous gilded edifices of their idols which they call *pagodes*:[384] and for everybody there are many large tanks made of bricks (in which one can sail boats) wherein the Moors and heathens bathe themselves.[385]

The language of Goa is Konkani, a tongue which, according to Pires,[386] does not resemble the languages spoken in the Deccan or Vijayanagar.

According to traditional history as related to the Portuguese "by the natives,"[387] the marshy territory near Goa was originally occupied by refugees from Kanara. After these first settlers had established themselves, they were subjected to the princes of Kanara and forced to conclude a perpetual contract with them. By the terms of this contract the thirty villages of the Goa area were required to pay annual tribute called "cocivarado" to the prince of Kanara.[388] Each village was obliged to contribute an annual tax according to its resources as determined by the headmen in council. The authority in charge of each village was a *tanadar*,[389] who apparently was charged with collecting revenues and making new assessments in those villages which defaulted. This "first population" founded the ancient Hindu city of Goa on the southern extremity

---

382 On this and other palm products see Orta's account in Markham (ed.), *op. cit.* (n. 4), p. 140.
383 See *ibid.*, p. 192, n. 1.
384 This word, obscure in its origins, is often used by the Portuguese to mean the "heathen" temples of India.
385 Castanheda in Azevedo (ed.), *op. cit.* (n. 17), II, 21.
386 Cortesão (ed.), *op. cit.* (n. 9), I, 54.
387 Account of Barros in Cidade and Múrias (eds.), *op. cit.* (n. 6), II, 192–93.
388 Albuquerque and his successors honored the special constitutions of these village communities. In 1526 a register, called *Foral de usos e costumes*, was compiled of their traditional usages and privileges, and it was subsequently employed in the sixteenth century as an administrative guidebook by the Portuguese rulers of Goa. An abstract of it in English may be found in R. S. Whiteway, *The Rise of the Portuguese Empire in India* (London, 1898), pp. 215–20. For the complete text, "rearranged so as to bring together all the orders relating to the same subject," and followed by a commentary, see B. H. Baden-Powell, "The Villages of Goa in the Early 16th Century," *Journal of the Royal Asiatic Society for 1900*, pp. 261–91.
389 Cf. discussion of this term in Cortesão (ed.), *op. cit.* (n. 9), I, 56, n. 1.

of the island and "from the appearance of its buildings" when the Portuguese arrived there, "it was a great place."[390]

Barros, who gives more details on Goa's history than any of the other Portuguese writers, is apparently not aware of the fact that the Hindu city of Goa was the capital of the Kadamba rulers until the latter part of the thirteenth century.[391] Nor does he seem to touch upon the first Muslim conquest of it in the fourteenth century. He and Albuquerque refer when they talk of Goa under its Hindu rulers to the century of Vijayanagar control from about 1370 to 1470. At this time, reports Albuquerque, Goa "was a very important place in these parts"[392] and was well staffed with troops to stand off the rising power of the Muslims in the Deccan. It had many Hindu temples "of a very good style of architecture" and remained a tributary of Vijayanagar until "about seventy years" before Albuquerque's conquest.[393] It was during these seventy years that a new city of Goa was built, according to Albuquerque, in the northern part of the island. The city was moved, he asserts, because the Juari River had become shallow and so was unable to accommodate the largest vessels. In the meantime the Mandavi had become broader and deeper and so a port was erected on its banks and Old Goa was left to die.[394]

As we have seen earlier, by this period the local rulers of the Deccan paid no more than nominal vassalage to the Bahmani sultan. The most powerful of these independent Deccan princelings in the Konkan was Yūsuf 'Ādil Khan, the ruler of Bijapur and lord of Goa who died in 1510. To the Portuguese he was known as the "Sabaio," his familiar name in common use at the time, which, Barros says, was derived from the name of his native town of Sava in northern Persia.[395] The Portuguese chronicler also gives two different stories derived from tradition concerning the Persian's decision to remain in India.[396] The "Sabaio" was reported by Albuquerque to be so pleased with Goa's beauty and strategic position that "he determined to take up his residence therein."[397] The "Sabaio" soon began to think in terms of using Goa as a base of operations for attacks upon Malabar and Gujarat. But all of these hopes came to nothing when Albuquerque wrested away his prize possession.

That Goa before 1510 was a great emporium, an impressive city, and a center of maritime activity on India's west coast is repeated time after time in the European sources. Barros even speculates that it once may have been populated by the Christians of St. Thomas. But more than anything else, the Portuguese

[390] Albuquerque in Birch (trans.), *op. cit.* (n. 116), II, 93.
[391] On Goa's history see Fonseca, *op. cit.* (n. 376), pp. 83, 119–23.
[392] Albuquerque in Birch (trans.), *op. cit.* (n. 116), II, 94.
[393] *Ibid.*, p. 92. Seventy years before 1510 would push the end of Vijayanagar control back to 1440 rather than the date 1470 which is usually accepted. For comments see Fonseca, *op. cit.* (n. 376), p. 125.
[394] Birch (trans.), *op. cit.* (n. 116), II, 93–94.
[395] Cidade and Múrias (eds.), *op. cit.* (n. 6), II, 197; see also Dames (ed.), *op. cit.* (n. 5), I, 172–73, n. 1.
[396] Cidade and Múrias (eds.), *op. cit.* (n. 6), II, 197. Orta claims that he was a Turk (Markham [ed.], *op. cit.* [n. 4], p. 72).
[397] Birch (trans.), *op. cit.* (n. 116), II, 96.

are impressed by the revenues which the "Sabaio" derived from trade and taxation. Arabian horses from Ormuz were sold in Goa at great profit to merchants from Vijayanagar and the Deccan. From the tax on these and other commercial items the "Sabaio" received substantial revenues. Barros gives figures on the taxes collected from the thirty villages, the mainland, and other Goan possessions of the "Sabaio."[398] The "Sabaio" is also reported to have large fleets, excellent fortifications, and a sizable army. Indeed, the strength and reputation of the "Sabaio" were so great that emissaries reportedly were sent to his court from as far away as Aden and Cairo.

Still, the Portuguese allege, the natives of Goa were restive under Muslim jurisdiction because of the high taxes and the tendency of the Moors to live apart and to treat the natives cruelly. Barros describes at some length how willingly the Goans after 1510 took to the Portuguese ways of trading, governing, and living. The Kanara women, unlike those of Malabar, were apparently quite willing to form alliances with or marry the Portuguese men, especially since newlyweds were given subsidies from the treasury of the city.[399] The non-Muslim population of the city was more willing to become converted to Christianity than the Malabars. But while the Portuguese describe the general receptivity of the Goans to Portuguese rule, they fail to comment in detail upon the customs of their Goan subjects. Much of what Orta has to say in his *Colloquies* is derived from his experience in Goa, but he has practically nothing to report on the customs of its inhabitants. His digressions into history, politics, and social practices almost always deal with some other part of India. In reporting on Goa after its capture, the Portuguese generally center their attention upon their achievements in the "Golden City" and their development of it as the administrative, episcopal, and commercial center of their Asiatic empire.

E. GUJARAT (CAMBAY)

North and west of the Deccan in the territory that surrounds the Gulf of Cambay lay the maritime state of Gujarat, which had been under Muslim rule since the end of the thirteenth century.[400] In 1342, Ibn Batuta visited several seaport towns of Gujarat and subsequently described the trade, prosperity, and

---

[398] Cidade and Múrias (eds.), *op. cit.* (n. 6), II, 198–99. According to rumor, the city of Goa alone paid him 500,000 *pardãos*, principally from taxes on the importation of horses. He also received taxes from the village communities (*tanadarias*) and the islands of Divar, Chorão, and Jua, as well as tolls paid for use of the fords to the mainland, port fees, and export duties.

[399] *Ibid.*, II, 199. On the marriage of Portuguese with native women see Danvers, *op. cit.* (n. 228), I, 217.

[400] The best general study, which utilizes some of the Portuguese sources, is M. S. Commissariat, *A History of Gujarat* (London, 1938), Vol. I. See also M. L. Dames, "The Portuguese and Turks in the Indian Ocean in the Sixteenth Century," *Journal of the Royal Asiatic Society* (1921), pp. 1–28; and the supplementary article by E. D. Ross, "The Portuguese in India and Arabia between 1507 and 1517," in *ibid.*, pp. 545–62. For earlier times see L. Stembach, "Gujarat as Known to Medieval Europe," *Proceedings of the Indian Historical Congress*, VII (1956), 292–95.

strategic location of the city of Cambay. With the appearance of the Portuguese in the Indian Ocean in the sixteenth century, the rulers of Gujarat, along with their Egyptian coreligionists, were quick to realize that the Christians would eventually threaten their vital maritime connections with the West. The Gujaratis therefore combined forces with the Egyptians to prevent the Portuguese from controlling the strategic ports of Ormuz at the entrance to the Persian Gulf and of Aden at the southern portal to the Red Sea. The Portuguese, on their side, soon came to realize that their position in southern India and their freedom to sail in the Indian Ocean and farther east depended upon their ability to check or overwhelm the Muslim powers whose leading representative in Asian waters was the Sultanate of Gujarat. Thus, the issue was joined between Portugal and Gujarat before the end of the first decade of European activity in India.

The Zamorin of Calicut in 1507 requested aid of the Sultan of Gujarat to help him wage war against those who were threatening to disrupt the profitable coastal and oceanic trade so vital to both of their states. However, the Gujaratis, who had suffered at the hands of the Portuguese the year before in the defense of Ormuz, were disinclined to engage the Europeans at too great a distance from their home bases. So it was not until 1507–8, when the Portuguese moved northward to the Deccan coast, that the combined Egyptian and Gujarati fleets descended upon them without warning at Chaul.[401] To avenge this defeat, Viceroy d'Almeida in 1509 brought a great new fleet northward, plundered Dabhul, and then proceeded to the island of Diu at the entrance to the Gulf of Cambay. Here he met and decisively defeated the combined fleets in a naval battle which halted the Muslim attack.[402] Among the spoils of victory the Portuguese acquired a number of books in various languages as well as the battle flags of the Egyptian sultan. The captured banners were taken to Portugal and hung from the walls of the Templars' church in Tomar, the headquarters of the crusading Order of Christ. D'Almeida did not feel strong enough to storm the fortress of Diu, and so after his victory he returned to Chaul, intimidated the ruler of Ahmadnagar, and forced him to pay tribute.

After Albuquerque's first victory at Goa in 1510, Sultan Mahmūd I of Gujarat sent an envoy to Cannanore to request peace and an alliance with Portugal. The envoy also carried two letters from the Sultan's capital at Chāmpāner addressed to Albuquerque; one was from Christians who were captive there, and the other from Malik Gopi, the minister of the Sultan. The Portuguese commander promised the envoy he would visit Gujarat to arrange terms for an alliance, and then he proceeded to his major task of preparing for the second descent on Goa. Once Albuquerque had clearly established Portuguese hegemony over Goa, diplomatic relations with the new ruler of Gujarat, Sultan

---

[401] On the date of this Muslim victory (January, 1508) see Ross, *loc. cit.* (n. 400), p. 547.

[402] Information on this battle is derived solely from Portuguese, Turkish, and Arabic histories. The contemporary Gujarati historians make no mention of this defeat in their annals. See Commissariat, *op. cit.* (n. 400), I, 247–48.

Muzaffar II (reigned 1511–26), became more regular.[403] At the end of 1512 Albuquerque received from Lisbon the terms which he should insist upon as the basis for an alliance. They involved permission to erect a fortress on the island of Diu, a request that Gujarati traders deal exclusively with Goa, and the requirement that the Sultan should have no further connections with the Egyptians or Turks.

After a few tentative efforts to feel out the Sultan, the Portuguese in 1514 sent an impressive embassy to the court of Muzaffar II. Even before the envoys arrived at the Sultan's court, it had become clear that Malik Ayaz, the governor of Diu, had convinced the government of Gujarat that it should not yield to the demand for a fortress at Diu. The Portuguese envoys, armed with gifts of cloth, silver, and horses, nevertheless proceeded to the Sultan's court which was then being held at Ahmadābād. In their negotiations with the royal officials, the Portuguese were offered various sites for a fortress but not Diu. The Sultan was apparently convinced, despite the tempting bait of increased revenues from trade which the Portuguese held before him, that the Europeans might use a fortress at Diu as a bastion from which to attack the mainland.[404] Upon the failure of these negotiations, the Portuguese envoys returned to Goa accompanied by a rhinoceros, the Sultan's gift to Albuquerque. (It was this rhinoceros that was sent on to Europe in 1514, and confined in the king's menagerie at Lisbon until 1517. The animal was finally dispatched to Rome as a gift to Pope Leo X. Though it perished in a shipwreck on the Mediterranean, the carcass was washed ashore. It was subsequently stuffed and sent on to the Holy Father.)

After negotiations broke down, a stalemate developed in Portugal's relations with Gujarat. The Portuguese stubbornly persisted in demanding permission to erect a fortress at Diu; the Sultan remained adamant and proceeded to fortify the island against a possible attack. Located off the southern shore of the Kathiawar Peninsula, Diu's trading prosperity was based on ease of access, a very good harbor, and freedom from the influence of the dangerous tides, currents, and shoals of the Gulf of Cambay which menaced shipping at other Gujarati ports. From the Portuguese viewpoint, Diu, in addition to its natural advantages as a trading center, was also a potential menace as a base for Muslim (Turkish–Gujarati) attacks. It was therefore primarily on strategic grounds that the Portuguese persisted in their efforts to establish an outpost at Diu.

Though the successors of Albuquerque sought through diplomacy and sporadic coastal raids to change the Sultan's mind, the Gujarati refused to budge. Finally, in the reign of Sultan Bahādur Shah (1526–37), the Portuguese managed to advance their position in northern India at the expense of Gujarat. While preparing to do battle with the Mughul emperor, Humayun, the ruler of Gujarat tried to obtain help from the Portuguese viceroy, Nuno da Cunha (in office 1529–38). In return for a promise of aid, Bahādur, by a treaty of 1534, ceded Bassein with all its territories and revenues in perpetuity to the Portuguese.

403 *Ibid.*, p. 293.
404 *Ibid.*, pp. 295–96.

The following year, despite Portuguese aid, Bahādur was defeated by the Mughuls. In return for their providing him with sanctuary, Bahādur was required to permit the Lusitanians to build a fortress at Diu. After Bahādur's death at their hands in 1537, the Portuguese assumed sovereignty over Diu and took over its entire administration. Shortly thereafter, a messenger was dispatched overland to carry the good tidings to Lisbon.[405] Portuguese troubles were not over, however, because the garrison at Diu was seriously besieged in 1538 and again in 1546. The success of the Portuguese in withstanding the second siege of Diu was one of the last of their great exploits in India, for thereafter their power began to wane in Europe and India, and, as we earlier pointed out,[406] this was related to the breakdown of their spice monopoly. Still, the Portuguese managed to retain their hold on Diu, and it remained a Portuguese possession to 1962.[407] Bassein, on the other hand, was lost to the Marathis in 1729.

A number of the European writers on India visited Gujarat before the middle of the sixteenth century and they subsequently relayed to Europe a substantial amount of data about it. Varthema, who visited the city of Cambay in 1504, describes it at greater length than he does most of the other places on his itinerary. Albuquerque, who actually spent six days at Diu in 1513 while waiting for ship repairs, wrote in considerable detail on his diplomatic relations with Gujarat, and a large part of this information was published in the *Commentaries.* Pires' description of Cambay based on his travels in India during 1511–12[408] was translated and published by Ramusio in 1550 as was the account by Barbosa, who traveled in Gujarat around 1515. The latter presents in his *Book* the most reliable and interesting account of the seaports of Gujarat ever to be printed. Castanheda, who accompanied Nuno da Cunha's unsuccessful expedition against Diu in 1531, describes at some length its position in trade and strategy before the Portuguese takeover.[409] But for his general description of Gujarat, Castanheda seems to rely heavily on Pires and Barbosa. Orta, who went to Diu in 1535 with the expedition that established a Portuguese fortress there, also visited the city of Cambay and the islands of Bassein, Salsette, and Elephanta.[410] In the first three *Décadas* by Barros there are only incidental references to Gujarat, presumably because Barros felt that he could add very little to Barbosa's account.[411] The systematic discussion of Gujarat which appears in the fourth *Década* was probably the work of the continuator, and since it was not published until the seventeenth century it will not be considered here.

[405] *Ibid.,* pp. 385–86.

[406] Above, pp. 128–29.

[407] For a history of the island during its Portuguese period see A. B. de Bragança Pereira, *Os Portugueses em Diu* (Bastorá, n.d.).

[408] For the dating of his travels see Cortesão (ed.), *op. cit.* (n. 9), I, xxiv.

[409] Azevedo (ed.), *op. cit.* (n. 17), IV, 242–54; also I, 385–87.

[410] On his travels in these regions see A. X. Soares, "Garcia d'Orta, a Little Known Owner of Bombay," *Journal of the Bombay Branch of the Royal Asiatic Society,* XXVI (1921–23), 204–7.

[411] Cf. the discussion in Dames (ed.), *op. cit.* (n. 5), I, xxxiii–vii.

In addition to the general accounts, a series of works was published in Portugal in the latter half of the sixteenth century which celebrates the triumphs of the Portuguese at Diu. Diogo de Teive (Jacobus Tevius), a Portuguese Humanist trained in Paris, published in 1548 at Coimbra a book containing two poems by friends of his which salute the construction and defense of Diu.[412] In 1556 an eyewitness account of the second siege of Diu appeared at Coimbra[413]; the author was Lopo de Sousa Coutinho, a *fidalgo* of the king's household, who wrote of this dramatic defense in "a grave and excellent style."[414] Jerónimo Côrte Real, a poet who specialized in rejoicing over naval victories such as Lepanto, published at Lisbon in 1574 a series of cantos honoring the heros of the second siege of Diu;[415] and, in 1589, Francisco de Andrade had printed at Coimbra a poem commemorating the fiftieth anniversary of the first siege of Diu.[416] Though none of these works was translated into other European languages, it is apparent from their number that they helped to keep alive Portugal's interest in Diu and Gujarat.

Gujarat, which is generally called Cambay by the Portuguese as it was by the Muslim authors, is considered to be one of the "chief kingdoms of India."[417] On the interior it is bounded by two other "great and rich kingdoms," Malwa and "Sanga" (actually the territory to the east and north ruled by Rana Sanga, the leader of the Rajput Confederacy). On the north Gujarat confines with "Dulcinde" (a combination of Diul, or the seaport of Dival, with Sind). The coastal jurisdiction of Gujarat, upon leaving Sind, begins at the city of Mangalor[418] on the southwest coast of Kathiawar and extends southward almost to Chaul in the Deccan. Such a geographical description, while it differs in a few details among the several Portuguese writers, seems to be typical of those written by the Europeans who comment on Gujarat.[419]

On the history of Gujarat before their arrival there, the Europeans are not well informed though they have a few vague ideas about it. Barbosa, after hearing tales in Gujarat of the exploits of Alexander the Great and Darius of Persia, concludes that Darius once ruled over this kingdom.[420] Originally, the Gujarati territory was controlled by "heathens," especially the Rajputs, who

---

[412] Entitled *Cōmentarius de rebus in India apud Dium gestis anno salutis nostrae M. D. XLVI*. For bibliographical detail see King Manuel II, *Early Portuguese Books* (3 vols.; London, 1929–35), II, 233–41.

[413] Entitled *Livro do cerco de Diu*. See King Manuel II, *op. cit.* (n. 412), II, 486–95.

[414] Estimate of Diogo do Couto as quoted in *ibid.*, p. 493.

[415] Entitled *Sucesso do segundo cerco de Diu*. See King Manuel II, *op. cit.* (n. 412), II, 79–81.

[416] Entitled *O primeiro cerco de Diu*. See King Manuel II, *op. cit.* (n. 412), III, 280–81.

[417] Geographical description based on Castanheda in Azevedo (ed.), *op. cit.* (n. 17), II, 313.

[418] Mangrol is sometimes used instead to distinguish the northern Mangalor from the city in the southern Konkan of the same name. See Dames (ed.), *op. cit.* (n. 5), I, 127–28.

[419] For a modern map which generally accepts these boundaries see C. C. Davies, *An Historical Atlas of the Indian Peninsula* (2d ed.; Oxford, 1959), p. 39. Also see Pires' description in Cortesão (ed.), *op. cit.* (n. 9), I, 33.

[420] Dames (ed.), *op. cit.* (n. 5), I, 108. For the latest scholarship on this debatable assertion see Commissariat, *op. cit:* (n. 400), I, xiv.

acted as "knights and wardens of the land."[421] About two hundred years before the Portuguese conquest (*ca.* 1300), Muslim forces based on Delhi began to expand into Gujarat.[422] They pushed the Rajputs out of its cities and into the hinterland. The Rajputs continued for a long time thereafter to harass the Muslim invaders from bases in the back country. The Muslim sultans of Gujarat, who were in power at the time of the Portuguese advent there, are said to have been truly independent for just a short time. Originally, Castanheda remarks,[423] they were captains in the service of the Delhi emperor, and only succeeded in establishing an independent dynasty by concerting with the other captains (of "Dulcinde," "Sanga," Malwa, etc.) in overthrowing the emperor's authority. The disintegration of the Delhi empire in northwestern India was followed, according to the Portuguese, by the establishment of the separate kingdom of Cambay whose ruler in the early sixteenth century was "the fourth of his line counting as the first the one who [had] revolted."[424]

The original rebel was Mahmūd I (reigned 1458–1511), the greatest of the Gujarati sultans and the conqueror of the Rajputs of Chāmpāner in 1484. Varthema, who visited Gujarat in 1504, remarks with surprising accuracy that Mahmūd "about forty years ago . . . captured this kingdom from a king of the Gujarati. . . ."[425] The Italian observer then goes on to describe Mahmūd's manner of living and seems particularly impressed by the elephants which do reverence to him. Varthema, Barbosa, and Castanheda, incredible as it may seem, report that Mahmūd was nourished from childhood on a daily ration of poison so that he would develop an immunity to it.[426] As a result of this regime, he became so poisonous that "when a fly touched him . . . it forthwith died . . . and as many women as slept with him perished."[427] Varthema also describes the Sultan as having "mustachios under his nose so long that he ties them over his

---

[421] Dames (ed.), *op. cit.* (n. 5), I, 110.

[422] Probably a vague reference to the Muslim conquest of 1298. See Albuquerque in Birch (trans.), *op. cit.* (n. 116), IV, 106.

[423] Azevedo (ed.), *op. cit.* (n. 17), II, 316; cf. Pires in Cortesão (ed.), *op. cit.* (n. 9), I, 36.

[424] Since Castanheda is writing during the reign of Bahādur (1526–37), he is probably referring to the sultans beginning with Mahmūd I (Azevedo [ed.], *op. cit.* [n. 17], II, 316). For a detailed history of Gujarat in the early sixteenth century, based on Persian and Gujarati sources, see the fourth *Década* of Barros (Cidade and Múrias [eds.], *op. cit.* [n. 6], IV, 258–65).

[425] Temple (ed.), *op. cit.* (n. 233), p. 45.

[426] Commissariat, *op. cit.* (n. 400), I, 230–31 appears to treat this story with more seriousness than it deserves; for a more plausible appraisal of it as a piece of folklore see Dames (ed.), *op. cit.* (n. 5), I, 121–22, n. 3. Pires (in Cortesão [ed.], *op. cit.* [n. 9], I, 40) gives a similar account and adds: "But I do not believe this, although they say it is so." Castanheda (in Azevedo [ed.], *op. cit.* [n. 17], II, 316) accepts this story and relays it without comment to posterity. Garcia de Resende in his *Commentaries* (1554) ascribes similar habits to the kings of Sumatra (see passage translated in Cortesão [ed.], *op. cit.* [n. 9], I, 40, n. 2). It also eventually got into Purchas and was apparently the inspiration that moved Samuel Butler in *Hudibras* (Pt. II, Canto 1,) to write:

> "The Prince of Cambay's daily food
> Is asp and basilisk and toad,
> Which makes him have so strong a breath,
> Each night he stinks a queen to death."

[427] Dames (ed.), *op. cit.* (n. 5), I, 122.

head as a woman would tie her tresses, and he has a white beard which reaches to his girdle."[428]

Mahmūd's son, Muzaffar II (reigned 1511–26), came to the throne when he was almost forty years of age and shortly before Pires visited Gujarat. The Portuguese traveler reports that he was then at war with the neighboring princes of Malwa, Sind, and the Rajput confederacy "and to some extent with Delhi."[429] Gujarat is protected from invasions by Delhi, however, by the high Malwa plateau which separates the two states, and by the activities of a "Gujarat Jogee" who controls the only pass connecting them.[430] Muzaffar is judged as being "given to all manner of vice in eating and lechery" and of spending most of the time "among his women stupefied with opium."[431] In all other matters he is said to be "judicious."[432] The Sultan is aided in governing by "Milagobim" (Malik Gopi, a Brahman of Surat and "friend of the Portuguese"), "Chamlc-malec" (Kiwam-ul-Mulk, title of the great noble, Malik Sarang), "Asturmalec" (unidentified),[433] and "Codandam" (possibly Khush-'adam, whose title was Imad'l-Mulk). Each of these emirs has a vast retinue of mounted followers, and, as great lords native to the kingdom, they share with the sultan in the administration of justice, government, and revenues. When the ruler dies, they are said to act as "the electors of the kingdom." In addition to his noble advisers, Muzaffar is reputed to possess "up to a thousand wives and concubines"[434] of whom the leading one was apparently a Rajput woman.[435]

The sultan with his court usually resides at Chāmpāner, a fortified mountain town whose ruins stand today a short distance northeast of Baroda. Captured in 1484 from the Rajputs, it remained the royal stronghold, minting center, and capital of Gujarat until its conquest by the Mughul emperor, Humayun, in 1535. At the time when Castanheda was in India (1528–38), the city is reputed to have had 130,000 hearths enclosed within seven strong walls. The royal palaces, warehouses, and arsenals, "which occupy as much space as Evora,"[436] are separated from the rest of the city by a wall that has iron gates at its three portals. The only persons permitted to go within the wall are the sultan, his wives, household officials, and tax collectors. The countryside around the city is "a land of broad plains which yield great store of food" so that "in the city

[428] Temple (ed.), *op. cit.* (n. 233), p. 45. For comment on this enormous mustache and the possible relationship of it to the sobriquet "Begada" (impotent) under which Mahmūd I is known to posterity see Commissariat, *op. cit.* (n. 400), I, 232–33.

[429] Cortesão (ed.), *op. cit.* (n. 9), I, 36. See below, p. 420.

[430] *Ibid.* For a more detailed account of "the king of the Ioghe" or Yogis see Varthema in Temple (ed.), *op. cit.* (n. 233), pp. 46–47. This is possibly a reference to the chief of a tribe known as the Gor. khnatha Gosains (Yule and Burnell, *op. cit.* [n. 10], p. 352). None of the Portuguese who visit Gujarat after Pires remarks on this ruler.

[431] Pires in Cortesão (ed.), *op. cit.* (n. 9), I, 40.

[432] *Ibid.* Commissariat, *op. cit.* (n. 400), I, 290–92 calls him the "clement" ruler and describes his regime as "liberal and tolerant."

[433] Listed also by Albuquerque in Birch (trans.), *op. cit.* (n. 116), IV, 108.

[434] Pires in Cortesão (ed.), *op. cit.* (n. 9), I, 41.

[435] Albuquerque in Birch (trans.), *op. cit.* (n. 116), IV, 107.

[436] Azevedo (ed.), *op. cit.* (n. 17), II, 319.

there is enough and to spare of all things." [437] In the mountains surrounding the plain there is much game, and Muzaffar II domesticates animals for hunting and collects wild animals from all over the world as a hobby. It was this ruler who sent the rhinoceros from his menagerie to Albuquerque. The *Commentaries* of Albuquerque record details on the reception accorded a Persian embassy at Chāmpāner in 1511–13 and on the difficulties which developed between the envoy's retinue and the retainers of a visiting prince from Malwa. [438] As on the occasion of the Portuguese embassy of 1514 to Chāmpāner, the Sultan sent the Persian envoys off with a gift rhinoceros.

Because of the constant threat of war from the Rajputs and other neighboring peoples, the Sultan of Gujarat must constantly be prepared for hostilities. In addition to powerful horse and elephant units, he maintains a large standing army, recruited mostly from foreign Muslim adventurers to whom he pays high salaries. [439] The horsemen are "so light and skillful in the saddle" [440] that they play polo for recreation. When girded for war, the foreparts of the horses are protected by stiff caparisons and their riders wear coats of mail or quilted cotton jackets and carry shields, swords, and a Turkish bow. [441] While the horses are native to Gujarat, the elephants have to be imported at high cost from Ceylon and Malabar. Still, the ruler of Gujarat maintains a standing force of four or five hundred fighting elephants who are outfitted for battle and used in combat as is customary in other parts of India. Like the armies of the Deccan, those of Gujarat are also using imported artillery by the beginning of the sixteenth century.

The general descriptions of life in Gujarat relate to conditions in 1515 and shortly before. [442] Even Castanheda's account of social organization appears to be based on the earlier eyewitness reports of Pires and Barbosa. All the Europeans, beginning with Varthema, remark on the mixed population of the country. In the interior the majority of the people are Hindu; in the seaports the Moors and their practices predominate. [443] The Hindus, who count for "almost the third part of the kingdom," [444] are divided into three major groups: Rajputs or the fighters, Banyā or the merchants, Brahmans or the priests. The Rajputs, who live in mountain villages, have no ruler of their own and they wage war constantly against the Sultan of Gujarat. [445] In addition to being excellent horsemen and archers, the Rajputs are distinguished from other Hindus by the fact that they "kill and eat sheep and fish and other kinds of food." [446]

[437] Barbosa in Dames (ed.), *op. cit.* (n. 5), I, 123–24.

[438] Birch (trans.), *op. cit.* (n. 116), IV, 82–85.

[439] Castanheda in Azevedo (ed.), *op. cit.* (n. 17), II, 316.

[440] Barbosa in Dames (ed.), *op. cit.* (n. 5), I, 119.

[441] Pires in Cortesão (ed.), *op. cit.* (n. 9), I, 33–34.

[442] Commissariat, *op. cit.* (n. 400), I, chap. xx uses the reports of Albuquerque and Barbosa as the basis for his description of Gujarat immediately following the long reign of Mahmūd I, which ended in 1511. He calls (p. 254) Barbosa's "a reliable and interesting account."

[443] Castanheda in Azevedo (ed.), *op. cit.* (n. 17), II, 314.

[444] Pires in Cortesão (ed.), *op. cit.* (n. 9), I, 39.

[445] Barbosa in Dames (ed.), *op. cit.* (n. 5), I, 110.   [446] *Ibid.*

The Banyā "dwell among the Moors with whom they carry on all their trade."[447] Barbosa and Castanheda describe at length the abhorrence felt by the Banyā about taking life of any sort. Actually the Portuguese writers seem to be describing practices of Jains who follow the doctrine of *ahiṃsā*.[448] Barbosa seems to delight in recounting how these devotees are forced—by Moors, beggars, and others—to ransom small birds, insects, and other living things to prevent them from being killed in their presence. But while revering life, the Banyā are still "great usurers, falsifiers of weights and measures . . . and great liars."[449] Tall, tawny, and well clothed, the Banyā restrict their diet to milk, butter, sugar, rice, fruit, and vegetables. The women, fair and dark alike, are slender, well shaped, and beautiful. Both men and women bathe twice each day to purify themselves of their sins. The men have long hair, "as women do with us,"[450] which they twist upon the head under a turban. Dressed in long cotton and silk shirts, or with short coats of silk and brocade, the men wear pointed shoes. The women, like their husbands, clothe themselves in long garments, as well as in silken bodices cut low at the back. On going outside they throw over themselves a cloak called a *chadar*. They always are barefooted and "on their heads they wear nought but their own hair well-dressed."[451] The women wear anklets of gold and silver as well as rings on their fingers and toes; the men ornament themselves with rings and earrings set with precious stones. The men do not carry arms, both out of predisposition and because the Moors protect them. A very amorous people, the women of the Banyā "are kept much at home and shut up."[452]

Certain Brahmans manage beautiful and large temples which have great revenues. Other members of the priestly caste beg for alms or act as couriers.[453] Though subject to the Moors, some of the Brahmans are among "the men who rule in the kingdom"[454] as, for example, the rich and renowned minister, Malik Gopi. Below the waist, the Brahmans wear cotton garments. They go about bare from the waist up, except that they wear "a cord of three strands [the sacred thread]" over their shoulder. Like the Banyā, the Brahmans marry just once in a lifetime, this rule applying to both men and women. Barbosa describes in some detail their wedding ceremony and the accompanying festivities. Adultery on the woman's part brings death by poisoning, "unless it be with the brothers of their husbands" with whom it is lawful to sleep.[455] The sons are the only legitimate heirs of the father's property and position, "for Brahmans must be sons of

---

447 *Ibid.*, p. 111. For a lengthier description of the Rajputs see Pires in Cortesão (ed.), *op. cit.* (n. 9), I, 32–33.

448 Commissariat, *op. cit.* (n. 400), I, 255.

449 Barbosa in Dames (ed.), *op. cit.* (n. 5), I, 112.

450 *Ibid.*, p. 113.   451 *Ibid.*, p. 114.   452 *Ibid.*

453 *Ibid.*, p. 117, talks about "Pateles" who are a lower order of Brahmans who act as messengers; Pires (in Cortesão [ed.], *op. cit.* [n. 9], I, 39, 42) refers to "Pattars" (presumably also messengers) whom he calls "the more honoured Brahmans." See for discussion of this term Dalgado, *op. cit.* (n. 44), II, 186–88. It would appear that both terms are derived from Sanskrit: *Patel* = governor.

454 Pires in Cortesão (ed.), *op. cit.* (n. 9), I, 40.

455 Castanheda in Azevedo (ed.), *op. cit.* (n. 17), II, 314–15.

Brahmans."[456] In their creed the Brahmans attach great importance to a God in three persons, and their teachings show "many resemblances to the Holy Trinity."[457] Upon entering a Christian church, they revere the sacred images and ask for Holy Mary. From this it is concluded "that they were once Christians" who "gradually lost the faith because of the Mohammedans."[458]

Moors from all over the Islamic world congregate in the cities of Gujarat to carry on trade or to find employment as soldiers of the sultan. In addition to the native Moors and their coreligionists of Delhi, a cosmopolitan flavor "is given to life by the presence of Turks, Mamalukes, Arabs, Persians, Khurasanis, Turcomans, Abyssinians, and a sprinkling of renegade Christians."[459] In this melting pot of peoples, many tongues are spoken, including Arabic, Turkish, and Gujarati. Fair of complexion, the members of the ruling class live a luxurious life. Attired in rich clothes of gold, silk, cotton and camlets, the Moors wear high turbans on their heads and leather boots up to the knee which are decorated with dainty devices. Unlike the Banyā, the Moors carry in their girdles short swords "finely damascened with gold and silver according to the rank of the wearer."[460] Of their women, who are beautiful, white, and well dressed, they may marry as many as they can support. Since they are extremely jealous of their wives, the women are transported from one place to another in enclosed carriages which are drawn by horses and extravagant to behold.[461] Divorce is possible, and may be initiated by either husbands or wives, on the payment of a sum of money the size of which is determined and agreed upon at the time of marriage.[462]

The Sultan of Gujarat is said to have jurisdiction over sixty thousand towns,[463] large and small, both along the seacoast and scattered throughout the interior. Many of these towns are enclosed with walls, divided into streets, and built up with "high houses of stone and mortar like those of Spain."[464] Aside from the capital at Chāmpāner already described, the only other interior cities noticed by the Portuguese are "Andava" (Ahmadābād), "Varodrra" (Baroda), and "Barnez" (Broach). Over these cities rule "grand viziers or captains, men by whom the whole kingdom is governed."[465] Ahmadābād, founded by Ahmad Shah in 1411 and capital of the Gujarati sultans until the conquest of Chāmpāner,

[456] Barbosa in Dames (ed.), *op. cit.* (n. 5), I, 117.

[457] *Ibid.*, p. 115, especially n. 1.

[458] Pires in Cortesão (ed.), *op. cit.* (n. 9), I, 39; Castanheda (in Azevedo [ed.], *op. cit.* [n. 17], II, 314), who wrote a generation later and long after the Portuguese had discovered that the Hindus were not former Christians, still arrives at this same conclusion.

[459] Composite list is derived from Dames (ed.), *op. cit.* (n. 5), I, 119–20; Cortesão (ed.), *op. cit.* (n. 9), I, 34; and Azevedo (ed.), *op. cit.* (n. 17), II, 316.

[460] Barbosa in Dames (ed.), *op. cit.* (n. 5), I, 120.

[461] For further detail on these carriages see Castanheda in Azevedo (ed.), *op. cit.* (n. 17), II, 315.

[462] On women having the liberty to divorce their husbands, Barbosa may be misinformed (Dames [ed.], *op. cit.* [n. 5], I, 121, n. 2).

[463] Castanheda in Azevedo (ed.), *op. cit.* (n. 17), II, 315.

[464] *Ibid.*

[465] Pires in Cortesão (ed.), *op. cit.* (n. 9), I, 35.

is the only one of these inland cities talked about at any length by the Portuguese. Evidently the sultans, even after 1484, continued to spend a good deal of their time in the larger and pleasanter city of Ahmadābād.[466] Barbosa, in commenting upon this city, notes that the all-powerful sultan punished an official guilty of malfeasance by forcing him to drink poison.[467]

The seaport towns, both on the mainland coast and on the nearby islands of the entire region from the Gulf of Kutch around the coast of the Kathiawar Peninsula and the Gulf of Cambay as far south as the Deccan frontier which runs between Mahim and Chaul, are listed by a number of the Portuguese writers. Pires names sixteen such ports and Barbosa comments on fourteen of them. Other maritime trading centers, such as "Betexagor" (Bate-shahr on Bate Island in the Gulf of Kutch),[468] attract the attention of Albuquerque. The principal coastal cities are clearly identified by all commentators as Diu, Cambay, Surat, and Randēr. In recent times, these seaport towns of Gujarat have declined as oceanic trade has increasingly concentrated at Bombay which was little more than a fishing village in the early sixteenth century.

The most important trading center west of the Gulf of Cambay is located on the island of Diu, a point of rendezvous before the Portuguese got there for ships from East Africa, the Red Sea, and the Persian Gulf, as well as from the ports of western India. Here the Malabars are accustomed by 1515 to bring coconuts and spices to exchange for silk and cotton cloth, horses, and opium, "both that brought from Aden and that which they make in Cambay, which is not so fine as the former."[469] Goods of India and the further East are also shipped from Diu to Arabia and Persia; the traffic at Diu is the greatest "of any found in these regions" and the returns from it are so great as to be termed "astonishing." Malik Ayaz, the governor of Diu for a number of years before his death in 1522, is a subject of interest to most of the Portuguese writers. Barros avers that he was a Russian by birth who was taken into slavery by the Turks and eventually became the ward of a merchant doing business in India. On a journey to Cambay, the merchant presented the young slave to Sultan Mahmud I to add to his corps of archers. The ruler was so pleased with Ayaz's skill that he soon freed him. Little by little he won further recognition and ultimately he was given the honorary title of Malik and the post of governor of Diu.[470] Citing the *Chronicle of the Kings of Gujarat*, Barros reports that Diu was built by the father[471] of Mahmud I on the ruins of an ancient settlement to celebrate a victory which he had won at sea against some Chinese junks which

---

[466] See Albuquerque in Birch (trans.), *op. cit.* (n. 116), IV, 108.

[467] Dames (ed.), *op. cit.* (n. 5), I, 125–26.

[468] Birch (trans.), *op. cit.* (n. 116), IV, 106–7.

[469] Barbosa in Dames (ed.), *op. cit.* (n. 5), I, 129. On opium see Orta's discourse in Markham (ed.), *op. cit.* (n. 4), pp. 330–34.

[470] Cidade and Múrias (eds.), *op. cit.* (n. 6), II, 93–95. For further details see Commissariat, *op. cit.* (n. 400), I, 213–15.

[471] Cidade and Múrias (eds.), *op. cit.* (n. 6), II, 94. Probably this was the brother rather than the father, the one who became Ahmad Shah (reigned 1451–58).

were operating to the north of their factory at Cochin. When Malik Ayaz first took over, Diu was no great trading center. It only became so under his regime as he built up there a small personal empire and heavily fortified the port which held out against the Portuguese until long after his death.

In the Gulf of Cambay between Diu and the city of Cambay, there are a number of active ports "where dealings take place in many kinds of goods,"[472] and where the sultan has custom houses and officials. But because of the dangerous tides in the gulf, navigation with keeled ships is very hazardous, and strangers dare not try to navigate these treacherous waters without native pilots to guide them. It is for this reason, Castanheda guesses,[473] that the small ships of Gujarat are constructed without keels. Ships approach the city of Cambay by way of "Guindarim" (Ghandar) close to the entrance of the Mahi River which flows by the metropolis.

As of 1512 the "great and fair city"[474] of Cambay is under the jurisdiction of "Sey Debiaa," a noble Moor of great repute.[475] This walled city is a great center of international trade; according to Varthema, "about three hundred ships of different countries come and go here."[476] But it is mainly the industries and crafts of Cambay which attract the eye of Barbosa. Skilled mechanics and craftsmen produce "cunning work of many kinds, as in Flanders."[477] They weave fabrics of all kinds: cotton, silk, velvets, satins, and carpets. Their artisans turn out ivory beads, bedsteads, dice, and chessmen, as well as inlaid productions of great variety. Lapidaries, goldsmiths, and counterfeiters of gems cut stones and produce finely wrought jewelry. Particularly striking is the great amount of work they do with corals and carnelians. In sum, "the best workmen in every kind of work are found"[478] in this city.

The people of Cambay are both Moors and Hindus, the tone of the city's life being set by the men of substance who have derived their wealth from trade and industry. The city boasts great buildings of stone and mortar, well laid out streets and parks, and "many fair houses, very lofty with windows and roofed with tiles in our [the Portuguese] manner."[479] The householders cultivate gardens and orchards, not only for the fruits and vegetables they produce but also for pleasure. Men and women alike wash and perfume themselves and wear jasmine flowers or other local blooms in their hair. In traveling about the city they go to visit their friends or attend functions in coaches drawn by oxen or horses, the richer coaches being enclosed like rooms and having windows decorated with silk hangings. In their coaches, as they go about the city, the

[472] Barbosa in Dames (ed.), *op. cit.* (n. 5), I, 136.
[473] Azevedo (ed.), *op. cit.* (n. 17), II, 315.
[474] Barbosa in Dames (ed.), *op. cit.* (n. 5), I, 139.
[475] Pires in Cortesão (ed.), *op. cit.* (n. 9), I, 35. I have not been able from other sources to confirm this statement or to identify the governor any further.
[476] Temple (ed.), *op. cit.* (n. 233), p. 46.
[477] Dames (ed.), *op. cit.* (n. 5), I, 141.
[478] *Ibid.*, p. 142.
[479] *Ibid.*, p. 140.

passengers sing and play instruments, for they are great adepts in music. These cosmopolites, who are "almost white," are "a people of great culture, accustomed to good clothing, leading a luxurious life, given to pleasure and vice."[480]

Cambay "lies in a pleasant district, rich in supplies."[481] As if to prove this assertion, Barbosa makes a short detour inland to talk about the town of Limodara on the banks of the Narbada in the vicinity of Ratanpur in the Rajput state. Here he locates the carnelian quarries and comments on the extraction and working of the stones. Dealers from Cambay buy the finished stones and market them to merchants from all over the world, even the Portuguese. Because the carnelians are plentiful, they do not bring high prices.[482] The Moors apparently believe in their power to help preserve chastity and to staunch blood.[483]

On the eastern shore of the Gulf of Cambay the town of Randēr stands on the northern side of the Tāpti estuary. Along with Damão and Surat, Randēr is within the jurisdiction of Dastur Khan, a native Moor.[484] Aside from the regular items of trade found in most of Cambay's ports, Barbosa advises "whosoever would have at his disposal things from Malacca and China, let him go to this place, where he will find them in greater perfection than in any other place soever."[485] In their houses the wealthy Moors keep on display their collections of "fair and rich porcelains of new styles."[486] The women of Randēr, unlike Moorish ladies elsewhere, go about the city freely with their faces unveiled. This departure from custom may possibly be accounted for by the fact that the Moors of Randēr, called *navāyāta* (newcomers), were Shiites from Arabia who had originally migrated to India to escape the persecutions of the numerically superior Sunnites.[487] Until the Portuguese sack of Randēr in 1530, Randēr clearly seems to have been the principal commercial center south of Broach. Surat, which was also a rich entrepôt with a customs house of its own in the early sixteenth century, outstripped Randēr in importance after 1530 as both towns strove to recover from the Portuguese onslaught.

The southernmost outposts of Gujarat bordering on the Deccan are the complex of island and mainland ports in the vicinity of modern Bombay. Barbosa, who visited the islands of Bassein and Mahim as well as the town of Tana at the head of the creek which encircles the island of Salsette, speaks of them as being active ports and fine Moorish towns.[488] He also remarks upon

480 *Ibid.*, p. 141.   481 *Ibid.*   482 *Ibid.*, p. 145.

483 Orta in Temple (ed.), *op. cit.* (n. 233), p. 360. For a more detailed discussion of Cambay's trade in semi-precious stones see A. Summers, "An Account of the Agate and Carnelian Trade of Cambay," *Journal of the Bombay Branch of the Royal Asiatic Society*, Vol. III (1851), Pt. II, pp. 318–27.

484 Pires in Cortesão (ed.), *op. cit.* (n. 9), p. 35; also see Albuquerque, in Birch (trans.), *op. cit.* (n. 116), IV, 94–96 for a discussion of Dastur's reception at Surat of the Portuguese embassy of 1514. Malik Gopi, a Hindu noble and friend of the Portuguese, was a person of particular consequence in Surat during the reign of Sultan Muzaffar II.

485 Dames (ed.), *op. cit.* (n. 5), I, 146–47.

486 *Ibid.*, p. 148.

487 Commissariat, *op. cit.* (n. 399), I, 264.

488 Dames (ed.), *op. cit.* (n. 5), I, 151–53.

these islands and inland waterways as lairs for the pirates who prey upon oceanic and inland waterway shipping. Orta, who toured some of these islands in 1535, clearly indicates that Bassein is the leading town of the region.[489] He also describes the extensive Buddhist caves at Kanhiri a few miles from Tana on the island of Salsette with their great underground houses and temples.[490] From his visit to the island of "Pori" (Gharapuri or Elephanta) the Portuguese herbalist describes the great cave-temple, concluding that it is a sight worth seeing, and reporting that "some say that it is the work of the Chinese when they navigated to this land."[491] The island later came to be called Elephanta by the Portuguese because a huge elephant cut from rock stood on a knoll near the port when they took over. The sculptured elephant gradually crumbled over the years, and in 1864 its rocky remains were removed to the Victoria Gardens in Bombay.

Orta, who is writing around 1560, has a good deal to say about the native populations of these islands.[492] Only a few Moors, essentially those who had intermarried with the Hindus, remained in the Bassein area after the Portuguese takeover in 1535–36. The natives are described as Hindus of the non-Brahmanical castes. Those who till and sow the ricelands are called "curumbis" (*Kutumbi* or cultivators). Those named Mālīs (a gardener caste) tend the gardens, raising flowers and fruits. Clerks and accountants known as "Parus" (Parsis) are great businessmen and they collect taxes and rents both for the government and private estate-owners. There are also those whose duty it is to bear arms and, as elsewhere in Cambay, many who engage in trade. Pariahs, who are universally abhorred, exist in every locality and are employed as executioners. The Parsis, whom many Portuguese apparently thought of as Jews, are correctly described by Orta as being originally from Persia, as having "special letters of their own," and as exposing their dead. Notable by their absence from this list are the Brahmans.

While the towns of Gujarat, especially the seaports, are described in some detail, the Portuguese have very little to say about the rural inland areas or about agriculture. Pires asserts that "the kingdom of Cambay does not extend far inland";[493] however, on its luxuriant flat coastal land enough wheat, barley, millet, rice, vegetables, and fruits are produced to feed its large population, to export, and to support in addition a substantial livestock industry. Gujarat, unlike many of the Indian states, breeds and raises small horses of its

[489] Markham (ed.), *op. cit.* (n. 4), pp. 443–45.

[490] For a more recent description see J. Ferguson and J. Burgess, *The Cave Temples of India* (London, 1880), pp. 348–66. For a translation of Do Couto's account see W. K. Fletcher (trans.), "Of the Famous Island of Salsette at Bassein, and Its Wonderful Pagoda Called Canari . . . ," *Journal of the Bombay Branch of the Royal Asiatic Society*, I (1841–44), 34–40.

[491] Markham (ed.), *op. cit.* (n. 4), p. 444. This rumor, which indicates the great respect which the Portuguese had for Chinese craftsmanship, was ill-founded. For a summary of contemporary scholarship on these Hindu caves see Commissariat, *op. cit.* (n. 400), I, 548–49. Also see Ferguson and Burgess, *op. cit.* (n. 490), pp. 465–75, and Fletcher (trans.), *loc. cit.* (n. 490), pp. 40–45, for a translation of Do Couto's description.

[492] Markham (ed.), *op. cit.* (n. 4), pp. 445–46.

[493] Cortesão (ed.), *op. cit.* (n. 9), I, 35.

own, some great lords having several hundred such horses regularly in their stables.[494] Among the other natural products of the country, the Portuguese list cotton, indigo, lac, wormwood, and opium poppies.[495] From their agricultural resources the Gujaratis produce at least twenty different types and colors of cotton cloth, soap, dressed hides, leather, honey, and wax.[496] Their lapidaries, as already mentioned, cut, shape and make jewelry from the local carnelians just as their potters shape crude pottery of various kinds from their native clay.[497]

But trade, rather than agriculture or industry, is deemed to be the life blood of Gujarat. Albuquerque remarks that the Gujaratis understand the navigation of the seas east of India "much more thoroughly than any other nation on account of the great commerce they carry on in those parts."[498] The Banyā, who dominate the foreign trade of Gujarat, are as prominent in all the seaports of the region from Aden to Malacca as are the Genoese in Europe's marts.[499] When Albuquerque stormed Malacca, he found the Gujaratis resident there to be among those who held out most staunchly against him. In the ports of Gujarat itself merchants congregate from all over the East. The products of Italy and Greece reach Cambay by way of Cairo and Aden. Merchants from Ormuz bring horses to Cambay and return with the same variety of items carried westward by Gujarati merchants on their regular trading missions to Malacca. Pires sums up the relationship of Gujarat to the eastern trade before the Portuguese interrupted it. He asserts that if they are to remain rich and prosperous "Malacca cannot live without Cambay, nor Cambay without Malacca."[500] Thus, it was the Gujaratis who suffered most severely by Albuquerque's conquest of Malacca,[501] for they were the main intermediaries in the trade of south Asia with the countries of the west.

F. FROM CAPE COMORIN TO BENGAL

Portuguese ships and factories straddled the traditional commercial routes of western India from Diu south to Colombo. But with the east coast of India the Portuguese had little direct contact and accumulated information mainly through hearsay in the years when they were hastily constructing their empire. Still the Portuguese established a few footholds on the east coast to the north of

---

[494] See Castanheda in Azevedo (ed.), *op. cit.* (n. 17), II, 314; Pires in Cortesão (ed.), *op. cit.* (n. 9), I, 33, 40.
[495] Orta (Markham [ed.], *op. cit.* [n. 4], p. 333) says that most of the opium sold in Cambay originates in Malwa.
[496] Pires in Cortesão (ed.), *op. cit.* (n. 9), I, 43–44.
[497] *Ibid.*, p. 44.
[498] Birch (trans.), *op. cit.* (n. 116), III, 58.
[499] See Pires in Cortesão (ed.), *op. cit.* (n. 9), I, 42, 45.
[500] *Ibid.*, p. 45.
[501] *Ibid.*

Madras in the first years after arriving in India. Alarmed by the inroads they had made, the ruler of Orissa forced them in 1514 to limit their activities to Pippli, a small town at the mouth of the Subarnarekha River. But such early settlements seem not to have endured and prospered.[502] Even Albuquerque apparently possessed very little knowledge of the maritime region of Coromandel or the rich double delta of the Godavari and Krishna rivers though he was aware that the people of these areas traded with Malacca, Bengal, Burma, and Sumatra.[503] Once Goa was in his hands, the great conqueror, ignoring eastern India, proceeded to attack Malacca itself by following the well traveled trade route from Ceylon directly eastward. Even after definite trade connections were established with Bengal, beginning in 1517, the main Portuguese trading fleets continued to bypass the eastern coast as they sailed directly from Ceylon to the delta of the Ganges. Still, from Malacca and Colombo the Portuguese were able to extend their authority over trade in the Bay of Bengal and to plant settlements at a few points on the Coromandel coast and in Bengal.[504]

Ptolemy takes notice of the ports of eastern India,[505] but most of the other writers of antiquity and the Middle Ages are not so well informed. Marco Polo, who uses the Arabic word "'Ma'bar'" for the Coromandel coast, discourses at some length on examples of the trade, traditions, enterprises, personalities, and ports of the Tamil country.[506] The friars who visited and worked in south India during the late thirteenth and early fourteenth centuries visited the shrine of St. Thomas at Mylapore and commented on Hindu and other native customs and practices. The Italian trader, Nicolò de' Conti, who visited Vijayanagar around 1420, remarked on several of the eastern seaports of that Hindu empire. But beyond these incidental references, there was very little more until the sixteenth century when connected narratives appeared which more clearly identified the coastal towns, their relationship to one another and to more distant places, and presented a few observations on the type of life prevailing there. The only European writers among those here under consideration to travel on the east coast were Varthema, Pires, and Barbosa, and none of them seems actually to have visited Bengal. The other commentators appear to derive their information from these early travelers and numerous unspecified sources.

Barros divides the coast facing the Bay of Bengal into three major areas. Beginning just north of Cape Comorin he indicates that the coastal region for 200 leagues (800 miles) is within the jurisdiction of Vijayanagar. The next large division of 110 leagues (440 miles) belongs to Orissa, and it is followed as he proceeds northward, by a segment of 100 leagues (400 miles) belonging to

---

[502] N. K. Sahu (ed.), *A History of Orissa* (Calcutta, 1956), I, 178–79.

[503] See, *inter alia*, the reference in Academia Real das Sciencias, *Cartas de Affonso de Albuquerque* (7 vols.; Lisbon, 1884–1935), II, 392.

[504] See general discussion in W. H. Moreland (ed.), *Relations of Golconda in the Seventeenth Century* ("Hakluyt Society Publications," Series II, Vol. LXVI [London, 1931]), pp. xx–xxi.

[505] See S. M. Sastri (ed.), *op. cit.* (n. 3), pp. 62–72.

[506] For evaluation of Polo's account see K. A. Nilakanta Sastri, "Marco Polo on India," in *Oriente Poliano* (Rome, 1957), pp. 114–17.

Bengal.[507] Like the other European writers, Barros notices that the ports at the tip of the peninsula and those on the east coast just north of the Cape lie outside the direct authority of Vijayanagar and that the local rulers maintain some sort of vassal relationship to Quilon.[508]

Comorin itself, which the Ptolemaic writers refer to as "Komar,"[509] is shown by most of the sixteenth-century authors to have intimate geographical, cultural, and commercial relationships with Malabar, Coromandel, the Maldives, and Ceylon. Barros lists many of the ports lying within each of his larger divisions of the east coast, but does not comment in detail on any of them except Mylapore.[510] Pires describes Comorin as a separate "kingdom" bounded on the west by Travancore and on the east by "Quaile" (Palayakayal or Old Kayal in the delta of the Tamraparni River).[511] Upon the death of the ruler of Quilon the prince of Comorin is said to succeed to the rāja's place. Aside from Travancore, the land of Comorin is held to be inferior to its other neighbors and almost without palm trees. The sterility of the land at the cape, Pires attributes to the fact that it lacks the wet winds which keep Malabar fresh and luxuriant.[512]

The port of Palayakayal is important for its intermediary position on the trade route linking Bengal, Cambay, and Malacca. Though technically within the territory of Quilon, at least until 1532 when Vijayanagar took it over, this town appears to have enjoyed a measure of independence. In Marco Polo's time, "Cael" (Kayal) was considered to be the most important city and seaport on the eastern coast of India.[513] Its relative commercial importance was probably not so great in Barbosa's day, for shortly thereafter its harbor silted up and its merchants and fishers moved to Tuticorin, now the principal seaport of Tinnevelly.[514] Still, when the Portuguese first arrived at Palayakayal, it is singled out as a great center of pearl fishing. The rāja of Quilon possesses the monopoly of these fishing rights which he farms out to a Moor. The Muslim fishers, who probably came originally from the pearl fisheries of the Gulf of Ormuz, had taken over at a somewhat earlier date from the native fisher caste of Paravans. In Barbosa's time, the Muslim fishers are said to work all week for themselves except for Fridays when they hand over their catch as rent to the owner of the fishing boat. In the last week of the fishing season their catch is paid to the chief pearl farmer in compensation for their fishing rights. Though the ruler of Quilon and his armed retainers are always close by the city, the real arbiters of justice in local affairs seem to be the wealthy Moors who run the fishery.[515]

[507] Cidade and Múrias (eds.), *op. cit.* (n. 6), I, 359–60.

[508] *Ibid.*, p. 358. See also Castanheda in Azevedo (ed.), *op. cit.* (n. 17), II, 404.

[509] S. M. Sastri (ed.), *op. cit.* (n. 3), p. 55. "Komar" is short for Kanyā Kumāri, the full name.

[510] Cidade and Múrias (eds.), *op. cit.* (n. 6), I, 360–61.

[511] Cortesão (ed.), *op. cit.* (n. 9), I, 81. Pires is not entirely consistent in his account of political control. At another place in his narrative (*ibid.*, p. 66) he talks about Cape Comorin as being "in the King of Quilon's land."

[512] *Ibid.*, p. 66.

[513] Yule and Cordier (eds.), *op. cit.* (n. 4), II, 370–75. For confirmation of this assertion see R. Caldwell, "Explorations at Korkei and Kayal," *Indian Antiquary*, VI (1877), 82.

[514] Dames (ed.), *op. cit.* (n. 5), II, 122–23, n. 1.   [515] *Ibid.*, p. 124.

Northward along the Fishery Coast, close to the narrows and Adam's Bridge in the Gulf of Manaar, is the small seaport of Kilakarai.[516] This town and the surrounding country are, according to Barbosa, still within the territories of the rājā of Quilon.[517] Moorish traders come here in sampans, bringing horses from Cambay and taking out cargoes of rice and cloth for sale in Malabar. Barbosa also reports that "in this province" there is a great temple with revenue-producing estates which is large enough to have its own ruler. Every twelve years a great jubilee is held to honor the god of the temple. On these festival occasions the ruler ritually kills himself on a platform in the presence of a great throng and his intended successor. The resemblance of this festival to the *Mahāmakka* celebration of Calicut is remarkable and deserves consideration from those who categorically deny, on the basis of tradition alone that self-immolation by the Zamorin after a twelve years' reign was customary.[518]

The Coromandel coast (*Choḷamaṇḍala* or country of the Cholas) is given different limits and a variety of place-names by the Portuguese chronicles, rutters, and maps. In general, however, they place it, along with Barros and any modern Admiralty Pilot, between Point Calimere in the south and the deltas of the Godavari and Krishna rivers in the north. All of this coastal stretch, peopled mainly by Hindus, is within the jurisdiction of Vijayanagar and separated from Orissa on the interior by a range of mountains called the "Odirguale-mado" (Udayagiri, south of the Krishna).[519] Barbosa, who is the only one of the European writers to attempt a general description of Coromandel, indicates that this coastal "land of open plains" produces an abundance of rice, meat, and wheat.[520] Ships from Malabar bring in the products of the west and carry out cargoes of rice and dispose of it in rice-deficit areas. Drought and famine sometimes sweep this normally fruitful land, and in those catastrophic years the ships from Malabar bring in rice and coconuts and take away shiploads of children whom their parents out of want sell into slavery. After the Portuguese made merchandising dangerous for Muslims on the west coast of India, Barbosa reports that the Arab traders concentrated their activities on developing commerce between the Far East and the marts of Coromandel.[521]

Both Pires and Barros give extended but dissimilar lists of the individual seaports of Coromandel.[522] The trader, Pires, lists five coastal towns northward as far as Pulicat, where he seems to think Coromandel ends. Barros, the research student, lists sixteen ports as coming under the jurisdiction of Vijayanagar but has almost nothing to say about them. Negapatam, the southernmost port of

[516] Identification in *ibid.*, p. 120, n. 2; for a slightly different identification see Cortesão (ed.), *op. cit.* (n. 9), II, 271, n. 1.

[517] Dames (ed.), *op. cit.* (n. 5), II, 120.

[518] See above, p. 356 and Raja, *op. cit.* (n. 67), pp. 28–31.

[519] See above, p. 372; also Dames (ed.), *op. cit.* (n. 5), II, 130 n.

[520] Dames (ed.), *op. cit.* (n. 5), II, 125.

[521] *Ibid.*

[522] See Cortesão (ed.), *op. cit.* (n. 9), II, 271, and Cidade and Múrias (eds.), *op. cit.* (n. 6), I, 360–61.

Vijayanagar, was visited in 1505 by Varthema. The Italian describes it as being located in rice-producing country and "on the route to very large countries."[523] Pires mentions a famous temple of Vijayanagar in connection with Negapatam. The probability is, since no temple exists within the city antedating 1777, that he is referring to the famous and rich temple in nearby Tiruvalur.[524]

Mylapore, today practically a southern suburb of Madras, is noticed by the Europeans primarily because of the tradition that St. Thomas died there. Isidore of Seville in 636 reported that the Apostle had been killed and buried in India.[525] In Europe this report was echoed by later travelers and commentators, and in India pilgrims visited the tomb at Mylapore long before the Portuguese arrived there.[526] Varthema in 1505 heard from some Indian Christians of Coromandel that the bones of St. Thomas were nearby and were being watched over by native Christians. Meanwhile, the Portuguese in Malabar were occupying themselves with the St. Thomas Christians whom they found there, and with the restoration of the church at Mylapore. But when Barbosa arrived at this spot around 1515 the ancient city "which erstwhile was very great and fair" is described as being "almost deserted." The body of St. Thomas lies buried "in a little ruined church near the sea" in which a "poor Moor" keeps lonely vigil over the tomb.[527] In 1516, a Franciscan mission and church were built at Mylapore[528] and in the next year a group of Portuguese and Indian Christians made a pilgrimage to the tomb. By 1521 the tomb had been opened by a Portuguese expedition[529] and eventually the bones found therein became sacred relics and Mylapore was elevated by the Portuguese to a holy place.[530] So by the time when Barros wrote, he is able to comment on the restoration of the city with magnificent houses and to note that since about 1545 it has been called St. Thomas.[531] Through Nuno da Cunha, Barros also received some native writings which gave him information on the customs of the people in these parts.[532]

The most active and richest port of the Coromandel coast is Pulicat.[533] Varthema arrived in this Vijayanagar city from Ceylon early in 1505, and he observes that it is an entrepôt in the trade with Ceylon and Burma.[534] Merchants from the inland marts of the great Hindu kingdom exchange goods,

[523] Temple (ed.), *op. cit.* (n. 233), p. 72. Probably meaning the provinces of Vijayanagar. For substantiation see Castanheda in Azevedo (ed.), *op. cit.* (n. 17), IV, 277.

[524] Cortesão (ed.), *op. cit.* (n. 9), I, 91–92.

[525] L. W. Brown, *The Indian Christians of St. Thomas* (Cambridge, 1956), p. 55.

[526] *Ibid.*, p. 56.

[527] Dames (ed.), *op. cit.* (n. 5), II, 126–29.

[528] See above, p. 235.

[529] Corrêa, *op. cit.* (n. 2), II, 724–25.

[530] Brown, *op. cit.* (n. 525), p. 58.

[531] Cidade and Múrias (eds.), *op cit.* (n.6), I, 360–61.

[532] *Ibid.*, p. 361. These were "um livro da escritura dos chis [possibly Shiites] e outro dos parseos. ..." Eventually they were forwarded to Paulus Jovius in Rome on the request of papal representatives in Lisbon.

[533] Cf. remarks of Castanheda in Azevedo (ed.), *op. cit.* (n. 17), I, 458.

[534] Temple (ed.), *op. cit.* (n. 233), p. 74.

especially precious stones, with the maritime traders. The rājā has a governor at Pulicat charged with collecting the duties of the trade.[535] The colored cotton goods produced as a specialty at Pulicat are exported to pay for the rubies of Burma and the elephants of Ceylon. The customs, dress, and laws of Pulicat, Varthema asserts, "are the same as at Calicut."[536] Bellicose, even though they possess no artillery, the people of Pulicat are said to be waging war in 1505 against "Tarnassari."[537] Though the Portuguese landed at Pulicat in 1521 on their way to Mylapore, their appearances at Vijayanagar's great eastern port seem to have occurred only at relatively infrequent intervals during the first generation of the sixteenth century.[538] Of the coastal strip from Pulicat to the Krishna, often known as the Northern Sircars, the Europeans say little beyond supplying the names of seven ports.[539] Indeed, it appears that most of what they have to report about the entire east coast to the north of Pulicat is derived from the accounts of others.

Orissa, the Hindu kingdom which was being pinched between Vijayanagar and Bengal, receives a bit of attention from Pires and Barbosa. Barros reports that the seaboard of Orissa is rough and concludes therefrom that this is the reason why the kingdom has so few ports. Then he goes on to give a list of ten of them, ending up with "*Cabo Segogara* to which we give the name 'das Palmeiras' [Point Palmyras]."[540] Orissa extends far inland, and has very little maritime trade.[541] The northernmost of its ports is Remuna, the chief town of northern Orissa, where the Europeans apparently traded by way of the Bura-balanga River. Orissa is separated from Bengal by a river that Barbosa and later European writers call the "Ganges" or the "Ganga," possibly confusing the Dhamura River with the authentic Ganges to the north.[542]

Ruled over by a "heathen" king, Orissa is constantly at war with one or the other of its neighbors.[543] Even though there are but a few Moors in Orissa, its Gajapati king still has a large and capable army of infantrymen.[544] Pires also indicates that Orissa's ruler pays tribute to Bengal, possibly in return for help in warding off the onslaughts of Vijayanagar.[545] While the Portuguese admit

[535] Barbosa in Dames (ed.), *op. cit.* (n. 5), II, 132.

[536] Temple (ed.), *op. cit.* (n. 233), p. 74.

[537] *Ibid.* The editor (Temple) of Varthema appears to think that a war was being fought with Tenassêrim across the Bay of Bengal. Dames (ed.), *op. cit.* (n. 5), II, 130, considers this improbable and thinks that Varthema was speaking of Orissa.

[538] For examples of these irregular contacts see Castanheda in Azevedo (ed.), *op. cit.* (n. 17), IV, 115, 116, 130.

[539] Barros in Cidade and Múrias (eds.), *op. cit.* (n. 6), I, 361.   [540] *Ibid.*

[541] Barbosa in Dames (ed.), *op. cit.* (n. 5), II, 133.

[542] *Ibid.*, pp. 133–34. Or for another interpretation of this disputed identification see C. R. Wilson, "Note on the Topography of the River Hugli . . .," *Journal of the Asiatic Society of Bengal*, LXI (1892), 112.

[543] Krishna Dêva Rāyya, ruler of Vijayanagar, had as one of his primary ambitions the capture of Orissa's eastern coast. He started his major campaign in 1512 and occupied the fortress of Udayagiri during the following year. These internal wars seem to be what the Portuguese hear most about, probably through Vijayanagar.

[544] Barbosa in Dames (ed.), *op. cit.* (n. 5), II, 132–33.

[545] Cortesão (ed.), *op. cit.* (n. 9), I, 89.

to having no first-hand knowledge of the people of Orissa "by reason of their dwelling away from the coast," [546] Pires unqualifiedly asserts that the best diamonds come from there and that "cowries are the current coinage." [547]

Most of what the Portuguese heard about Orissa evidently came to them through Vijayanagar and their outposts in Bengal, Colombo, and Malacca. In Malacca the merchants native to the Telugu coast were usually called "Klings," a Malay form of the territorial name Kalinga. Pires states that Orissa is within "the province of the Klings" [548] and he appears to understand that their languages (Oriya and Telugu) are different from the Kanarese spoken in Vijayanagar. [549] The "Klings," who are particularly prominent in the cloth trade at Malacca, are reported to marry their daughters at an early age to the merchants of other nationalities in the great Malay port. In the total trade of Malacca the "Klings," before the influx of the Portuguese, have a greater share than any other foreign group and live there under a special administration. [550] The generic term "Kling," as used in Malacca, probably included most of the merchants who originated in the ports of eastern India south of Bengal, and so it would seem logical to assume that those from the Telugu country constituted no more than an influential minority.

Individual Portuguese certainly got as far north as Bengal in Albuquerque's time, but no evidence exists of a Portuguese vessel arriving there before the visit of João Coelho in 1516–17. [551] This initial contact was followed by the expedition of 1518 sent from the Maldives under João de Silveira to ask for trading facilities and permission to erect a factory. Silveira landed at Chittāgong on the extreme eastern side of the delta on May 9, [552] but the ruler of Bengal, Mahmūd Shah, refused to receive the Portuguese envoy, and the governor of the city finally turned him away. Though rebuffed, the Portuguese hereafter continued annually to send a trading ship to Chittāgong. [553] It was not, however, until Nuno da Cunha's period as viceroy (1529–38) that the Portuguese renewed

[546] Barbosa in Dames (ed.), *op. cit.* (n. 5), I, 229.

[547] Cortesão (ed.), *op. cit.* (n. 9), I, 89, 94, 224.

[548] *Ibid.*, p. 4; for the relation of Orissa to the ancient term "Kalinga," see R. M. Chakravarti, "Notes on the Geography of Orissa in the Sixteenth Century," *Journal of the Asiatic Society of Bengal*, XII (1916), 34.

[549] Cortesão (ed.), *op. cit.* (n. 9), I, 64–65.

[550] *Ibid.*, p. 281. Also see below, p. 513.

[551] Early Portuguese documents indicate that ships were being sent to Bengal before 1516, but they do not tell of the success or failure of these missions. For a summary of early references see A. Cortesão, "The 'City of Bengala' in Early Reports," *Journal of the Royal Asiatic Society of Bengal* (*Letters*), XI (1945), 13, n. 2. See also J. J. A. Campos, *History of the Portuguese in Bengal* (Calcutta, 1919), p. 26. And for general historical background see J. N. Sarkar (ed.), *The History of Bengal* (Dacca, 1948). Unfortunately, the authors of this otherwise excellent history rely almost entirely upon the general secondary accounts of the Portuguese in Bengal and they do not refer to either Castanheda or Barros.

[552] Castanheda in Azevedo (ed.), *op. cit.* (n. 17), II, 441; also Barros in Cidade and Múrias (eds.), *op. cit.* (n. 6), III, 68. For a summary of the story which Silveira told about Bengal after his return to Cochin see the letter of Dom João de Leyma to the king (December 22, 1518) as summarized in S. N. Sen, "An Early Portuguese Account of Bengal," *The Calcutta Review*, LXVI (1938), 21–25.

[553] Campos, *op. cit.* (n. 551), p. 30.

their efforts to establish a trading settlement in Bengal. Attempts in 1529 and 1533 failed to establish cordial relations with the ruler of Bengal and the Portuguese suffered many losses at his hands. Largely as a result of the war in 1535–36 between Mahmūd Shah and Sher Shah, the Portuguese were able to wring concessions from the obdurate Bengal ruler. As a reward for aid rendered to Mahmūd Shah in the war, the Portuguese were permitted in 1536 and 1537 to build factories at Chittāgong and at Sātgāon in western Bengal. In both places, which they occupied almost simultaneously, the Portuguese possessed land, owned houses, and administered customs.[554] It was not until the port of Sātgāon silted up that the Portuguese in 1580 founded Hugli (or Hoogly), just a little to the southeast of their earlier settlement.

It was mainly as a result of commercial contacts in places as widely separated as Malacca, Goa, and Lisbon, that the European writers on India were able to learn about Bengal. Varthema is the only one of them who even pretends to have set foot on the soil of Bengal.[555] That part of his account which deals mainly with trade and personal relations is less valuable and more confusing than many of his other descriptions. Pires and Barbosa seem to have learned most of what they recount from reports current in Malacca and the ports of India before 1515. Castanheda is the only one of the chroniclers to publish in the sixteenth century a general description of the land and people at the lower reaches of the Ganges.[556] Barros, who clearly collected important detail on the geography and history of the delta region, is not able in his lifetime to summarize this material in print. His collection of information, like his manuscript maps, he left to be completed and published by Lavanha in *Década IV* (1613).[557] Orta confines his remarks to noticing that flax and elephants are native to Bengal.[558] It is therefore Pires, Barbosa, and Castanheda who furnish the most coherent and reliable accounts of Bengal, even though they are all based on the reports of others.

Barros, who usually revels in listing the names of ports, humorously remarks that describing the jagged and island-lined seacoast from Point Palmyras to Chittāgong is a task much more suited to the art of the painter than to that of the writer.[559] The Ganges, which empties into the Bay of Bengal (the Ptolemaic *Gangeticus Sinus*), is the overwhelmingly prominent geographical feature of the region to the Portuguese even as it had been to the Ptolemaic geographers. Though its source is unknown to Castanheda, the Ganges is described as emptying into the sea through two great mouths. In the interior its banks are

---

[554] Castanheda in Azevedo (ed.), *op. cit.* (n. 17), IV, 410–11.

[555] For an interpretation of his remarks based on the visit of 1505 see Temple (ed.), *op. cit.* (n. 233), pp. lxvi–lxix.

[556] Azevedo (ed.), *op. cit.* (n. 17), II, 439–41.

[557] Cidade and Múrias (ed.), *op. cit.* (n. 6), IV, 501–5.

[558] Markham (ed.), *op. cit.* (n. 4), pp. 54, 181.

[559] Cidade and Múrias (eds.), *op. cit.* (n. 6), I, 361. He defers this listing to his *Geografia* which has never been found. In the map of Bengal published in 1613 by Lavanha, presumably on the basis of Barros' notes and drawings, a large number of towns appear. See illustrations.

said to be lined for many leagues with towns.[560] The great Gangetic plain which covers a vast expanse is surrounded by hills. The mountainous state of Orissa borders Bengal on the south and Arakan fronts it on the east or the "Pegu (Burma) side."[561] In the interior towards Delhi it is bounded by the bellicose states of Coos and Tipura. The lords of all these surrounding territories are said to be vassals of the ruler of Bengal.[562] The principal city of the kingdom is "Bengala" (Gaur),[563] and its most important ports, when Castanheda wrote, are recognized to be Chittāgong and Sātgāon.[564]

Gaur is located on the Ganges one hundred leagues (400 miles) from the sea,[565] two days being required to make the journey upriver.[566] A city of forty thousand hearths, it is a long narrow metropolis which stretches out along the river for four leagues (16 miles).[567] Though it is located on level ground, Gaur is surrounded by rivers (the Ganges and the Mahānanda) in which seagoing vessels of four hundred tons lie anchored. That Gaur was accessible to seagoing vessels is clear from all the Portuguese accounts. On the east the city is protected by a great marsh backed up by a dense jungle populated by ferocious beasts; and because the jungle helps to protect the city from invasion, the rulers of Bengal forbid that it be cut down. Upriver more than twenty leagues (80 miles) from Gaur is a fortress town called "Gori" (Garhi) which controls the passes to the mountains separating Bihar from Bengal and was known as "the gate of Bengal."[568]

Within the city there stand many elegant mosques and fine houses. The royal residence includes many sumptuous palaces spread over as much of an area as the entire city of Evora.[569] Constructed of sun-dried bricks,[570] the

---

[560] Azevedo (ed.), *op. cit.* (n. 17), II, 439–46.

[561] Pires in Cortesão (ed.), *op. cit.* (n. 9), I, 89. [562] *Ibid.*, pp. 89–90.

[563] On the much disputed question of the identity of the "city of Bengala" see Cortesão, *loc. cit.* (n. 551), pp. 10–14. He concludes that the writers of the early sixteenth century are talking about Gaur when they refer to "Bengala." Later, after the Portuguese actually had settlements in Bengal, they usually equate Chittāgong with "Bengala." It may be pointed out that in Bengali sources Gaur and Bengala are considered to be separate towns.

[564] Azevedo (ed.), *op. cit.* (n. 17), II, 441. For a later effort to describe the political geography of Bengal in this period see H. Blochmann, "Contributions to the Geography and History of Bengal," *Journal of the Asiatic Society of Bengal*, Vol. XLII, Pt. I (1873), pp. 209–307.

[565] Castanheda (in Azevedo [ed.], *op. cit.* [n. 17], II, 440) greatly exaggerates the distance, for it was actually only 200 miles upriver.

[566] Pires in Cortesão (ed.), *op. cit.* (n. 9), I, 90.

[567] A change in the course of the Ganges River and the pillaging of war brought Gaur to ruin and desolation in 1575. According to calculations by modern archaeologists, the city with its suburbs covered an area of from 20 to 30 square miles. The city proper, enclosed by a continuous embankment, ran about 7.5 miles in length and 1 to 2 miles in width. See Hunter, *op. cit.* (n. 46) V, 37. Barros (in Cidade and Múrias [eds.], *op. cit.* [n. 6], IV, 505) estimates its population as running as high as 200,000. For a map of Gaur see M. Martin, *The History . . . of Eastern India* (London, 1838), facing p. 72.

[568] This description by Castanheda (in Azevedo [ed.], *op. cit.* [n. 17], IV, 408) is similar to that given by certain Muslim historians (Blochmann, *loc. cit.* [n. 564], p. 213); for its identification with Garhi see Campos, *op. cit.* (n. 551), p. 38.

[569] Castanheda in Azevedo (ed.), *op. cit.* (n. 17), II, 440.

[570] Pires in Cortesão (ed.), *op. cit.* (n. 9), I, 91. For confirmation see Hunter, *op. cit.* (n. 46), V, 37, who writes: "Countless millions of small, thin bricks were used in building Gaur."

splendid houses of the city have only ground floors, are decorated in gold and blue, and enclose beautiful patios and gardens.[571] The poorer people live in palm-leaf huts.[572]

Most descriptions of life in Bengal given by the European writers appear to be based on observations made at Gaur. The population of the city includes Moors, Hindus, and many foreigners. Most Bengalis are "sleek, handsome black men, more sharpwitted than the men of any other known race."[573] The European writers denounce the Bengalis for being overly wary and treacherous, and Pires reports that in Malacca it is an insult to call a man a Bengali.[574] The women of Bengal are beautiful and clean; they live in luxury and are forced to remain indoors. Moors of the upper class have three or four wives or as many as they can maintain. It is obviously an advantage in sixteenth-century Bengal to be a Moor inasmuch as the Hindus "daily become Moors to gain the favor of their rulers."[575]

Life in Gaur is opulent and it centers around the royal residence whose occupant is esteemed to be a "faithful Muslim and much richer in treasure than any other king in India."[576] The betel he chews is mixed with camphor of Borneo which is so expensive that the royal chamberlain makes a tidy sum annually by recovering the camphor from the ruler's golden cuspidor![577] Being extremely fond of music, the ruler imports singers and musicians from as far away as Vijayanagar and Gujarat. To one of his Moorish singers he pays an enormous annual salary.[578] Husain Shāh, who was ruling when Pires wrote, is reported to have many daughters and twenty-four sons by his various wives.[579] He also maintains a large military establishment of both cavalry and infantry, for he is almost constantly engaged in war with his vassals and neighbors, especially Delhi.[580]

The government of Bengal is correctly reported to have been taken over by Muslims about three hundred years before the arrival of the Portuguese in India. Pires also contends that "for seventy-four years" before the date of his writing the succession in Bengal was systematically achieved by murder. This system, which he claims was borrowed from Pasay in Sumatra, he calls "the Pase practice."[581] Regicide was mainly the task of a Pretorian band of Abyssinians and, as a result, the Abyssinian eunuchs closest to the throne were considered

[571] Castanheda in Azevedo (ed.), *op. cit.* (n. 17), II, 440.

[572] Pires in Cortesão (ed.), *op. cit.* (n. 9), I, 91.   [573] *Ibid.*, p. 88.

[574] *Ibid.*, p. 93; also Castanheda in Azevedo (ed.), *op. cit.* (n. 17), II, 440. Campos (*op. cit.* [n. 551], pp. 20–21) apologetically contends that the Portuguese were giving this bad character to the rulers rather than the people of Bengal. Such a contention holds no water, because Pires clearly means for his defamatory remarks to apply to Bengali fishermen and tailors working in Malacca.

[575] Barbosa in Dames (ed.), *op. cit.* (n. 5), II, 148; also Castanheda in Azevedo (ed.), *op. cit.* (n. 17), II, 441.

[576] Castanheda in Azevedo (ed.), *op. cit.* (n. 17), II, 441.

[577] *Ibid.*   [578] *Ibid.*

[579] Cortesão (ed.), *op. cit.* (n. 9), I, 95.

[580] *Ibid.*, pp. 89–90.

[581] *Ibid.*, pp. 88–89. For a description of the practice at Pasay see Barros in Cidade and Múrias (eds.), *op. cit.* (n. 6), III, 234–35. Also see below, p. 578.

by Pires as being the real governors of the land. Though Pires' dates for the Abyssinian ascendancy may be suspect, his description of the role which they played in the late fifteenth century corresponds extremely well with what is known from other sources.[582] According to the Muslim histories, it was Bārbak Shāh (reigned 1460–74) who first maintained a large number of Abyssinian slaves as protectors of the throne. Between this ruler's death and the accession of Husain Shāh in 1493, the very names of the rulers during the interregnum proclaim that they were Abyssinian eunuchs.[583] In Bengal, Pires avers, "they are more in the habit of having eunuchs . . . than in any other part of the world."[584] Aside from the Abyssinian eunuchs at the court, it is common for eunuchs to act as harem guards and domestic servants in the houses of the wealthy.[585] Others receive administrative appointments as city governors and they are "called 'lascars' in the language of the land."[586] Traffic in young boys, taken particularly from the non-Muslims of the back country, apparently prevails in the early sixteenth century as it did in the time of Marco Polo. While many of the enslaved youths die from castration, those who survive are held in high regard and often become rich and influential in their own right.[587]

In addition to Abyssinians, Bengal plays host to other foreigners, especially merchants from Arabia, Egypt, Turkey and other parts of India. In Husain Shāh's time, however, many were said to be going elsewhere because he is antagonistic to them.[588] Still, some foreign merchants, mostly Muslims, decide to remain in Bengal because "this land is large, fruitful, and healthy."[589] Wheat, rice, and sugar are produced in great quantities. Cattle, both large and small varieties, are innumerable; sheep, horses,[590] fish, and poultry are all in excellent supply; and wild game and birds exist in profusion. The land also yields citrus and a multitude of other fruits, long pepper, ginger, cotton, and flax. But what is evidently most attractive to the foreign merchants and astounding to the Portuguese is the cheapness of food.[591]

Native industries based on the produce of the field are also numerous. From cotton and flax the Bengali men make thread on a spinning wheel. This is woven by the same men into white and colored materials for the domestic

---

[582] Majumdar *et al.*, *op. cit.* (n. 6), pp. 345–46.

[583] Blochmann, *loc. cit.* (n. 564), p. 286.

[584] Cortesão (ed.), *op. cit.* (n. 9), I, 88.

[585] Barbosa in Dames (ed.), *op. cit.* (n. 5), II, 147.

[586] Castanheda in Azevedo (ed.), *op. cit.* (n. 17), II, 441. Ordinarily, as used in Luso-Indian works, "lascar" means "soldier" or "sailor" and is of Persian derivation. With reference to Bengal it roughly means "the governor of a city." See Dalgado, *op. cit.* (n. 44), I, 514–15.

[587] Barbosa in Dames (ed.), *op. cit.* (n. 5), II, 147.

[588] Pires in Cortesão (ed.), *op. cit.* (n. 9), I, 95.

[589] *Ibid.*, pp. 140–41.

[590] Castanheda (in Azevedo [ed.], *op. cit.* [n. 17], II, 440) compares the horses of Bengal in size to "the little horses of England."

[591] Castanheda (*ibid.*) gives prices for cattle, poultry and rice with the obvious intention of impressing his reader with how inexpensive they are. Also see Pires in Cortesão (ed.), *op. cit.* (n. 9), I, 88.

and export markets. These cloths are especially fine for making ladies' head-dresses and turbans. Others are turned into rich canopies for beds, fancy pieces of cutwork, and tapestry-like hangings. Numerous fruits and vegetables for both domestic and foreign consumption are preserved in ginger, and sugar, and sometimes in vinegar. Sugar, since they do not know how to press it into loaves, is wrapped for export as a powder in sewn, leather parcels.[592]

The foreign trade of Bengal in the early years of the sixteenth century seems to have been concentrated at Gaur and Sātgāon. Chittāgong does not attract the notice of either Barbosa or Pires, perhaps because it was the seaport serving Gaur.[593] Sātgāon, a good port with a satisfactory entry, is a city of ten thousand hearths where many merchants concentrate.[594] Writing later on in the century, Castanheda describes Chittāgong as a kind of Venice in Bengal with its numerous waterways and bridges. A city of great commercial activity, Chittāgong is governed by a "lascar" who is a vassal of the ruler in Gaur.[595] Bengali trading vessels, both ships like those of Mecca and junks like those of China, sail annually to Malacca and Pasay.[596] In the Malay port they market Bengali cotton and muslin materials at a great profit; in Sumatra the Bengalis buy mainly pepper and silk.[597]

Ships sailing from Malacca to Bengal (presumably Sātgāon) usually depart around the first of August and arrive there at the end of the month. The merchants then stay in Bengal until the first of the following February to catch the monsoon back. In the interim they sell Borneo camphor and pepper in large quantities as well as other spices, porcelains, silks and damasks, and the swords and krises of Java. Foreign merchants trading in Bengal have to pay duties of "three on every eight."[598] Gold in Bengal is worth one-sixth more than it is in Malacca; silver is from 20 to 25 per cent cheaper. The local currency is primarily in silver, but for smaller units cowrie shells are commonly in use. In Bengal the cowries are larger than those circulating elsewhere, and are further distinguished by a yellow stripe down the middle. These special cowries originate in the Maldive Islands and are accepted as coinage in all of Bengal and Orissa, but not elsewhere. Goods are weighed in the ports of Bengal on a balance stick called a *dala* and duties are apparently assessed in terms of the weight so determined. Pires clearly feels these duties are excessive, an opinion which he probably derived from his contacts in the merchant community of Malacca.[599]

Little is reported by European writers about the Hindu population of Bengal beyond remarks to the effect that their children are sometimes sold to be

[592] Barbosa in Dames (ed.), *op. cit.* (n. 5), II, 146.
[593] Pires in Cortesão (ed.), *op. cit.* (n. 9), II, 13.
[594] *Ibid.*, I, 91.
[595] Castanheda in Azevedo (ed.), *op. cit.* (n. 17), II, 441.
[596] Pires in Cortesão (ed.), *op. cit.* (n. 9), I, 92.
[597] *Ibid.*, pp. 92–93.
[598] *Ibid.*, p. 93.
[599] *Ibid.*, pp. 94–95.

eunuchs, that many of them become converts to the Muslim faith, and that they constitute the majority of the population outside of the port cities. Castanheda, in talking about the Ganges, reports that for some unknown reason the "gentiles" of Bengal believe that its waters are holy and its source is in heaven. He reports that they make pilgrimages from near and far to bathe in its waters and so become cleansed of their sins. The king of Vijayanagar is said to have a cask of holy water from the Ganges brought to him each week so that he may bathe in it regularly. Orta, who claims to have proved the efficacy of its waters, records that the Bengalis go to the Ganges so that they may die with their feet in the holy river.[600]

G. HINDUSTAN AND THE AFGHAN–MUGHUL STRUGGLE FOR SUPREMACY

None of the European writers seems to have penetrated personally very far into the interior of northern India, aside from a few excursions inland from one seacoast town or the other. Gaur was probably as far into Bengal as the Portuguese merchants were ever able to penetrate in any numbers. On the west coast Portuguese adventurers from Diu went as far inland as Chitor, the leading city of Mewar, when they fought with the armies of Gujarat. It does not follow, however, that the Portuguese were uninformed about the Indo-Gangetic plain. From native informants, as well as the reports relayed to them by their own countrymen, the Portuguese writers from Pires to Barros are conscious that Delhi is the imperial city of northern India and that its ruler is an "emperor" who irregularly exacts obedience from a number of vassal "kings." Barros, as mentioned earlier, refers to the region between the Indus and western Bengal as Hindustan. South of the Himalayas, Barros includes within Hindustan the states of "Maltan" (Multan), Delhi, western Bengal, Orissa, "Māndū" (Malwa), "Chitor" (Mewar), and Gujarat, a political definition which corresponds closely to the conclusions of modern scholars working from Muslim sources.[601] But neither Barros nor the other Portuguese writers are able to comment on this entire list. Their observations on interior places are restricted to Delhi, Mewar, Malwa, and Bengal west of Gaur.

Pires and Barbosa report about the Delhi sultanate in the time of Sikander Lodi, the last ruler of the Lodi (Afghan) sultanate who died at his capital of Agra in 1517.[602] The rulers of Delhi were originally Hindus, according to the two Portuguese reporters, and about a century and a half before Vasco da Gama

---

[600] Markham (ed.), *op. cit.* (n. 4), pp. 401–2.

[601] See K. M. Ashraf, "Life and Conditions of the People of Hindustan (1200–1550 A.D.)—Mainly Based on Islamic Sources," *Journal of the Asiatic Society of Bengal* (*Letters*), I (1935), 105–6. The most notable omissions in Barros' list are the Punjab and Oudh. Also see above, p. 341 and Orta in Markham (ed.), *op. cit.* (n. 4), p. 293.

[602] The Lodis were Sultans of Delhi from 1451 to 1517.

arrived in Calicut the Muslims took over in Delhi.[603] At its apogee the Muslim sultanate of Delhi was clearly the greatest state of India with dominion over Sind, the Rajputs, Cambay, Malwa, and part of the Deccan. With the decline of central authority the captains of these provinces set themselves up as independent princes. In Delhi itself, which is described as a large and mountainous country far in the interior, there lived at the time of the Portuguese arrival many Hindus and Muslims. The sultans of Delhi, however, made life extremely difficult for the non-Muslims in their jurisdiction.[604] Many of the northern Hindus, especially the Yogis, emigrated to a more favorable political climate:

Barbosa reports that the Yogis, being "unwilling to stay under the power of the Moors,"[605] left Delhi and became wanderers to atone for their failure to take up arms against the invading Muslims. These pilgrims, who migrate from place to place in small bands, have no desire for property after having lost all their worldly possessions. Naked except for brass girdles, they smear their bodies and faces with ashes and carry heavy iron chains around their necks. The Yogis abide by no dietary laws, hold no pollution beliefs, and perform no purification ceremonies. Still they are held in great respect by the Hindus and even by some Moors. As they go about begging for alms, they bless their devotees by streaking them with ashes, and to the kings and lords who protect them they give antidotes against poison.[606] Orta, who evidently knew Barbosa's account, remarks a generation later that the Portuguese "are very little conversant with things in the kingdom of Delhi" and that what they know about it has come to them through the Yogis.[607]

Essentially this assertion is correct, for the Portuguese limit themselves to very general statements about life in Delhi. It is described as a cold and heavily populated country rich in horses, elephants, and food. The horses, which are born and bred there, are used mainly in war. The warriors of Delhi, Moors and Hindus alike, are good archers and well equipped with a variety of spears, swords, battle-axes, and maces.[608] Most of them carry steel quoits with razor-like outer edges called *chacora* (in Sanskrit, *cakra*) which they hurl at their enemies with skill and great effect.[609] The products of Delhi, like those of other inland states, are distributed to the outside world through Cambay.[610]

Aside from Delhi, the only other inland states of the north referred to by the

[603] See Pires in Cortesão (ed.), *op. cit.* (n. 9), I, 36. Possibly this is a reference to the establishment of the Khalji sultans in Delhi around 1290.

[604] Barbosa in Dames (ed.), *op. cit.* (n. 5), I, 230.

[605] *Ibid.*

[606] *Ibid.*, pp. 233–36.

[607] Markham (ed.), *op. cit.* (n. 4), p. 483. Some writers (for example, Ficalho [ed.], *op. cit.* [n. 369], II, 186) contend that Barbosa sees the Yogis as leading a Hindu reaction against the Muslim usurpation of power. In my reading of Barbosa I have not been able to discover this assertion.

[608] For confirmation and greater detail see William Irvine, *Army of the Indian Moghuls: Its Organization and Administration* (London, 1903), pp. 73–112.

[609] Barbosa in Dames (ed.), *op. cit.* (n. 5), I, 232–33. Also see the account of Varthema for a description of Yogis throwing quoits of this sort in Calicut in 1505 (Temple [ed.], *op. cit.* [n. 233], p. 101).

[610] Pires in Cortesão (ed.), *op. cit.*, I, 37.

early Portuguese writers are "Indo" (Sind), the Rajput territories, and the Muslim state of Malwa. At the beginning of the sixteenth century Sind, to the west of the Rajput country,[611] is already Muslim. Through its territories runs the Indus, "where India begins."[612] At its mouth there is a large port city whose governor is a Hindu of Sind. The products of Sind are indigo and, in small quantities, lac. Though it was once a famous kingdom, it is in Pires' day a small, mountainous, landlocked territory far removed from the centers of greatest activity in India.[613] The Rajput territories to the north of Gujarat are the homeland of Hindu warriors who obey no master and constantly prey upon their richer Muslim neighbors. To the east of Gujarat on the edge of the Vindhyan hills is the state of Malwa, whose king had but recently become a follower of the Prophet.[614] In olden times the warriors of this rocky plateau country were Amazons. And its king, in Pires' day, was said to have about two thousand women who rode out to battle with him.[615]

It is from Castanheda that Europe first learned in some detail about the Mughul advent in India, and about the subsequent struggle for supremacy between the Afghans and the Mughuls which occurred over the next generation. Upon arriving at Goa in 1528, Castanheda heard of the great victories being won by Babur in the north. The Mughul conqueror, who had spent the early years of the sixteenth century in winning dominion over central Asia, began his march from Kabul against the heart of Hindustan in 1525, after subjugating the Punjab. With the connivance of discontented nobles in Delhi, Babur proceeded against the forces of Ibrāhīm Lodi, the nominal sultan, and defeated them at Pānipāt in 1526. Routing of the Lodi forces led to the occupation of Delhi and Agra by the Mughuls, but Babur still had before him the task of pacifying the Rajputs under Rana Sanga and the provincial Afghan military chieftains. In 1527 he defeated Rana at Khanua, a town to the west of Agra, and brought an end to the Rajput national revival and the loose political confederacy led by Mewar. Then he turned eastward to hunt down the allied Afghans of Bihar and Bengal, whom he successfully defeated on the banks of the Gogra in 1529. With most of Hindustan at his mercy, Babur died at Agra in 1530 before he could organize and consolidate his conquests. Humayun, the son and successor of Babur to the Delhi sultanate, was thus confronted from the beginning of his reign with holding down hostile populations over an extended area with nothing at his command but military force. The Afghans in the east soon

---

[611] *Ibid.*, p. 37, n. 4.

[612] *Ibid.*, p. 38.

[613] *Ibid.*, pp. 37–38. In fact, it may almost be said that the Arabs and the Portuguese did not usually consider this Indus state to be within what they called India. See Yule and Burnell, *op. cit.* (n. 10), p. 634.

[614] Pires in Cortesão (ed.), *op. cit.* (n. 9), I, 37. The first Muslim king was the founder of the house of Ghori, an Afghan, Dilawar Khan, who ruled from 1387 to 1405.

[615] *Ibid.* This is a reference to the harem government which developed in Malwa and had its own army. See Ashraf, *loc. cit.* (n. 601), p. 150. Ferishta and other Muslim writers refer to Māndū, the capital, as the "city of joy" and they include in their accounts references to armed women. See Commissariat, *op. cit.* (n. 400), I, 288.

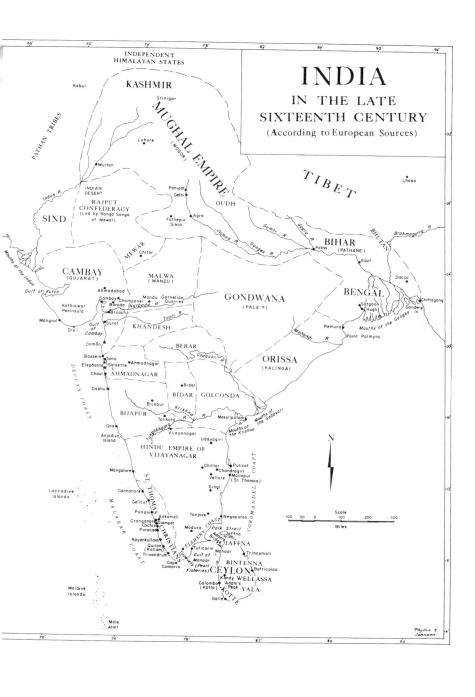

INDEPENDENT
HIMALAYAN STATES

INDIA
IN THE LATE
SIXTEENTH CENTURY
(According to European Sources)

Kabul

KASHMIR

Srinigar

PATHAN TRIBES

Lahore

TIBET

Lhasa

MUGHAL EMPIRE
(MOGOR)

Multan

Indus R.

INDIAN
DESERT

Panipat
Delhi

RAJPUT
CONFEDERACY
(Led by Ranga Sanga
of Mewar)

OUDH

SIND

Gumti R.

Gogra R.

Brahmaputra R.

Fathepur
Sikra
Agra

Juana R.

Ganges R.

BIHAR
(PATHANE)

BHUTAN

Patna

MEWAR

Chitor

Gaur

Dacca

Mouths of the Indus

CAMBAY
(GUJARAT)

MALWA
(MANDU)

GONDWANA
(PALE ?)

BENGAL

Satgaon
Hugli

Chittagong
Sandwip

Gulf of Kutch

Ahmadabad

Cambay
Baroda
Champener
Mandu
Carnelian
Quarries

Narbada R.

Mouths of the Ganges Is.

Kathiawar
Peninsula

Broach

Tapti R.

Remuna

Point Palmyra

Mangrol

Gulf
of
Cambay

Surat

KHANDESH

Mahandi R.

Diu I.

Damao

BERAR

ORISSA
(KALINGA)

Godavari R.

Bassein
Tana
Elephanta Salsette
Ahmadnagar

AHMADNAGAR

Chaul

DECCAN COAST

Dabhul

BIDAR
GOLCONDA

Bidar

Bijapur

Krishna R.

BIJAPUR

Talikota

Masulipatam

Mouths of
the Gadavari

Goa

Tungabhadra R.

Anjadiva
Island

Vijayanagar

Udayagiri

Mouths of
the Krishna

HINDU EMPIRE OF
VIJAYANAGAR

N

Chittor
Chandragiri
Mailapur
(St. Thomas)

Pulicat

Mangalore

Vellore

CORMANDEL COAST

Gingi

Laccadive
Islands

Cannanore

Calicut

Ponani
Ankamali
Cranganore
Cochin
Puracad
Diamper

Tanjore

Negapatam

Scale
100 50 0   100   200   300
Miles

ST. THOMAS CHRISTIAN

MALABAR COAST

Kayankullam
Quilon
(Kollam)
Trivandrum

Madura

Tuticorin

Manaar

Palk Strait
Jaffna

Adam's
Bridge

JAFFNA

Trincomali

FISHER COAST

Cape
Comorin

Gulf of
Manaar
(Pearl
Fisheries)

BINTENNA

CEYLON

Botticaloa

WELLASSA

Colombo
(Kotta)

Kandy Adam's
Peak

YALA

KOTTE

Galle

Maldive
Islands

Male
Atoll

Phyllis S.
Johnson

Cannanore at the beginning of the sixteenth century.

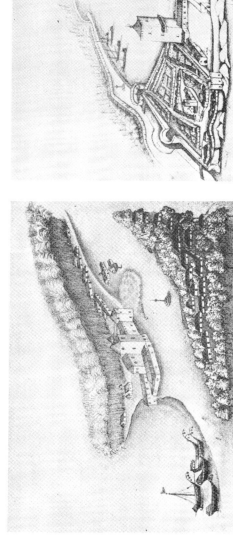

Quilon at the beginning of the sixteenth century.

Both illustrations from Agência geral do ultramar, *Fundacão do estado do India em 1505* (Lisbon, 1955).

The king of Cochin with his attendants. Woodcut in Balthasar Springer's *Meerfahrt* (published 1509) attributed to Hans Burgkmair, the famous engraver of Augsburg. Reproduced here from Franz Schulze, *Balthasar Springers Indienfahrt* (Strassburg, 1902).

Die Coninck van Guttchin met finen hoffluyden

DER GOSOI SIDE GUTSMIN

The "famous rhinoceros" of Cambay. Woodcut by Albrecht Dürer (1515). A copy of this woodcut is in the Albertina Museum in Vienna. The original drawing was based on a description sent to Dürer

the East (*a.* 1538–46). Original in the Biblioteca Casanatense (Rome). This and the two illustrations on the following page are from G. Schurhammer's "Desenhos orientais do tempo de S. Francisco Xavier," *Garcia da Orta*, Special Number (Lisbon, 1956).

"Baneanes" (Bānyas) of Cambay. Watercolor.

Dɛ funere in demortui cremandique Brachmani honorem inſtituto: in
quo ſimul eorum vxores viuæ in rogum ardentem
inſiliunt.

Os eſt Brachmanis, vt aliquo ex ipſis demortuo propin-
qui foueam parent, in quam ligna Sandali, herbas odo-
ratas, cibaria, oriʒam, ſiliginem atque oleum inflam-
mando rogo infundant, quibus incenſis cadauer ſuper-
imponunt. mox procedit vidua, comitata inſtrumentis
muſicis, quam cognatæ alacres exhortantur, vt virum fideliter inſequa-
tur, quo in altero mundo cum ipſo inter mille gaudia exultet. ipſa vero a-
nimo paratiſſimo, lætabunda veſtes & clenodia depoſita inter pro-
ximas diſtribuit, mox ridens rogum inſilit viua cum
mariti cadauere concremanda.
vid. cap. 36.

C 2   Rɪᴛᴠs

Sati, or widow-burning. From Theodor de Bry, *Indiae orientalis* (Frankfurt, 1599).

Gujarat. This and the map on the facing page are from João de Barros, *Décadas da Ásia* (Madrid, 1615). Courtesy of the Cornell University Library.

Bengal.

Juggernaut and ceremonial religious suicide in the *Rath-játra*, a Hindu procession. This and the illustration on the facing page are from G. Schurhammer's "Desenhos orientais do tempo de S. Francisco Xavier," *Garcia da Orta*, Special Number (Lisbon, 1956).

A Portuguese fidalgo in India.

Ships and boats of India. From J. van Linschoten, *Itinerario* (Amsterdam, 1596). Courtesy of the Newberry Library.

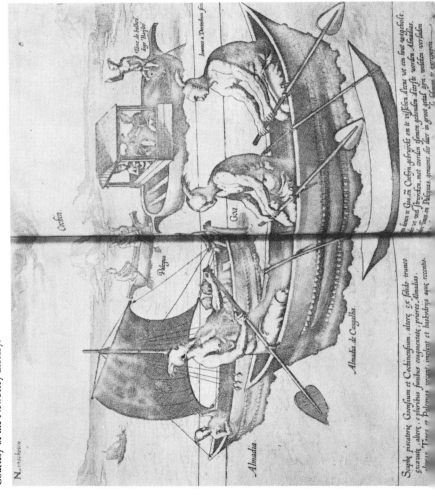

received the support of Bengal, and in the west Gujarat openly offered refuge and aid to the victims of the Mughul expansion into Hindustan.[616] When Gujarat and Bengal joined the resistance to the Mughuls, the Portuguese began to take more than an academic interest in the events transpiring in Hindustan.

Castanheda discusses at some length the expansion of the "Mogors" (Mughuls) into India and the resistance which formed against them. In connection with these discussions he also deals at greater length than the earlier writers with the states and peoples of north central India. He begins with a general account in which he describes how the Mughuls entered India from their own kingdom which borders on Persia and was called "Parchia" (Parthia) in antiquity.[617] The Mughuls, on the basis of testimony by Portuguese who had been in their company, are said to be white,[618] full-bearded, and to wear Moorish caps on their shaved heads. The nobles dress themselves in silken gowns and eat their dinners in great luxury at tables bedecked with elegant silver services and lighted by wax tapers. When traveling, camels carry their effects in large trunks and each night they pitch their own tents when they make camp. The Mughuls, who fight mainly from horseback, carry suspended from the pommels of their saddles a variety of weapons: bows, arrows, machetes, iron maces, and small axes.[619] Their cavalcades also include pieces of light artillery mounted on carts.[620] The Mughul warriors are accompanied by Tartars, Turcomans, and Khurasanis, and other peoples. The ruler of the Mughuls (presumably Babur) is highly respected by his Moorish retainers, and they salaam to him twice each day for they consider him to be holy. It is reported that he shuns women and so refrains from overly luxurious living.[621] But, even in peacetime, the Mughul ruler maintains a large personal bodyguard paid directly from his private funds and fed from his own kitchen.[622]

After Humayun became ruler of the Mughuls in 1530, Bahādur Shah of Gujarat shortly became involved in hostilities with him. The Gujarati ruler had provoked Humayun by giving sanctuary to certain Afghan refugees and by having taken advantage of the breakdown of the Rajput confederacy to annex Malwa in 1531, thus bringing to an end the Ghori dynasty which had ruled there since 1387. He then gradually made its capital city, Māndū, into a base of operations for an attack upon the Rajput fortress of Chitor. And, preparatory

---

[616] Majumdar *et al.*, *op. cit.* (n. 6), pp. 425–34. Also see Ishwari Prasad, *The Life and Time of Humayun* (Bombay, 1956), pp. 66–67.

[617] Castanheda in Azevedo (ed.), *op. cit.* (n. 17), IV, 337–39.

[618] Later European travelers use the word "Mogor" to mean white peoples. For a short summary of such references see E. Maclagan, *The Jesuits and the Great Mogul* (London, 1932), p. xxi, n. 1.

[619] On the offensive arms of the Mughuls see Irvine, *op. cit.* (n. 608), pp. 73–89.

[620] Cf. *ibid.*, pp. 133–51.

[621] Actually Babur, unlike most Muslim rulers in India, appears to have been a devoted family man, although perhaps a bit more inclined to wine which he renounced at least twice during his career in India on the eve of decisive battles. For an account of his life see L. F. Rushbrook Williams, *An Empire Builder of the Sixteenth Century* (London, 1918).

[622] Cf. Ashraf, *loc. cit.* (n. 601), p. 154.

to the campaign against Chitor, Bahādur Shah in 1534 concluded peace with those Portuguese who had been harassing shipping in the Gulf of Cambay and enlisted their help for his inland expedition. Castanheda, who participated in the unsuccessful expedition of 1531 against Diu, acquired his information about the Gujarati war of 1534–35 from those same Portuguese and perhaps the other Europeans who accompanied Bahādur Shah. Consequently, his account relates many of their experiences and reflects their bias.

According to Castanheda,[623] Bahādur Shah assembles at the entry of Māndū in 1534 an army of 150,000 cavalrymen, of whom about 30,000 are mounted on good horses, the rest of the horses being only mediocre. Of the 500,000 infantry under Bahādur's command about 15,000 are foreign mercenaries: Fartakis from the Arabian peninsula, Abyssinians, 300 Rumes (Turks or Egyptians) including the engineer Rumi-Khan of Constantinople, 50 Portuguese, 15 captive Christians who were released to aid in the war, and 30 "Franceses" (probably Christian Europeans) who were being held at Diu on the Portuguese ship, the "Dobrigas."[624] Among the Portuguese are four artillerymen whom Nuno da Cunha, the viceroy, had sent out from Portugal. Capable gunners familiar with European guns are essential to the effective functioning of the artillery, inasmuch as Bahādur manages to assemble, so Castanheda reports, 1,000 pieces of artillery mounted on four-wheel ox carts. The final contingent is an elephant brigade of 800, all of them saddled with wooden turrets on which are mounted either short cannons or muskets. To finance this army, Bahādur fills 500 great copper coffers with gold and silver pieces which are transported in individual carts. Additional money is also forthcoming from the great lords and merchants who accompany the army.

From the city of Māndū, Bahādur set out in 1534 on the road to Chitor, a name "which means in the language of the land, 'the sombrero of the world.'"[625] Situated upon a very high mountain, Chitor is described as a fortress surrounded by strong walls and bulwarks within which there stand many sumptuous temples and dwellings. Orta, who never visited there himself, says that he is told that the city is a picture.[626] The queen, who resides in this hill fortress is a young and beautiful widow called "Cremeti" (Hadi Karmeti, the Rani [queen] and widow of Rana Sanga). Energetic as a man, she is said to have at her command 2,000 cavalry and 30,000 swordsmen for the defense of the city. Castanheda then describes the encirclement of the city in 1535, the destruction of its walls, and the final desperate sortie of the queen. Defeated, the queen flees from the city with her sons and a vassal whom she calls her friend. And the Portuguese chronicler concludes his account with the observation that Bahādur Shah,

---

[623] Castanheda in Azevedo (ed.), *op. cit.* (n. 17), IV, 355–56.

[624] On Europeans in the service of Indian rulers also see Irvine, *op. cit.* (n. 608), pp. 152–53.

[625] Castanheda in Azevedo (ed.), *op. cit.* (n. 17), IV, 355. It is also called Chattrapura, or "the city of the royal umbrella." For further comment on this derivation see Orta in Markham (ed.), *op. cit.* (n. 4), p. 462. For a different etymology see W. Crook (ed.), *Tods Annals and Antiquities of Rajasthan* (Oxford, 1920), III, 1647, n. 2.

[626] Markham (ed.), *op. cit.* (n. 4), p. 462.

being so delighted with the capture of Chitor, remarked that "nobody hereafter would wear this sombrero if he did not." [627]

While the Gujaratis besieged and captured Chitor, Humayun, en route to meet Bahādur Shah, remained strangely inactive. [628] According to Castanheda, [629] the Mughul emperor, when he departed from Delhi, had under his command 200,000 horsemen, one-fourth of whom are armored and the rest of whom are light cavalry. In addition, there are in this cavalcade many female archers on horseback. His foot soldiers are beyond count, though he possesses at least 10,000 swordsmen and 1,000 pieces of artillery. This great and mobile Mughul force occupies the road to Māndū without a fight, probably in 1535, and so places itself between Bahādur Shah and the road back to Gujarat. Three days after investing Chitor, Bahādur Shah, learning of Humayun's actions, moves his forces back towards Māndū. Arriving at a place called "Dacer," [630] Bahādur entrenches himself in a level field along the bank of a river. He encircles his camp with palisades, trenches, and much artillery to await the onslaught of the Mughuls. The army of Humayun being only seven leagues (28 miles) away, Bahādur, contrary to his usual custom of making his own decisions, consults with Rumi-Khan as to whether or not he should venture out to attack the Mughuls. On the advice of the Turk, Bahādur decides to try to extricate himself from his situation by means other than direct attack. [631] It seems that Rumi-Khan felt that with the onset of the rainy season only about a month away, rains, floods, and swollen rivers would make unlikely a victory in the field for either party. In the meantime his troops, suffering from famine and exposure, begin to desert and ultimately Bahādur himself flees from the camp at the riverside. Humayun follows him, and ultimately Bahādur takes refuge at Diu. From Castanheda's viewpoint, the defeat of Bahādur is providential because, had the Gujarati ruler won a victory over Humayun, "all his power would then have been directed against the Portuguese and he would not have let up until they had been driven from India." [632]

While Humayun overran Gujarat in 1535 and while the Portuguese were beginning to build their fortress at Diu, events were transpiring in eastern Hindustan which required the Mughuls' attention. The victory of Babur at Gogra had not resulted in the complete pacification of the Afghan chiefs in and around Bihar. Even in the reign of Sultan Nasrat Shah (1519–32) of Bengal, an alliance with the Lohani rulers of Bihar directed against the Mughuls was

---

[627] Castanheda in Azevedo (ed.), *op. cit.* (n. 17), IV, 356. For a similar account of the siege based on Persian, Sanskrit, and Rajput sources see G. N. Sharma, *Mewar and the Mughal Emperors* (A.D. 1526–1707) (Agra, 1954), pp. 55–57.

[628] The reason usually given is that he did not want to engage a fellow Muslim while he was fighting an infidel army. But for further discussion of this debated issue see Sharma, *op. cit.* (n. 627), pp. 51–53, and Prasad, *op. cit.* (n. 616), pp. 70–71.

[629] Azevedo (ed.), *op. cit.* (n. 17), IV, 356–57.

[630] Probably near Mandsur, northwest of Māndū, the capital city, on the bank of the Sipra River, where the two armies first made contact.

[631] Cf. account in Prasad, *op. cit.* (n. 616), p. 72, and see insert maps.

[632] Azevedo (ed.), *op. cit.* (n. 17), IV, 357.

basic to Bengali foreign policy. The anti-Mughul confederation was, however, constantly being endangered by the internal feuds of the Afghan chiefs, some of whom, probably out of self-interest, favored co-operation with the Mughuls. Among these chieftains there was one bearing the title of Sher Khan who sought to take over the leadership of the Afghan revival from the Lohanis and to check the growing influence of Bengal in the affairs of Bihar and other Afghan-ruled states. In 1533, Sher Khan defeated the Lohani–Bengali forces at Surajgarh on the banks of the Kiul River. Then, taking advantage of Humayun's preoccupation in western Hindustan, Sher Khan suddenly invaded Bengal by an unusual route and appeared at Gaur before Mahmūd Shah (reigned 1532–38) realized what was happening. The Bengali ruler immediately sued for peace, paid the Afghan tribute, and ceded him territory. As a consequence of this victory, many Afghan leaders, who hitherto had been reluctant to accept Sher Khan's supremacy, joined forces with him. While Humayun lingered in Agra, Sher Khan gathered his forces in 1537 for another descent upon rich Bengal. He besieged, occupied, and plundered Gaur in 1538 and escaped from the city with his loot before Humayun could bring it succor. Shortly after the Mughul ruler reached Gaur, Sher Khan transferred his plundering activities to the Mughul territories in Bihar and Jaunpur. Within the following two years Sher Khan consolidated his gains, defeated Humayun in two major battles, and forced the Mughul ruler in 1540 from the throne of Delhi.[633]

The Portuguese, being as involved in the affairs of Bengal as they were in those of Gujarat, followed these events closely and so were able to take advantage of Mahmūd's plight to wring concessions from him. Castanheda,[634] in particular, tells how "Xercansur" (Sher Khan Sur) seized the kingdom of the "Pathanes"[635] (Afghan kingdom of Bihar) from the grasp of Bengal in the time of "Mahumedxa" (Mahmūd Shah). The Portuguese chronicler further relates that after the Mughuls had been defeated by the joint efforts of the "Pathanes" and Bengalis, probably around 1530, the Bengal ruler occupied Bihar and seized its king. This area was then turned over to a governor, "Cotufoxa,"[636] a vassal of Bengal who maintained a large army in which the services of "Xercansur" were enlisted. It was not long before "Xercansur" deserted, raised his own army, killed the governor appointed by Bengal, and set up in his place a man of his own choice, "Sultan Halamo" (Jalal Khān). Shortly thereafter, in 1532, "Nancarote Xa" (Nusrat Shah) died, and his successor, Mahmūd, quickly instructed "Sultan Halamo" to restore the kingdom of the "Pathanes" to Bengal's control or accept the consequences. In the ensuing war of 1534, Sher Khan emerged victorious and Bihar was lost to Bengal. Though Castanheda's story is not entirely consistent with the accounts based on other sources,

[633] Account based upon chapters by A. B. M. Habibullah and N. B. Roy in Sarkar (ed.), *op. cit.* (n. 55), pp. 152–76, and upon Majumdar *et al.*, *op. cit.* (n. 6), pp. 434–38.

[634] Azevedo (ed.), *op. cit.* (n. 17), IV, 379–80.

[635] Derived from Hindustani, *Pathan*. See Dalgado, *op. cit.* (n. 44), II, 188.

[636] Possibly Khatif Shah.

it depicts, in their essentials, the original alliance of Bengal with the Afghans against Babur, the ensuing effort of Bengal to control Bihar, and the rise of Sher Khan as a new power to be reckoned with in eastern Hindustan.

It was as a result of the military services that the Portuguese rendered Mahmūd Shah in this campaign that they were permitted, in 1536–37, to establish their first settlements in Bengal. The Portuguese, through their emissary, Affonso Vaz de Brito, let Mahmūd know in 1538 that, all of their available forces then being involved in Gujarat, they would not be able to send the military aid which they had earlier promised him until the following year. To make certain that the Portuguese would finally live up to their promise of aid, Mahmūd held Affonso Vaz de Brito and four other Portuguese as hostages in Gaur. It was apparently from the reports of these eyewitnesses that Castanheda and the continuator of Barros were able to reconstruct the campaigns of Sher Shah and Humayun in Bengal during 1538. So far, however, no historian of Bengal has seen fit to incorporate the detail from the Portuguese chroniclers into their accounts of these wars, depending as they do almost too exclusively on the scantier Muslim sources.[637]

Castanheda's report of the crucial events of 1538 in Bengal are not so full as those published in 1613 in the fourth *Década* of Barros.[638] In his eighth book,[639] however, first published in 1559, Castanheda reports that when Affonso Vaz de Brito arrived in Gaur news was already abroad in the capital that Sher Shah with 100,000 cavalry and 300,000 infantry was advancing on the city. Mahmūd thereupon inquired at once to learn if Martim Affonso de Mello and the other released Portuguese prisoners had left the city. After hearing that they had gone, the sultan dispatched Nuno Fernandes Freire to Chittāgong with orders to acquire 1,000 "munchuas" (little boats like those of Malacca) with which he hoped to obstruct Sher Shah's advance down the Ganges. Even before the Portuguese emissary left, however, the "Pathanes" had begun to encircle Gaur, and so he was forced to make his way through their blockade in a small boat rather than in a "parão" (warship). Downriver, Nuno Fernandes Freire met the "lascar" (governor) of "Carnagão"[640] who was on his way to Gaur with 600 "almadias" (Indian rafts) loaded with provisions. When he learned from the Portuguese that the city was already under siege, the governor refused to go on; consequently there was so great a famine in Gaur that the fathers ate their children. When the "Pathanes" finally entered the city, they killed the majority of its inhabitants and Sultan Mahmūd was sorely wounded while fleeing his ravaged capital. The fugitive ruler soon met with a Mughul captain who had 40,000 cavalry at his command. This contingent, accompanied by Mahmūd,

---

[637] See the comment in Campos, *op. cit.* (n. 551), p. 41n. The writers of Bengali history for this period in Sarkar (ed.), *op. cit.* (n. 551) utilize Campos and other secondary works based on the Portuguese chroniclers but they fail to exploit the chronicles themselves.

[638] Cidade and Múrias (eds.), *op. cit.* (n. 6), IV, 507–34.

[639] Azevedo (ed.), *op. cit.* (n. 17), IV, 486–87.

[640] "Sornagam" on Lavanha's map in Barros. A river town near Dacca called "Sonagam" on D'Anville's map of 1752. Possibly identical to Sonārgāon the capital of eastern Bengal.

joined the main body of Humayun's army and immediately proceeded towards Gaur. Before they could reach the capital, Sher Khan evacuated it and escaped with all its treasure. Mahmūd meanwhile had died of his wounds and so Sher Khan immediately proclaimed himself the monarch of Bihar and Bengal. Exalted by these successes, Sher Khan then met and defeated the Mughuls, killed many great lords of the land, seized control of Delhi, Chitor, and Malwa, and established Afghan supremacy throughout Hindustan.

The profile of India as it emerges from the major Portuguese literary sources of the sixteenth century is an uneven outline resembling an artist's preliminary sketch for a monumental fresco. The west coast, especially the two maritime states of Malabar and Gujarat, stand out in bold relief, in good perspective, and with some of the shadings already suggested. The east coast is chalked out vaguely as far north as the delta of the Ganges where the representation again becomes more graphic and studied. Vijayanagar, especially its capital city, dominates the piece in the interior of India south of the Krishna River. The Indo-Gangetic plain of the north is sharply defined along its eastern and western extremities, in Bengal and Gujarat, but then the details and the firm lines fade out towards the interior. In the extreme north of the subcontinent no interior demarcations can be seen at all between Delhi and the brooding mountains which divide India from the rest of Asia. Though stark in its outlines, the basic pattern of India's geography can be clearly perceived here; it is left for subsequent generations to give it better form, substance, and tone.

The Portuguese perspective on India is distorted somewhat by the limits of the observers' experiences and by the preconceptions and prejudices which they brought with them. Concerned with trading and building an empire, the Portuguese naturally overstress the importance of maritime activities and related enterprises. And because they are also thinking of conquest, the writers tend to look at the states of India too exclusively in terms of military potential. The Europeans also persist in believing that the Hindus adhere to some early form of Christianity which they were either forced to give up or modify under pressure from the Muslims. Consequently, they seek to associate Hindu practices with Christian beliefs rather than trying to understand Hinduism for itself. Though they remark upon the religious tolerance of both the Hindus and the Moors, they categorically relegate many of the native beliefs to the limbo of superstition. Literary conventions also make some of their comparisons pointless, as when on almost every occasion they contrast the cities of India with Evora. And being gallant Latins, the Portuguese almost always describe the women as attractive and desirable. They do not, however, express universal admiration for the men, though they do generally admit, except in the case of the Sinhalese, that the Indians make good soldiers. Nonetheless, in the final analysis, a handful of valiant Portuguese can usually overwhelm extremely large armies without suffering heavy casualties.

Like travelers of practically any era, the Portuguese record what interests them and see only those things which they are prepared to see. Except for Barbosa, they show no interest in the languages spoken in the places which they visited or heard about. Pires, Orta, and Castanheda were obviously men of education, and they clearly evince, on the basis of their Asian experiences, a consciousness of the limits of European knowledge about the East. Barros, who never visited India himself, systematically collected, checked, and collated information on India, not only from Portuguese informants and writings but also from Persian and Arabic literary sources. The simple fact that the Portuguese observers in India were intellectually curious and open-minded (or prejudiced) enough to record the obvious and sometimes the superficial gives particular value to certain of their observations. They remark, for example, on everyday activities, customs, and particularly inhuman practices which rarely appear in the Indian writings, either Hindu or Muslim.[641] And, as we have seen, when their statements can be checked against available native records, they are generally, though not unexceptionably, shown to be accurate and reliable.

2

THE JESUIT NEWSLETTERS AND HISTORIES

In an earlier chapter, we surveyed the Jesuit system of epistolary communication and observed how it systematically helped to disseminate in Europe a substantial amount of information about the East.[642] The newsletters published at intervals between 1545 and 1601 supply documentation on India for the period after 1542, or *that part of the century which is not covered by the Portuguese histories.* Both the published letterbooks and the unpublished Jesuit letters available in southern Europe also provided those sixteenth-century historians writing on the mission with some of their best primary sources. But, like most sources, the newsletters and the histories based on them must be subjected to rigorous historical criticism if they are to be used intelligently by the modern scholar. That they were designed to be letters of edification is a fact never to be forgotten. In the case of the "Indian letters" particularly, the Jesuits, soon to find that there was very little edification for ecclesiastic or layman to obtain from their arduous and disagreeable experiences in India, were not particularly inclined to view India's religions, customs, or people with the clear eye of impartiality. Nonetheless, the Jesuit letters and histories extend in time the European sources available on sixteenth-century history, and add dimensions on Indian languages and religions which the lay historians of Portuguese expansion treated only sketchily.

[641] Cf. comments in Ashraf, *loc. cit.* (n. 601), pp. 121–22.
[642] See above, pp. 314–28.

India

As an example of how complicated it is to trace the evolution of the European image of India from the Jesuit sources, let us look at the publication history of Xavier's letters during the sixteenth century. Two of his general letters from Goa of 1542 were published in Paris in 1545, presumably in an effort to inspire the students in that seat of learning to volunteer for service in Asia, and these were among the first missionary letters about India to be printed.[643] In them he paints a rosy picture of the state of Christianity in India. Two personal letters of the same date addressed to Loyola from Goa did not appear in print until the end of the century, perhaps because they were less edifying and much more descriptive of the hardships recruits might expect to suffer in India; they were finally published by Tursellinus in 1596 as part of the documentation then being prepared by the Jesuits for the anticipated canonization of Xavier.[644] The Apostle's letter of October 28, 1542,[645] which was penned to Loyola from Tuticorin on the Fishery Coast, was included, at least in part, in the publications of 1545. Here Xavier, who had just barely arrived at his new post, tells of how he made conversions among the gentiles and of how the Portuguese governor had helped the Paravans in their struggle against the Muslims. His letter from Cochin of January 15, 1544 (also published in a French collection of 1545),[646] gave Europe the first of his detailed and optimistic reports on the progress of evangelizing along the Fishery Coast and in Travancore. It was this hopeful letter which was republished more frequently in the sixteenth century than any of his other dispatches.[647]

The fleet which landed at Lisbon in September, 1545, brought four letters from Xavier written in Cochin, as well as Miguel Vaz, the Vicar-General of Goa.[648] From these letters and the personal testimony of Vaz and his companions, the European sponsors of the Christian enterprise in India received the happy impression that a complete conquest for the faith was in the making if only the Portuguese rulers of India would co-operate more effectively and sincerely and if only more able recruits could be sent to gather in the harvest. Once Xavier's letters arrived at Lisbon, they were immediately dispatched to the court which was then in Evora. Simão Rodriguez opened and read them and, after making copies of the letters, had them forwarded to the Roman Fathers for local distribution. King John responded immediately to the Jesuits' appeal

643 For the titles of these pamphlets see John Correia-Afonso, S. J., *Jesuit Letters and Indian History* (Bombay, 1955), p. 176, Appendix D. This author also notes a German translation published at Augsburg in 1545.

644 H. Tursellinus, *Francisci Xaverii epistolarum libri quatuor* (Rome, 1596).

645 G. Schurhammer and J. Wicki (eds.), *Epistolae S. Francisci Xaverii aliaque eius scripta* (Rome, 1944), I, 129–43.

646 *Ibid.*, pp. 152–77.

647 R. Streit, *Biblioteca missionum* (Aachen, 1928), IV, 126.

648 G. Schurhammer, "Xaveriusforschung im 16. Jahrhundert," *Zeitschrift für Missionswissenschaft*, XII (1922), 130–33.

for funds and likewise acted at once to draw up directives for the authorities in India in an effort to establish better working relationships between the secular arm and the missions. Many Portuguese volunteered to join the Society to carry on the work in India, and with the fleet of the next year nine Jesuits and six Franciscans were sent to Goa.

At the Jesuit College of Coimbra, Xavier's letters of 1545 created a sensation and in the midst of the fervor the Rector wrote to Rome "that there would be no difficulty in transplanting this College to there [India!]." [649] Xavier's general letter to the brothers of Europe created a similar stir in other Jesuit centers. Copies of it were received and read at Jesuit stations as widely separated as Valencia and Cologne just one year after Xavier had penned it. At the German center additional copies were made and distributed to high ecclesiastics in the surrounding areas. A Dutch Jesuit, Jacobus Lhoost, commented after reading it that the firm faith of the Indians compensated the church for the losses suffered at the hands of Luther and Melanchthon. [650] Finally it was translated into Italian and published in pamphlet form at the Eternal City in 1546 as *Copia de una lettera. . . .* [651]

Though it was apparently not reprinted again until 1596 (Tursellinus), Xavier's general letter of 1545 awakened hopes in Europe that great progress was to be expected in India and it was even the subject of discussion at the ecumenical Council of Trent (1545–63) which was then beginning to meet. [652] After reporting that he baptized more than 10,000 people in Travancore during a single month, Xavier explains his simple method of reciting the articles of the faith to the assembled multitude in Tamil and how he considered their affirmation of them as constituting conversion. [653] Through such mass conversions, he hoped that more than 100,000 could be baptized in a year. [654] The text printed in the *Copia de una lettera . . .* contains conversion figures which far exceed in size all previous statistics, it being alleged that to 1545 there had been 635,000 conversions in the various parts of Portugal's Asian empire. [655]

Thirty-two of Xavier's letters dated from India are still extant. Of this number, twenty-two were published for the first time in Tursellinus' collection of 1596 appended to Xavier's biography. Seven of his other letters were first published at intervals between 1545 and 1570; the only ones which appeared before his death in 1552 are those published in 1545 already discussed. Of the seven letters published before 1596, just four of them were printed more than once: the two missives of 1542 (printed in 1545 in two editions) and two others of 1559 (first printed in 1569 and 1570). And most of the Xavier letters written in the last three years of his life (1549–52) have more to say about Japan and China than India. The letters printed before the appearance

[649] Schurhammer and Wicki (eds.), *op. cit.* (n. 645), I, 264.   [650] *Ibid.*, pp. 266–67.

[651] The sole surviving copy of this newsletter exists in the library of the Historical Society of Würzburg. Published in *Serapeum*, XIX (1858), 180–85.

[652] Schurhammer and Wicki (eds.), *op. cit.* (n. 645), I, 267.

[653] *Ibid.*, pp. 273–74.   [654] *Ibid.*, p. 277.

[655] See Schurhammer, *loc. cit.* (n. 648), p. 133.

of the Tursellinus collection in 1596 stress the successes of Christianity in the East and the need for more missionaries to bring in the great harvest of souls awaiting Christian enlightenment; there is no hint in them of the problems which he anticipated in India or little mention of his dissatisfaction with the secular arm. Tursellinus, eager to stress the hardships overcome by the first great Jesuit missionary, naturally has no hesitation in putting into print Xavier's more critical and pessimistic letters.

In trying to reconstruct the channels by which information subsequently filtered into Europe through the Jesuit letters, it is necessary to isolate for analysis the published writings of Xavier's successors in India. From their correspondence at least 120 separate letters were published in whole or in substantial part during the latter half of the sixteenth century. These missives were penned from the Indian stations by at least forty-seven different correspondents, some of whom are represented in the published books by just a single letter. A number of the letters, however, were printed in several different collections, and a handful of them appeared in as many as five to seven different editions. From the first published letters of 1545 to the end of the century, fifty separate collections were printed which included substantial numbers of letters from and about India and the state of the Christian enterprise there.[656] These compilations were produced mainly in the cities of Italy, Portugal, and Spain, but a few originated in the printing shops of Paris, Louvain, Dillingen, and other Jesuit centers in northern Europe. Certain of the collections were derivative, in the sense that they seem to have been compiled wholly or in part from earlier letterbooks. A substantial number of the letters which recount the trials of evangelizing in India or complain about the relationship between the Society and other agencies of church or government, were not printed at all during the sixteenth century.

In approaching the complicated problem of dealing with the printed letters, it seems best to divide them and our consideration of them into two distinct chronological periods: 1552–1570; 1571–1601. The first epoch begins with the systematic publication in southern Europe almost annually of collections of missionary letters. Normally, in this period, the letters were compiled, edited, and printed shortly after their arrival. It closes with the publication of several massive Latin collections prepared for distribution in northern Europe. The second epoch commences with a decade (1571–81) of decline in publication. It is followed by the issuing of the "true" annual letters (beginning in 1581) and concludes with the appearance of the first of the Jesuit histories (beginning in 1588). The last decade is concerned with the revival of interest in India inspired by the hope of converting Akbar, and with the publication of Tursellinus' collection of Xavier letters and Guzman's Spanish history of the Society's activities in the East.

---

656 The list of "principal editions" compiled by Correia-Afonso (*op. cit.* [n. 643], pp. 176–79) includes just thirty-five separate items for the sixteenth century. The list of editions referred to here is longer because it includes a few items missed by Correia-Afonso and a number of editions of "Japan Letters" which contain significant Indian materials.

B. THE FIRST IMPRESSIONS, 1552–70

In the two decades of this period three great series of letterbooks were being published. At Coimbra, beginning first in 1551 or 1552, appeared those which are referred to variously as *Copia de unas cartas* or *Copia da diversas cartas*. After the initial publications, new compendiums in this series were printed in 1555, 1561, 1562, 1565, and 1570. To facilitate their circulation they were issued from Coimbra in Spanish rather than in Portuguese versions; even so, several of them were later reissued in Spain in somewhat more elegant Spanish versions. At Rome (and beginning in 1559 at Venice) the series known as *Avisi particolari* or *Nuovi avisi* also began to appear in 1552, and subsequent editions came out in 1553, 1556, 1557, 1558, 1559, 1562, 1565,[657] 1568, 1570, and thereafter. More comprehensive compilations soon began to be published in Latin. The first of these was an unauthorized collection of *Epistolae Indicae* . . . published at Dillingen in 1563. Provoked to action, the Jesuits published similar Latin collections of their own at Louvain in 1566 and 1570. Occasionally one volume or the other of these three series was translated into German or French, but the trend even in this period was towards issuing the letters in the more universally acceptable Latin. The separate letters were often reproduced in more than one of these volumes, but at times the versions printed are quite different from one another. The "Indian letters" in the publications of 1552 to 1570 were all written between 1548 and 1561. For some unexplained reason there was no effort to publish the letters written from India between 1561 and 1568.[658] The following generalizations are therefore based on the letters *actually published* in the period from 1552 to 1570 (though all are dated as of 1561 or before) as we have extracted them from the versions reproduced in the first five of the critically edited Wicki volumes entitled *Documenta Indica*.

The newsletters, which began to be published in books contemporary with the appearance of the works of Ramusio, Castanheda, and Barros, are very sketchy and unorganized when compared to the secular books. Like many lay commentators, the Jesuit writers dwell on the great length, hardships, and uncertainties of the sea voyage. "The experience of traveling from Portugal to India," concludes the Provincial Dom Gonçalo da Silveira, "cannot be related except by those who have undergone it, cannot be understood or believed except by those who have observed it. . . ."[659] The major ports of India

---

[657] This collection of twenty-six letters (printed in Venice), almost all of which are dated 1561, includes five from Japan, one from China, thirteen from India, one each from the Moluccas and Ethiopia, and five from Brazil.

[658] Examination of the sixth volume of J. Wicki (ed.), *Documenta Indica* (Rome, 1960), which includes letters written between 1563 and 1566, reveals that not a single one of the letters from these years was published during the sixteenth century.

[659] Letter from Cochin to Father Gonçalo Vaz de Melo at Lisbon (January, 1557) in Wicki (ed.), *op. cit.* (n. 658), III, 622.

receive little more than mere mention, though occasionally the Jesuits give approximate distances from one place to the other. The letters of Henrique Henriques give considerable detail not to be found elsewhere on the place names of the Fishery Coast and Travancore.[660] Michael Carneiro, the first Jesuit to penetrate the Serra of the Malabar Christians, gives some descriptive material on the hilly country of the interior behind Cochin.[661] Of particular interest is the account by Gonçalves Rodrigues of his overland journey in 1561 from Belgaum, inland from Goa, to the court of Bijapur. This part of the Deccan he describes as "excellent country" with "many fine streams, large towns, much livestock . . . and many different foods." He goes on to make a few more specific observations:

The land . . . is very black and fertile, and very flat. Seldom are stones found in the earth, and it seems to be the most fertile soil imaginable for grains, that is, if it were in the hands of our Portuguese farmers. As it is such excellent land, all foods grow abundantly with only the dews [for moisture]. The natives make poor use of the land, and many parts lie unused, for the land is too large and there is much left over.[662]

Rodrigues speaks less favorably about living conditions in the towns of the Deccan. In the five or six places he passed through on the road to Bijapur, he found the people to be living in "little huts worse than what the cows have in our country."[663] Bijapur itself is situated in a fertile plain where irrigated orchards produce fruits in splendid abundance. Though he concludes that Bijapur is larger than Goa and very strongly fortified, Rodrigues summarizes his unfavorable impression of the interior of the town by asserting that it "does not contain ten servicable houses."[664] In an earlier letter from Bassein,[665] Rodrigues, who clearly had an eye for agriculture, tells how the Jesuits bought land and houses at Trindade and Tana and started farms to give their converts employment and income.

Surprisingly, the Jesuits give only cursory descriptions of the major centers of their activities,[666] though occasionally they make revealing incidental remarks. For example, we learn that in 1550 "many parts of Pesquaria [the Fishery Coast] were barren because of drought."[667] Mortality of adults on the Fishery Coast is not abnormally high, but the children, particularly the infants, seem

---

[660] See especially his letter to the General from Manakkudi in Travancore (January 13, 1558) in *ibid.*, IV, 31–36.

[661] Letter from Goa to Luis Gonçalves de Câmara at Lisbon (December 24, 1557) in *ibid.*, III, 795–801.

[662] Letter from Bijapur (April 7, 1561) to Quadros in Goa as reproduced in *ibid.*, V, 138–39.

[663] *Ibid.*, p. 139.

[664] *Ibid.*, p. 143.

[665] To the Fathers in Portugal (September 5, 1558) in *ibid.*, IV, 100–104.

[666] The only effort to give brief background summaries on each of the Jesuit centers from Goa to China is contained in Barzaeus to Loyola (January 12, 1553) in *ibid.*, II, 581–600; in two earlier letters Barzaeus also gives fine descriptions of Ormuz and surrounding areas. See his letter of December 10, 1549, in *ibid.*, I, 644–47, and his letter of November 24, 1550, in *ibid.*, II, 77–79.

[667] Henriques to Rodrigues (January 12, 1551) from Cochin in *ibid.*, II, 156.

to have more trouble surviving than they do elsewhere in India.[668] Cochin is said to have "houses like those of Rome" and to be serviced by a "large river of salt water."[669] In September, 1557, Goa suffered from an epidemic of what it seems from the description of symptoms we would now call influenza.[670] And, of the places further to the East, the Jesuits report that Japan is cold and unpleasant,[671] and notice that the people of Amboina "live on high hills that can be reached only crawling up on hands and feet."[672] Scattered throughout the letters are numerous references to the names of coins, prices, and the availability of products, particularly foodstuffs, in the various localities.

A European reader of the earliest published newsletters would not receive a general perspective on Asia's political organization. Most of the missionaries are content merely to mention that the overlord is either a heathen or a Moor, and that he is either a friend or an enemy of the Portuguese. They relay some slight information on general political conditions in the *padroado* generally by references to the joint attacks of Calicut and the Turks on the Portuguese outposts in south India during 1553, to the power of the Muslims in Travancore subsequently, or to rumors of an outbreak of war between the Turks and Abyssinians in 1557.[673] Gaspar Barzaeus, who is somewhat more politically conscious than his colleagues, discusses in a letter to Loyola dated 1553 the extent of Malay political dominion in southeastern Asia and observes that China is said to include a land inhabited by Jews, to border on its land side with Germany, and to "allow no commerce except at the seaports."[674] Three years later the Jesuits from India optimistically report to Europe that the ports of China are open to trade and that a letter was received at Canton from a ruler in Japan who promised to become a Christian.[675]

On India itself the letters are most specific on events transpiring along the Fishery Coast. Beginning in 1549 the Jesuits begin to complain about the attacks of the Badagás upon Punical, the Portuguese fortress and trading center.[676] Repeatedly, Henriques complains about the meddling of the Portuguese captains in the politics of the Fishery Coast. Troubles with the Badagás and hostilities within Paravan factions leads Henriques in 1556 to act as a political mediator,[677] probably because of his abilities in both Tamil and Portuguese. Proposals were meanwhile being made in Goa suggesting that the Paravan Christians should be transplanted to the friendlier and more accessible territory

---

[668] Henriques to the General (January 13, 1558) from Manakkudi in *ibid.*, IV, 29.
[669] Antonius de Herédia to Loyola, from Cochin (January, 1552) in *ibid.*, II, 291.
[670] Fróis to Portuguese fathers from Goa (December 12, 1557) in *ibid.*, III, 749.
[671] For example, see Barzaeus to Loyola from Goa (January 12, 1553) in *ibid.*, II, 600.
[672] Fróis to Fathers of Coimbra from Goa (November 30, 1555) in *ibid.*, III, 716.
[673] Fróis to Fathers of Coimbra from Goa (November 30, 1557) in *ibid.*, III, 712.
[674] From Goa during January, 1553, in *ibid.*, II, 586.
[675] See especially Soveral to Coimbra Fathers from Cochin (January 20, 1556) in *ibid.*, III, 451, and Brandão to Portuguese Fathers from Goa (November, 1556) in *ibid.*, III, 579–80.
[676] Jesuits of the Fishery Coast to the Bishop of Goa written from Punical (January 19, 1549) in *ibid.*, I, 482.
[677] Henriques to Loyola from Punical (December 31, 1556) in *ibid.*, III, 595.

across the Straits of Manaar in northern Ceylon. Events going from bad to worse at Punical in 1557, Henriques, who was blamed both by the Portuguese and local factions for his political meddling, was sent to Cochin and Travancore until the situation at Punical could be brought under control. He was replaced on the Fishery Coast for a time by Father Francisco Peres who helped the Governor's agent, Francisco Alvares, to restore temporary order.[678]

Shortly thereafter the new Viceroy, Dom Costantino de Braganza, decided early in 1560 to transplant the Paravans to the territories of the ruler of Jaffna by force if necessary. This decision was apparently taken because Viśvanātha, the *Nāyaka* (viceroy) of Madura and Hindu overlord of the region, had demanded from the Christians the proceeds from one day's pearl fishing and threatened, if not obeyed, to imprison the women and children. When the Portuguese began to remove the Christians in large numbers, Viśvanātha in 1560 attacked and overwhelmed their garrison at Punical.[679] Father Pedro Mesquita was captured and taken to Madura as a hostage. With the aid of a Christian boy, he escaped in September, 1560, and arduously made his way to Henriques and the transplanted Christian community on the island of Manaar and ultimately got to Cochin.[680] Since the project of moving the Paravans to Jaffna could not be carried out successfully, they returned gradually to their former homes, particularly after the death of Viśvanātha in 1561.[681]

Conditions in Travancore are generally described as being worse for the Europeans than those prevailing on the Fishery Coast because "the Moors lord it over this coast."[682] Henriques reports that Mārtānda Varma, the prince of Travancore, died in 1554 and that disorders followed.[683] While in temporary exile in Travancore, Henriques comments on the hostility of the new ruler to the Christian "macuas." They cannot be protected adequately by the secular arm because the Portuguese captain at Quilon is much too far away from their centers to act effectively in their behalf.[684] Clearly, here as elsewhere in continental south India, the mission is still on the shakiest of foundations.

Little is said about the political relations between the Portuguese at Goa and Adil Khan of Bijapur until 1557, even though the Portuguese had been endeavoring for over a decade to replace Adil Khan by his brother, Meale Khan. The latter had conspired and revolted against Adil Khan in 1545, and, his plot failing, was forced to seek refuge in Goa. A series of Portuguese governors thereafter sought to use him as a political pawn in their efforts to acquire control

---

[678] Henriques to the General from Manakkudi on January 13, 1558, in *ibid.*, IV, 23–24.

[679] Henriques to Lainez from Manaar (January 8, 1561) in *ibid.*, V, 6–10.

[680] For the conditions of his imprisonment see Mesquita to Henriques from Madura (?) on August 29, 1560, in *ibid.*, IV, 604; for his escape see Mesquita to Coimbra Fathers from Cochin (January 16, 1561) in *ibid.*, V, 77.

[681] Probably died in October, 1561. See Henriques to Lainez from Manaar (December 19, 1561) in *ibid.*, V, 378. For further details see above, pp. 270–71.

[682] Francisco Durão to Rodrigues from Thêngâppattanam (November 22, 1557) in Wicki (ed.), *op. cit.* (n. 18), III, 695.

[683] Letter to Loyola from Punical (December 25–31, 1555), *ibid.*, III, 423.

[684] Henriques to the General from Manakkudi (January 13, 1558) in *ibid.*, IV, 32.

over the Deccan territories under Adil Khan's control. The Jesuits only begin to recount details of these enterprises beginning with the spring campaign of 1557.[685] Even then they give military and political data only as background to the conversion of Meale Khan's daughter at the end of 1557[686] and to the more repressive policies then being inaugurated at Goa to wipe out the Hindu and Muslim resistance to Christianity. Peace finally being concluded with the Portuguese in 1560, Adil Khan sent a request in 1561 to the Archbishop of Goa for the dispatch to his court of two or three learned priests.[687] The Muslim ruler, who was apparently curious about Christianity, received Fathers Gonçalves Rodrigues and Francisco Lopes in state at Bijapur in April, 1561. While accomplishing little in the way of religious instruction, the fathers interviewed the ambassador from Vijayanagar and requested him to ask his rājā for permission to let the Christians visit his domains. They also saw at Bijapur the brother of the Nizamu 'l-Mulk of Ahmadnagar whose kingdom had recently been invaded by a coalition of Bijapur, Golconda, and Vijayanagar. Particularly interesting are the identifications the Jesuits give of Adil Khan's leading advisers and of the ceremonies then prevailing at his court.[688]

The close working relationship between church and state during Dom Costantino de Braganza's term as viceroy (1558–61) was carried over to the military and diplomatic activities of the Portuguese in northwestern India. In the attack and capture of Damão and the island of Bulsar during 1559,[689] the Viceroy was accompanied by the Provincial of the Jesuits, Dom Gonçalo da Silveira, and the Vicar of the Dominicans, Friar Antonio Pegado, and a delegation of Franciscans. The Jesuit superior was accompanied by a lay brother who had in his charge some youths from the college at Goa. The enemy withdrew from Damão without a serious struggle, and when the Portuguese landed, the Provincial went to the city's leading mosque to celebrate mass. The boys from the College helped to pave the way for the capture of Bulsar, for the residents received them warmly. On this island, possibly because the Portuguese came with youths from the region, "the Viceroy found the natives to be tractable, willing to deal with and talk to the Portuguese, . . . [a quality] rarely met with in the nations of these parts."[690]

From Damão the Jesuits probed further northward to Surat by the end of 1560. Father Marcus Prancudo, a native of Valencia who was at Damão from 1558 to 1565, corresponded with the ruler of Surat, Khudāband Khan.[691] The young prince, then twenty years of age, was the son of parents who had once

[685] Fróis to Coimbra Fathers from Goa (November 30, 1557) in *ibid.*, III, 708–9.

[686] Celebrated as the first conversion of an aristocratic Muslim woman. For details of her conversion, see the remarkably frank letter of Fróis to the Fathers in Portugal from Goa (December 12, 1557) in *ibid.*, III, 731–35.

[687] Fróis to the Fathers in Portugal from Goa (December 1, 1561) in *ibid.*, V, 280.

[688] Rodrigues to Quadros from Bijapur (April 7, 1561) in *ibid.*, V, 140–43.

[689] A description of this action in Fróis to the Coimbra Fathers in *ibid.*, IV, 278–80.

[690] *Ibid.*, p. 280.

[691] Prancudo to Fathers in Goa from Damão (February 28, 1561) in *ibid.*, V, 110.

been Christians and who had reconverted to Islam. The Jesuit apparently got in touch with him through merchants who traded at Damão and Surat. With the help of these merchants Prancudo obtained an invitation to visit the court in order to explain the tenets of Christianity to Khudāband Khan. On the trip to Surat, Prancudo was accompanied by Diogo Pereira, a Portuguese merchant and faithful friend of Xavier, and by Abraam the Jew, both of whom are described as being "great friends" of Khudāband Khan. While Prancudo failed to convert the young ruler, he was apparently satisfied that his explanations and admonitions had not fallen on deaf ears. About secular matters the Jesuit remarks only on the rundown condition of the city's fortress (probably built around 1540) and on the young ruler's comment that a war was in the offing for which Surat could accept no blame.[692]

The key to the understanding of India, the Jesuits realized, lay in the mastery of the native languages and the opening of their literatures. Only a few missionaries working in the Portuguese-controlled ports troubled to learn Konkani or Marāthī in these early years.[693] Usually at Goa and in the Bassein area they relied upon professional interpreters and native boys from the College. The problem was further complicated for them in the trading centers by the fact that they worked with people of diverse backgrounds (Muslims, Jews, and heathens) who were themselves foreigners to the local languages. This problem was sometimes met in the Portuguese centers by communicating in "pidgin Portuguese."[694] It was only in the areas outside of Portuguese control that the Jesuits successfully attacked the local languages. In Japan, the Moluccas, and in south India, including Ceylon, the Jesuits from Xavier's time onward made serious efforts to speak, read, and write the native tongues, to prepare grammars and vocabularies, and to translate Christian prayers, catechisms, and songs into them. Occasionally in this period, the missionaries also acquired literary works in the native tongues for the purpose of understanding local beliefs in order to refute them in public disputations.

The greatest progress in India was made in the Tamil and Malayālam regions at the southern tip of the peninsula. Following the lead of Xavier, the Italian, Antonio Criminale, the first superior of the Fishery Coast, had learned by 1548 how to communicate and read in Tamil (or "Malabar," as the missionaries generally called it).[695] After Criminale's martyrdom in 1549, the lead in the study of Tamil was taken over by Henrique Henriques who reports that he learned to speak it in five months by studying day and night with the aid of a native youth.[696] He learned to speak and write it correctly, according to his own claims,[697] by organizing it according to the principles of Latin grammar and

---

[692] *Ibid.,* pp. 115–16.

[693] Brother Francisco Anes preached in Marāthī during 1556 at Tana (*ibid.,* III, 591), but as late as 1561 Fróis wrote that only a few fathers in Goa knew enough Kanarese to listen to confessions in that language (*ibid.,* V, 274).

[694] Teixeira to Portuguese Fathers from Goa (December 25, 1558) in *ibid.,* IV, 168.

[695] Henriques to Loyola from Bembay (October 31, 1548) in *ibid.,* I, 280.

[696] *Ibid.,* p. 285.   [697] *Ibid.,* pp. 287–88.

by working out a system of transliteration by which he and others could learn to pronounce it.[698] From remarks scattered throughout his letters, it is clear that Henriques and his associates found the pronunciation and accent of Tamil to be among their knottiest problems. As a product of his own experience in learning the language, Henriques prepared by 1551 a "Malabar" grammar and some translations of prayers. He sent a manuscript copy of the grammar to Portugal and notified the fathers there that all of the missionaries on the Fishery Coast were learning the language and talking in it with one another. "We hope," he comments, "that within a few days we can make a rule that no one is to write in Portuguese, only in Malabar."[699]

For his own translations and correspondence in Tamil, Henriques soon employed an interpreter and a secretary. He wrote out his texts in Portuguese, a boy then read them aloud to the interpreter, who then dictated them to the secretary, who wrote them down in "Malabar." Henriques would read the Tamil translations over, and then correct the mistakes in the *olas* (writings inscribed on palm leaves) before completing or dispatching them.[700] Like other missionaries after him, Henriques found it particularly difficult to convey through Tamil the precise meaning of Christian words and concepts, and so he was constantly revising his grammar, vocabularies, and translations to render them more accurate. Though hampered in carrying on his linguistic work by the unsettled conditions of life on the Fishery Coast, Henriques finally completed a revision of his "Malabar" grammar, compiled a vocabulary, and translated several Christian tracts into Tamil. In 1576, Henriques' *Doutrina Christão*, a translation of Xavier's brief Catechism, was printed in Tamil characters at Quilon. In the following year his lengthier *Doutrina Christão* was printed at Cochin.[701] And, in 1586, Henriques' *Flos Sanctorum* was printed in Tamil characters on the Fishery Coast, probably at Punical.[702]

Henriques did not confine his linguistic ambitions to Tamil. He believed that with the help of an interpreter and a secretary, and by following the method used in constructing the "Malabar" texts, he could "devise a grammar for the learning of any language in these parts in less than four months, even if it be a tongue of Japan, or China, or Prester John, or any other."[703] While reveling in his naïve optimism, Henriques soon learned that even Malayālam could pose

---

[698] For the kinds of linguistic difficulties which must have faced the missionary pioneers in learning Tamil see G. Moraes, "St. Francis Xavier, Apostolic Nuncio, 1542–1552," *Journal of the Bombay Branch of the Royal Asiatic Society*, New Series, XXVII (1950), 293.

[699] Henriques to Rodriguez from Cochin (January 12, 1551) in Wicki (ed.), *op. cit.* (n. 658), II, 158.

[700] Henriques to Loyola from Punical (November 6, 1552), in *ibid.*, II, 395. Later on he remarks that he receives from four to eight *olas* each day (*ibid.*, III, 239).

[701] Anant Kakba Priolkar, *The Printing Press in India* (Bombay, 1958), p. 11.

[702] A copy of this book is in the Vatican Library. See Xavier S. Thani Nayagam, "Tamil Manuscripts in European Libraries," *Tamil Culture*, III (1954), 225. For a sample page see Priolkar, *op. cit.* (n. 701), p. 319. The *Flos Sanctorum* (*Flower of the Saints*) is the *Golden Legend* prepared by the thirteenth-century Dominican, Jacobus de Voragine. See above, p. 27.

[703] Henriques to Loyola from Punical (December 31, 1556) in Wicki (ed.), *op. cit.* (n. 658), III, 598.

problems for the unwary. During his stay at Cochin for three months (September–November, 1557), he found that he could not work effectively on the west coast without an interpreter. From this experience he concluded that Malayālam and Tamil have "many points of similarity though they differ more than Spanish does from Portuguese."[704] Tamil, he asserts, is the "better language" and is more widely spoken; Malayālam is the language of Quilon, Cochin, the St. Thomas Christians, and others.[705] Still, he persisted in hoping that persons acquainted with both languages could, in conference with the religious authorities, prepare versions of the same prayers and other Christian writings in both languages so that they could be used everywhere in south India by the missionaries. During his visit to Cochin in 1560, he continued to make arrangements for the preparation of a Malayālam grammar and vocabulary.[706] While this project of training the missionaries in the languages of south India failed to produce fruit, Henriques' concern with it highlighted for Europe the importance of studying independently each of the many languages of India. A further complication was added to the language picture by the suggestion that instructors in Chaldean should be sent to Cochin to train the missionaries to the Serra in the sacred language used in the rituals and writings of the St. Thomas Christians.[707]

Though the early Jesuits knew next to nothing about the other languages of India, they were interested enough in them to notice inscriptions, to send copies of books written in them to Europe, and to have translations of some of the sacred Hindu texts made by their Indian converts. For example, Gonçalvo Rodrigues, while visiting Bijapur, tells of seeing an inscription on a newly constructed gateway "in a language I believe to be Persian."[708] In 1549, while Barzaeus was at Ormuz, he acquired a copy of the New Testament "written in [the] Gurzi script"[709] of Persian which he sent to Europe. While trying to root out Hinduism in Goa, the Jesuits in 1558 ransacked a Hindu home and confiscated two books "which they call *Anadipurana* [*Ananta-purāna*, or the history of Vishnu]."[710] A portion of this which related to the origins and creation of the Hindu gods was translated. In the following year, a Brahman convert "with the permission of the Viceroy" went to the mainland from Goa, accompanied by two or three men, and seized the library of a Brahman who "had spent eight years in copying out and gathering together several ancient authors."[711] Among the books seized and taken to the Jesuit College were eighteen books of the epic, *Mahabharata*, attributed to Vyāsa. Translations of

---

[704] Henriques to General from Manakkudi (January 13, 1558) in *ibid.*, IV, 28.

[705] *Ibid.*

[706] Henriques to Lainez from Manaar (January 8, 1561) in *ibid.*, V, 19.

[707] Melchior Nunes Barreto to European Fathers from Cochin (December 31, 1561) in *ibid.*, V, 416.

[708] Letter to Quadros from Bijapur (April 7, 1561) in *ibid.*, V, 140.

[709] Barzaeus to European Brothers from Ormuz (December 10, 1549) in *ibid.*, I, 698.

[710] D'Almeida to Portuguese Fathers from Goa (December 26, 1558) in *ibid.*, IV, 203.

[711] Fróis to Portuguese Fathers from Goa (November 14, 1559) in *ibid.*, IV, 335–36.

this work were made for the Jesuits in Ceylon and Europe by the youths in the College. When they were dispatched to Europe, translations of some of the land grants made by the rājā of Vijayanagar to the St. Thomas Christians were sent along with them.[712]

From their informants, both heathen and Christian, and from the translations of the confiscated texts, the Jesuits learned next to nothing about Hindu doctrine. Even Henriques, who clearly had more appreciation of Tamil culture than his fellow missionaries had of the native beliefs in their areas of India, remained completely untouched by Hindu thought. "After I had begun to learn the language," he comments, "I heard many of the stories and fables of the Gentiles, and . . . I shall one day write in Malabar against their fables."[713] While he apparently was too preoccupied otherwise to carry out this intention, he likewise never bothered to acquire and translate Tamil writings. From the translations made from the *Ananta-purāna*, D'Almeida relayed to Europe (in awkward Portuguese transliterations) the names of numerous Hindu gods, the reincarnations (*Avatars*) of Vishnu, and the knowledge that Vishnu, Shiva, and Brahma constituted the *Tri-mūrti* of Sanskrit teachings.[714] Fróis, on the basis of the *Mahabharata*, recounts the story of the marriage of Shiva and Pārvatī (whom he calls Adam and Eve) and the birth of Ganeśa from the sweat of Pārvatī's body.[715] Such information was relayed, not for its intrinsic interest, but rather as confirmation of the assertions that the Jesuits never tired of making about the hopeless superstitions which they met in India. "[Francisco] Rodrigues understands something of the question," Fróis writes, "for he has many translations from their books and has preached against their religion every Sunday for about one year."[716] Teixeira puts the unbending hostility of the Jesuits into an even more somber light by his gloating admission that "sometimes we spend our time making fun of their gods, of their eating and drinking habits, and of the errors in their religion, so that they will grow less fond of them."[717]

Limited by their cultural and religious hostility to Hinduism, the Jesuits were naturally unable to penetrate beneath the surface of Hindu life. Consequently, most of their letters, even when dealing with religious questions, are concerned primarily with outer trappings. Writing from Ormuz about the "superstitions of the Gentiles," Barzaeus remarks that they worship cows who are given "*cartas d'alforia* [patents of freedom]"[718] which allow them to walk unmolested around the streets of the city. The humble Hindus of this rowdy port city on the Persian Gulf refuse to take life or eat anything which has been killed. While living austerely on vegetables and harming nobody, these people barbarically sacrifice themselves to their gods by slashing each other with razors,

[712] *Ibid.*, p. 339.
[713] Henriques to Loyola from Bembay (October 31, 1548) in *ibid.*, I, 288.
[714] Letter to Portuguese Fathers from Goa (December 26, 1558) in *ibid.*, IV, 204.
[715] Letter to Portuguese Fathers from Goa (November 13, 1560) in *ibid.*, IV, 669–70.
[716] Letter to Portuguese Fathers from Goa (December 8, 1560) in *ibid.*, IV, 801.
[717] Letter to Portuguese Fathers from Goa (December 25, 1558) in *ibid.*, IV, 171.
[718] Letter to European Brothers from Ormuz (December 10, 1549) in *ibid.*, I, 646.

hurling themselves under carts, and burning widows alive.[719] Even in the "jungles of Cambay" they sacrifice to their gods by burning offerings of sugar, butter, and silk.[720] They have many rituals for purifying themselves, and feel polluted when they have relations with Christians. Father Prancudo complains about the Hindus of Damão:

They regard us as being so accursed that if we set foot, not in their houses, but merely on the porch, they tear down the house and build another one in some place we have not touched. If they give us something to drink, they will not use that vessel again. . . .[721]

Clearly, from these and similar references, the Jesuits saw the Hindus as humble folk who irrationally esteem their gods and cows while despising Christians as being polluted and "as bearing the curse of God."[722]

The Jesuit letters are dotted with references to the adoration of the Hindus for their *pagodes*. The Christian writers use the word to mean both "temples" and "gods,"[723] and in certain letters it is used in both senses by the same author within the same paragraph.[724] The Hindu temples of Travancore are described as being "very large houses, all of stone and marble" which contain images of bulls, cows, elephants, monkeys, and men.[725] Some of the more ethnocentric Jesuits, who were plainly astonished by the massiveness and beauty of the Hindu temples, believed that they were the creations of Alexander the Great or the Romans.[726] A great temple in Cochin, where pilgrims came from as far away as Cambay, was destroyed by the Christians as early as 1550.[727] Eight years later a luxurious temple located near Tana was converted into a Christian chapel and its entrance was destroyed and replaced by a Roman archway.[728] Statues of the gods were likewise ruthlessly destroyed by the Jesuits and their converts, even though these statues were "highly honored by the people" who treated them as living beings that eat, urinate, and perform numerous miracles.[729]

The island of Divar, just north of the island of Goa, is regarded by the Hindus as a "holy land" or as something like "Rome in Europe."[730] Divar is described as a center consecrated to temples and idols to which pilgrims come from many places to obtain indulgences and forgiveness for their sins. Every year in August at least thirty thousand believers are reported to be in the habit of coming to bathe in the purifying waters of the river facing Divar, near the temple of

719 *Ibid.*
720 Teixeira to Portuguese Fathers from Goa (December 25, 1558) in *ibid.*, IV, 169–70.
721 Letter to Portuguese Fathers from Damão (November 15, 1560) in *ibid.*, IV, 697.
722 *Ibid.*
723 For the very complicated history of this word see Dalgado, *op. cit.* (n. 44), II, 130–37.
724 As an example see Nunes Baretto to Coimbra Fathers from Travancore (November 18, 1548) in Wicki (ed.), *op. cit.* (n. 658), I, 320.
725 *Ibid.*
726 Barzaeus to European Brothers from Ormuz (December 10, 1549) in *ibid.*, I, 648; and Gonçalves Rodrigues to Portuguese Fathers from Bassein (September 5, 1558) in *ibid.*, IV, 100.
727 Melchior Gonçalves to Portuguese Fathers from Cochin (January 20 [?], 1551), *ibid.*, II, 184.
728 Rodrigues to Portuguese Fathers from Bassein (September 5, 1558) in *ibid.*, IV, 100.
729 Nunes Barreto to Coimbra Fathers from Travancore (November 18, 1548) in *ibid.*, I, 320–21.
730 Fróis to Portuguese Fathers from Goa (November 13, 1560) in *ibid.*, IV, 671.

Sapta-nātha.[731] The Portuguese, beginning in 1557, sought by force to halt these pilgrimages. The Christian converts, supported by Portuguese arms, were sent out to pollute the holy places on the island. On one occasion, at least, they cut up a cow and threw pieces of its carcass into the river to prevent the Hindus from bathing there.[732] Roadside shrines, at Divar and elsewhere, were callously pushed over to show the Hindus the error of their ways.

The effort at Goa to force the Hindus to abandon their rites and ceremonies resulted in the publication in Europe of information about native processions and festivals. After the secular authority began to break up public celebrations, the Hindu faithful sought to follow their traditional rites covertly. The Jesuits, who took a "special interest in stopping the feasts and ceremonies,"[733] obtained advance information through their Christian converts about the festival dates on which secret celebrations were almost certain to be held in private homes and at odd hours of the night. By this indirect route, we also learn that around mid-December, 1558, feasts were held in honor of the god who is variously called Gaṇeśa, Vighnaśāka, and Vināyaka. These feasts were held at various locations in Goa and some of them, at least, were invaded by the Jesuits and their converts.[734] On a later occasion when Hindus from Divar wanted to celebrate the feast of Gaṇeśa they tried to escape the vigilance of the Christians by sending their sons to the mainland where they were apparently free to carry on their festivals in Muslim territory.[735] The feasts of "Divalli" (Divālī) and of Sita, the god of fortune, are celebrated at the same time in Goa,[736] usually during the month of October, and are attended by the most honorable in the Hindu community. In writing from the Portuguese territories outside of Goa, where the Christians were not strong enough to forbid the celebrations, the Jesuits content themselves with giving graphic descriptions of Hindu processions but without really understanding what is being celebrated.[737]

The Hindus, according to the Jesuits, have three sorts of priests: Brahmans, Yogis, and Gurus. While the letterwriters recognize that the Brahmans manage the temples and are dominant in religious affairs, they have no admiration for them unless they become converts. Repeatedly they charge them with insincerity, duplicity, and with having "no aim except to collect money"[738] from the Hindu laity. When asked why they intentionally deceive their own people, the Brahmans reply, "What can we do, for this is how we earn our living? We beg you not to reveal our affairs to the people."[739] Fróis discourses

[731] D'Almeida to Portuguese Fathers from Goa (December 26, 1558) in *ibid.*, IV, 205–06.
[732] Fróis to Portuguese Fathers from Goa (December 1, 1561) in *ibid.*, V, 279–80.
[733] D'Almeida to Portuguese Fathers from Goa (December 26, 1558) in *ibid.*, IV, 201.
[734] *Ibid.*, p. 202.
[735] Fróis to Portuguese Fathers from Goa (November 13, 1560) in *ibid.*, IV, 669.
[736] D'Almeida to Portuguese Fathers from Goa (December 26, 1558) in *ibid.*, IV, 203.
[737] See, for example, Brother Luis de Gouveia to Goa Fathers from Quilon (April 7, 1560) in *ibid.*, IV, 545–46.
[738] Henriques to Loyola from Bembay (October 31, 1548) in *ibid.*, I, 284. See also his comparison of the Brahmans and the Christian priests (*ibid.*, p. 295).
[739] *Ibid.*, p. 292.

learnedly about the sacred threads of the Brahmans which are "worn around the neck next to the skin from the age of seven onwards." This ceremonial symbol "has three strands each of which has been twisted several times with a knot covering where the ends meet." Each thread honors a particular god and the "knot which joins the ends represents the oneness of the three persons, and thus they try to claim that they have a Trinity like ours." After showing the falsity of this assumption, Fróis concludes "that they only speak of three persons [*Tri-mūrti*, Sanskrit for three forms] because they learned it from the Christians" [740] Though the Brahmans pretend to be vegetarians, Nunes Barreto believes that "in secret . . . they will eat anything." [741] The Brahmans, though they are priests, marry "as many women as they want" [742] and entice young girls to prostitute themselves for the honor and revenue of the temples.

The ascetic Yogis are men of a different sort, and the Jesuits show marked respect for their spirituality, abstinence, learning, and willingness to listen. Fróis distinguishes two types of Yogis: mendicants and hermits.[743] They seem to "obey a superior" and are "regarded as saints" by the common people.[744] Barzaeus is so impressed with the influence they wield that he suggests that he might dress like them and live with them.[745] One of those whom he converted he sent to Europe in 1551, and later on this Christianized Yogi worked at the College of Goa. Two others, who were studying in the College, are reputed to know eighteen native languages.[746] Another, converted by Henriques on the Fishery Coast, was held to have great influence through the purity of his life among the *patangatins*, the village heads of the Paravans.[747] While the Gurus are recognized as being authorities on Hindu teachings, the Jesuits have very little to say about them as a group. They are more intent upon telling about sorcerers who are able to conjure up with their incantations "five hundred phantasmagoric elephants," [748] and about "jousi" (*jyotisī* or astrologers) who tell *fula* (fortunes) [749] by attaching leaves to both shoulders of an idol and waiting to see from which side they first fall before making a prediction,[750] or about the nocturnal demons and devils which plagued the Paravans at sea until they became Christians.[751]

On social questions, the Jesuit letters concern themselves mainly with those institutions and ideas which made the problem of conversion more complex.

[740] Fróis to Portuguese Fathers from Goa (December 8, 1560) in *ibid.*, IV, 803–4.
[741] Nunes Barreto to Coimbra Fathers from Travancore (November 18, 1548) in *ibid.*, I, 321.
[742] *Ibid.*
[743] *Ibid.*, p. 801.
[744] Barzaeus to European Brothers from Ormuz (December 10, 1549) in *ibid.*, I, 676; see also Nunes Barreto to Coimbra Fathers (November 18, 1548) in *ibid.*, I, 321.
[745] *Ibid.*, I, 676.
[746] Melchior Dias to Miron from Goa (January 4, 1555) in *ibid.*, III, 210–11.
[747] Henriques to Rodrigues from Cochin (January 12, 1551) in *ibid.*, II, 159–60.
[748] D'Almeida to Portuguese Fathers from Goa (December 26, 1558) in *ibid.*, IV, 204–05.
[749] Possibly from Sanskrit: *phala* = fruits of an act, hence fate.
[750] Fróis to Portuguese Fathers from Goa (November 14, 1559) in Wicki (ed.), *op. cit.* (n. 658), IV, 344–45.
[751] Henriques to Loyola from Bembay (October 31, 1548) in *ibid.*, I, 290.

The caste divisions of southern India interest them particularly. In addition to giving the names of a number of south Indian castes, Henriques advised Loyola that "...it is better in India to baptize all those of one caste than different individuals taken from various castes."[752] He talks mostly about the practices common to the Paravans and of the related groups of the interior called the "Chavallacars" and the "Taquanqutes," inhabitants of the region called Thekkumkur to the east of Lake Vampanad.[753] From Quilon the Jesuits of Europe learned about the castes of blacksmiths, carpenters, tailors, coconut workers, and other occupational groups. Very little specific information is given on the castes of Goa and those of the northern settlements. Fróis, who knows a great deal about the Brahmans and several of the lower castes of Goa, condemns the cruel custom by which the rich men of India cast their slaves into the streets to die when they become too ill or too old to work. Slaves and refugees from caste discipline often found sanctuary in the convents and schools of the Christian settlements in India.[754]

Marital practices and death customs intrigue and perplex the Jesuits. Henriques writes that there are "many people married to cousins, sisters and sisters-in-law, and it would make a great scandal to separate them because there are many of them, and they have many sons and daughters."[755] Always generous himself in allowing dispensations to the natives, Henriques repeatedly asks for a papal dispensation which would permit marriage within the third and fourth degrees of affinity and consanguinity, a concession already permitted in New Spain.[756] Instead of prayers and candles at the deathbed, "they bring in a live cow to the patient and put its tail into his hands and this for them is to die in the most devout manner."[757] In Travancore, it was the custom for all men to cut their beards at the death of a king; those who refused were usually arrested or done away with.[758] On the death of a king in southern India, it was also customary for his retainers to run amuck in order to avenge his death or to die in the attempt.[759] Even the St. Thomas Christians threatened to run amuck to avenge their bishop when the Portuguese tried to capture him.[760]

At Cape Comorin the people have a diet made up mainly of rice, wheat, flour, chicken, fish, milk, butter, eggs, figs, and the coconut and its milk.[761] The adults, who walk about in semi-nudity, ordinarily wear a loin cloth of slightly over two feet in width. Their children under the age of ten usually walk about

[752] *Ibid.*, III, 599.
[753] Henriques to Loyola from Punical (November 6, 1552) in *ibid.*, II, 397, and Silveira to Torres from Goa (December, 1557) in *ibid.*, III, 754.
[754] Fróis to Portuguese Fathers from Goa (December 8, 1560) in *ibid.*, IV, 793.
[755] Henriques to Loyola from Punical (December 31, 1556) in *ibid.*, III, 595–96.
[756] Henriques to Loyola from Punical (November 6, 1552) in *ibid.*, II, 396–400.
[757] Fróis to the Portuguese Fathers from Goa (November 14, 1559) in *ibid.*, IV, 344.
[758] Henriques to Loyola from Punical (December 25–31, 1555) in *ibid.*, III, 420.
[759] Carneiro to De Câmara from Goa (December 24, 1557) in *ibid.*, III, 796.
[760] *Ibid.*, p. 801.
[761] Nunes Barreto to Coimbra Fathers from Travancore (November 18, 1548) in *ibid.*, I, 319–20.

in nothing at all.⁷⁶² A commonplace sign of friendship is the companionable habit of chewing betel and areca, and a royal indication of good will is the sending of a branch of figs.⁷⁶³ Whenever traveling in south India, even in hostile territory, a stranger, if accompanied by a local guide, is understood to be under the ruler's protection.⁷⁶⁴ The climate of the island of Manaar is reported to accentuate sensuality, and Henriques wrote to the Jesuit General requesting permission to take certain tranquilizing drugs commonly employed by the Yogis "to mortify the flesh."⁷⁶⁵

In the judgment of the Jesuits, the non-Christian peoples of India, even when most advanced and learned, are very inferior to the peoples of eastern Asia. The Chinese are described as being wise and just, while the Japanese are esteemed for their industry, intelligence, and cleanliness. The Malabars and Kanarese are held to be much less acute, very weak and superstitious, and completely lacking in standards of cleanliness.⁷⁶⁶ The natives of Tana are brutish and troublesome to the missionaries, but "full of astuteness and worldly wisdom . . . in looking after their own interests."⁷⁶⁷ While the lower classes in Indian society are sometimes given credit for mildness and docility, the Brahmans, unless they become converts, are criticized for their obstinacy, arrogance, and unwillingness to listen to reason.

Even the implacable foes of the Jesuits, the Moors and Jews, are accorded greater respect than the Hindus. While the Jesuits condemn them for practicing sodomy and usury, they also admire their business acumen and their understanding of the faiths of their fathers.⁷⁶⁸ They recognize that most of the Muslims are Sunnites, and complain that their "casizes" (Muslim teachers) are sometimes able to win native Christians over to the faith of the Prophet.⁷⁶⁹ While Muslim women are ordinarily kept indoors, they apparently escaped surveillance enough of the time to cause the Jesuits to attack them for their immoral association with Christian men.⁷⁷⁰ G. Rodrigues remarks that in Bijapur "the Moors are as innumerable as insects" and extends his remarks to include a description of a Muslim festival and an estimate of Adil Khan.⁷⁷¹ With regard to the Moors, in particular, the Jesuits seem to be on the defensive. "We are here on a battlefield," Barzaeus writes from Goa to Loyola, "in constant struggle with Turks, Moors, and Gentiles, and we have no peace."⁷⁷²

⁷⁶² *Ibid.*, p. 320.
⁷⁶³ Carneiro to De Câmara from Goa (December 24, 1557) in *ibid.*, III, 799.
⁷⁶⁴ *Ibid.*, p. 797.
⁷⁶⁵ To Lainez from Manaar (December 19, 1561) in *ibid.*, V, 382. For the General's reaction see his reply of December 11, 1562, in *ibid.*, p. 661.
⁷⁶⁶ Gonçalves to Portuguese Fathers from Cochin (January, 1551) in *ibid.*, II, 185.
⁷⁶⁷ G. Rodrigues to Goa Fathers from Tana (December 1, 1558) in *ibid.*, IV, 116–17.
⁷⁶⁸ For example see Barzaeus to European Brothers from Ormuz (December 10, 1549) in *ibid.*, I, 657.
⁷⁶⁹ Durão to F. Rodriguez from Thêngâppattanam (November 22, 1557) in *ibid.*, III, 694–95.
⁷⁷⁰ Barzaeus to European Brothers from Ormuz (December 10, 1549) in *ibid.*, I, 663.
⁷⁷¹ Letter to Quadros (April 7, 1561) in *ibid.*, V, 143–44.
⁷⁷² Letter of January 12, 1553, in *ibid.*, II, 589.

The embattled Jesuits were by no means uncritical admirers of their secular Portuguese cohorts in India. In commenting about the Portuguese soldiers at Ormuz, Barzaeus complains that they seem "like men without law, king, or captain—all savages, renegades, blasphemers." [773] Many Portuguese men, already married at home, contract "secret" marriages in India and refuse to have the banns of their new marriages proclaimed in church. [774] In Goa, one street was famed for its Portuguese prostitutes, [775] some of whom were sent back to Europe by the missionaries from time to time. The Portuguese, like the Moors, shock the Jesuits by their addiction to sodomy, and in 1559, as part of a strict moral and religious rehabilitation campaign a number of Portuguese were executed, exiled, or imprisoned for unnatural sexual practices. [776] Indeed, the Jesuits repeatedly charge the Portuguese with making their mission difficult and of undoing their good works by the bad moral example they set and by the injustices which they tyrannically perpetrate upon the natives. [777] Friction was probably inevitable in the settlements, since, as in Goa, the Jesuits "were so surrounded by Portuguese that it is like living in Portugal." [778]

But the picture of the Portuguese painted by the Jesuits is not completely black. Portuguese youths are praised for remaining firm in their faith even while serving "in the armies of the Gentiles along with Moors and other Gentiles." [779] Their elders contribute to the mission, take pleasure in working in the confraternities, and lend aid in the construction of churches and schools. In 1557 an "honorable" Portuguese provided the paper for printing confessional manuals so that they could be distributed free of charge in all of the settlements. [780] Many Portuguese and Luso-Indians sought admission to the Society even though the Jesuits discouraged them because proper training was not available in India. [781] Naturally exceptions were made, one of the most notable being the admission of Fernão Mendes Pinto to the Society in 1554. [782] Occasionally it seems that the Jesuits won devotion from Portuguese officials who hoped to win Jesuit support in India and Europe for advancing their careers. Barzaeus writes about a captain working in Ormuz: "He is devoted to the Company and wants to be governor of India one day. Pray for him!" [783] Or, when Henriques speaks well of a captain at Punical, the Jesuit comments: "He takes our advice on everything. . . ." [784]

[773] Letter of December 10, 1549, in *ibid.*, I, 663.

[774] For example, see Henriques to Loyola from Punical (December 25-31, 1555) in *ibid.*, III, 419.

[775] Dias to Society in Europe (December 15, 1554) in *ibid.*, III, 158.

[776] Fróis to Coimbra Fathers from Goa (November, 1559) in *ibid.*, IV, 285-86.

[777] Quadros to Miron from Goa (December 6, 1555) in *ibid.*, III, 347.

[778] Da Costa to Portuguese Fathers from Goa (December 26, 1558) in *ibid.*, IV, 178. At Ormuz there always were 800 to 1000 Portuguese in the city. See Brandão to Coimbra Fathers from Goa (December 23, 1554) in *ibid.*, III, 191.

[779] Henriques to Loyola from Bembay (October 31, 1548) in *ibid.*, I, 297-98.

[780] Fróis to Coimbra Fathers from Goa (November 30, 1557) in *ibid.*, III, 711.

[781] Barzaeus to Loyola from Goa (January 12, 1553) in *ibid.*, III, 158.

[782] Brandão to Coimbra Fathers from Goa (December 23, 1554) in *ibid.*, III, 178-82.

[783] Letter to European Brothers (December 10, 1549) in *ibid.*, I, 673.

[784] *Ibid.*, III, 419.

The first impressions summarized here are, as we have said, based on letters written from India between 1548 and 1561, and so they necessarily relate events and describe practices from the first years of the Jesuit experience in the subcontinent. In Europe all of the letters quoted were available in printed form by 1570, and these letters, as well as others which remained unpublished, were likewise circulated in manuscript. From 1554 onward, voices were raised in criticism of the published letterbooks both in Europe and India. The letterwriters were attacked, particularly by the Portuguese in India, for exhibiting bias and for not always giving all the facts relating to certain questions. It was even rumored that a book had been compiled to point out the factual errors and inconsistencies in the letterbooks.[785] Within the Society the demand was also being made for more careful and comprehensive editions of the letters and for the preparation of an official history of the mission. It was these considerations, among others, which probably help to account for the lacuna of 1561–68 in the published letters. From the perspective of today, while giving due weight to the shortcomings of the letters as historical sources, the Jesuit writings are unique among European writings for this period in the information which they give on Indian languages and literature and for the way in which they point up the disdain of the missionaries for the Indian peoples, particularly the Brahmans, and for their religions. Blinded by their cultural and religious hostility, the Jesuits contented themselves with superficial or incidental references to Hindu practices.

C. THE SECOND GENERATION, 1570–1601

Between 1570 and 1588 very little information about India appeared in Europe in published form. Though several of Xavier's letters from India were published in 1566 and 1570, they deal with the Far East and say practically nothing about India. The *Nuovi avisi* published at Rome in 1570 included five new letters from India written between 1568 and 1570. From 1570 until 1585, just nine brief letters or extracts about India got into print, the most notable of which was a notice published in the *Nouveau advis* (Paris, 1582) telling about Aquaviva's departure for the court of Akbar in 1580. The *Litterae annuae* published at Rome in 1585 includes a detailed letter from Valignano which deals exclusively with the Salsette martyrs—those five Jesuits, including Rudolph Aquaviva, who were murdered in July, 1583. The other annual letters of this decade are notable for their failure to include news from India.

Not only was there a blackout of India during these years; those letters which actually saw light contributed almost nothing to the European image

---

[785] J. Wicki, *Alessandro Valignano, S. I., Historia del principio y progresso de la Compañía de Jesús en las Indias Orientales* (Rome, 1944), pp. 36*–37*.

and are little more than letters of edification. A letter from Goa of 1568 [786] stresses the dangers to the missionaries from the growing power of the Moors in the waters and seaports of India. "The Malabar nation is Muslim," it asserts, "and they are almost all pirates and hostile to the Christians." [787] While this was certainly not literally true, it brings out how seriously the Portuguese were under attack from an alliance of the Turks and Malabars. [788] The "pirates of Malabar," after the Zamorin in 1559 denounced his treaty of 1540 with the Portuguese, made the seas unsafe for the Europeans along the entire coast of western India—from Diu to Ceylon. Jesuits were killed, captured, or held for ransom. Even the Christian communities in the vicinity of Goa itself were preyed upon by plunderers from the sea. But, fascinatingly, even as the Europeans are forced on the defensive by the renewed Muslim and Malabar attacks, they begin to find that the Brahmans, whom they had so roundly condemned in their earlier letters, now come forward to help them in their hour of need.

The published reports on the status of the missions in Quilon (1569), Goa and its environs (1569), and Cochin (1570) take what must be described as a more appreciative attitude towards the Brahmans, whether converted or not. [789] The converted sons of leading Brahmans are praised for traveling about with the Jesuits and for their aid in bringing other Indians into the Christian fold. In many of the outlying territories of Goa the Jesuits are successful in converting Brahmans who are also *gancars*, [790] or members of the native councils which rule the village communities. In the attacks upon the Christians of Salsette, Brahman youths fought along with the other converts and some of the *gancars* secretly aided and gave sanctuary to the hard-pressed missionaries. In fact, the Hindu converts of all castes are described as standing sturdily beside the Europeans who are seeking to preserve their foothold in India.

These reports also give somewhat more statistical data than most of the Jesuit letters. Quilon "lies at the foot of a mountain and is back from the ocean by about 11,000 paces." [791] In its environs are twenty-three villages, all except four of which possess Christian churches. These are heavily populated places, but the necessities of life are available in abundance and the climate is healthy. Near the city of Cochin, about three thousand paces (yards) from its outskirts, there are a number of villages around Palurt, all of which are under the jurisdiction of the state of Cochin. The small principality of Porakád "which lies

---

[786] Organtino da Brescia to Europe (December 28, 1568). Text reproduced in German translation in Anton Eglauer (ed.), *Die Missionsgeschichte späterer Zeiten; oder, Gesammelte Briefe der katholischen Missionäre aus allen Theilen der Welt. Briefe aus Ost-Indien* (3 vols.; Augsburg, 1794-95), II, 290-309.
[787] *Ibid.*, p. 278.
[788] For a survey of these hostilities see Danvers, *op. cit.* (n. 228), I, chap. xix; also K. M. Panikkar, *A History of Kerala, 1498-1801* (Annamalainagar, 1960), pp. 116-20.
[789] J. de Gouvea to Society from Quilon (January 15, 1569) in Eglauer (ed.), *op. cit.* (n. 786), II, 313-17; Sebastian Fernandes to General from Goa (November, 1569) in *ibid.*, pp. 333-66; G. Ruis to General from Cochin (January 15, 1570) in *ibid.*, pp. 366-79.
[790] See Dalgado, *op. cit.* (n. 44), I, 416-17.
[791] Eglauer (ed.), *op. cit.* (n. 786), II, 313-15.

twenty miles from here"[792] is apparently also a fief of Cochin. But while the Jesuits enjoyed good relations with the rulers of Quilon and Cochin as well as some of their vassals, the missionaries continue to rail against their blindness in refusing to accept Christianity.

Despite the obvious difficulties faced by the Europeans, the missionaries continued to make converts in the Portuguese settlements. On Salsette Island, the converts numbered 2,000 in 1568 out of a total population of 200,000.[793] In the following year Sebastian Fernandes reports a total of 3,200 conversions in the Goa area, "a smaller number than in previous years, but large enough considering how progress was limited by war and unrest."[794] The College at Goa in 1569 housed 88 Jesuits, some of whom taught in the school which had 720 students.[795] In Cochin during 1570 the two Jesuit elementary schools together had a registration of 270 students. Mass baptisms continued in all of the coastal settlements of India, and in Goa they were still celebrated with great pomp and often with the viceroy in attendance.

News of Aquaviva's visit to the court of Akbar was published in Europe by 1582.[796] Three years later it became known that he, the nephew of the Jesuit General, had dispiritedly returned to Goa and was shortly thereafter killed on the island of Salsette.[797] The other letters from these years are also full of the hardships being suffered in India, even though the missions to Akbar apparently raised hope for a time that real achievements in India were in the offing. Contrast this bleak picture to the bright successes that the Jesuits were celebrating or anticipating in the Far East around 1585, and it is no longer hard to understand why the letters from India were not more frequently printed in the letterbooks of these years.

Maffei's Latin history which appeared at Florence in 1588 includes in chronological order a systematic discussion of the Portuguese enterprise in India from Vasco da Gama to about 1557. Though often classified as a Jesuit history, Maffei's work, as it relates to India, resembles in organization and emphasis the books of Castanheda and Barros. In fact, he explains at one point that it is his object to describe "the conquests of the Portuguese, and not the manners and customs of other nations."[798] The Jesuit historian, perhaps intentionally, has relatively little to say about the missions in India, though he does laud the great successes of Xavier and refers to him as a "saint." While Maffei fails to fill in systematically the gap (1561–68) in our information on India, it is clear from his discussion of particular subjects, whenever he examines them closely, that he was

[792] *Ibid.*, p. 376.   [793] *Ibid.*, p. 301.

[794] *Ibid.*, p. 364.   [795] *Ibid.*, pp. 333–34.

[796] Extracts from his letter of 1580 from Fatehpur Sīkrī appeared in *Nouveau advis* (Paris) and in the annual letter published at Rome in 1582.

[797] Valignano's letter of January, 1584, published in *Litterae annuae* (Rome, 1585).

[798] G. Maffei, *Historiarum Indicarum libri XVI* (Florence, 1588), I, 255. Apparently, he used two documents prepared in 1568 and 1569 on the fortresses, ports, and mission stations of India. These two reports have recently been edited and published in J. Wicki, "Duas relações sobre a situação da India portuguesa nos anos 1568 e 1569," *Studia* (Lisbon), VIII (1961), 133–220.

probably acquainted with many of the Jesuit letters from India which remained unpublished during the sixteenth century, and that he used some of them as well as special reports in the preparation of his digressions on social classes and religious practices.[799]

For Maffei, the political and social organization existing in Malabar, especially in Calicut, is the norm for India as a whole. The Zamorin, who is the chief ruler or "emperor" of Malabar, governs four kinds of people: magistrates or governors called "Caimales,"[800] priests called "Brachmanes," a military aristocracy called "Naires," and a great host of artisans and farmers. In addition to his own people, the Zamorin tolerates Muslim and Jewish merchants within his realm and they derive great profits from trading in his port cities. Such a description and emphasis was obviously derived by Maffei from the secular accounts rather than the missionary letters.

In his generalized descriptions of the Brahmans, Nāyars and working classes of Malabar, Maffei combines the secular sources with material from the missionary letters and the writers of antiquity. "There are several types of Brahmans," he asserts, "those who marry and raise children and the others who profess celibacy and are today called yogis. In former times the Greeks called them Gymnophistes." He then goes on to repeat what was said about the Brahmans and Yogis by the earlier writers, including the assertion that the Yogis live under a supreme general "who enjoys great revenues and who sends certain of these imposters at particular times to preach in divers countries their impious errors and their dreams."[801] He also notes that the Yogis believe that by their renunciation of things of the flesh they will eventually be "received in great glory among the '*Abdutes*' [Avadhūtas], which is one of their Orders."[802] The Yogis, with their "spiritual exercises," monastic hierarchy and organization, and evangelizing spirit seem to remind Maffei, as they did some of the Jesuits in India, of the regular Orders of the Catholic church.

Like the letterwriters, Maffei writes in wonderment about the Hindu temples "which are able to compete in magnificence with the most superb of ancient Rome."[803] And, like his colleagues, Maffei dismisses Hindu teachings as a mass of fable and superstition. The Jesuit historian saw some of the Brahmanical translations which had been prepared in India and sent to Portugal.[804] He admits that these books show "incredible care and labor" and that their teachings are "similar in some ways to the fables of ancient Greece or the '*Augurale*' [Auguria] discipline of the old Etruscans."[805] But, the good

---

[799] In the appendix of letters at the end of Maffei's *Historiarum Indicarum* just three of those included relate to the affairs of India. Most of those reproduced were written from Japan. See below, pp. 706–9.

[800] See above, p. 375n.

[801] Maffei, *op. cit.* (n. 798), I, 255.

[802] *Ibid.*

[803] *Ibid.*

[804] *Ibid.*, p. 56. Cf., above, pp. 438–39.

[805] *Ibid.* The Etruscans were famous even in the late Roman empire for their ability to discover by signs (auguries) whether a proposed act met with divine approval.

Christian Humanist concludes that it is of "little importance to give space at this point to these bagatelles and to these tales of old."[806] It is of more importance to reflect that God in his goodness is now ready to remove the scales from the eyes of those who have so long lived in darkness.

Maffei, perhaps more than any other writer of the century, gives considerable detail on the preparation of the Nāyars for military service, their equipment, and their conduct in battle. As the hereditary warrior caste, the Nāyars are in constant training from the age of seven until death, and Maffei is clearly impressed by the rigor of their physical training program and the bodily agility which it gives them. While they previously relied upon bows, pikes, and swords, the Nāyars quickly learned how to make, burnish, and aim all the firearms, large and small, that were to be found in the arsenals of the Portuguese. Still they went almost nude into battle and without the protection of breastplate or helmet. In battle with armored Europeans the Nāyars show themselves to be less firm when meeting the shock of attack than their enemies, but much nimbler and extremely well-outfitted for hit-and-run tactics. Their ability to strike quickly and effectively and then melt into the interior while harassing their pursuers with javelins and metal quoits thrown with deadly accuracy clearly made them formidable foes to the Portuguese. Though all Nāyars pride themselves on their aptitude for war, an elite exists among them called "Amoques" who pledge their lives, family, and children to avenge their masters or their fellows. Reckless and impetuous warriors, the "Amoques" are held universally in great esteem and the strength of a king is measured by the number of "Amoques" who have pledged themselves to him.[807]

While Maffei contents himself with denouncing the marital and inheritance customs of the Nāyars, he reserves his full wrath for their impossible pride, insolence, and pollution beliefs. Artisans and farmers live most miserably, a condition which the Nāyars seem to do their utmost to maintain. Men of the working classes are unable to better their conditions by changing their jobs for better ones. Evidently he was under the impression that the individual chose his occupation and was then frozen in it. Maffei, while referring to Arrian's Greek history of India, concludes that groupings based on occupation is one of the oldest of India's customs. The Nāyars and other Indian nobles who have been responsible for maintaining this system since antiquity quite naturally hate Christianity vehemently for its emphasis on moderation and brotherly love.[808]

Certain general impressions about Portuguese India emerge from Maffei's pages. The motivation for the Portuguese enterprise is primarily trade. In India, the Portuguese ruined themselves by overindulging in the debilitating luxuries of the Orient. The Franciscan missionaries, who dominated the Christian enterprise in India until the advent of the Jesuits, are depicted as

---

[806] *Ibid.*
[807] *Ibid.*, pp. 56–58. For a detailed discussion of the "Amoques" consult "Amouco" in Dalgado, *op. cit.* (n. 44), I, 33–36.
[808] Maffei, *op. cit.* (n. 798), pp. 58–59.

being well-intentioned and sincere but not overly effective.[809] Maffei finds that the St. Thomas Christians exhibit similarities in rites and traditions to the Latin faith, and he seems completely untroubled by their alleged predilection for Nestorian heresies. About India itself, and on those areas beyond the Portuguese outposts, Maffei has practically nothing to say and in this regard is less informative than the secular writers. While Maffei refers constantly to the classical authors of Greece and Rome, he indicates on more than one occasion that he feels that their descriptions of India must be modified in the light of what his contemporaries learned from actually being there.[810] And, like the secular historians, Maffei interrupts his narrative of the Portuguese conquest from time to time to titillate his readers with stories—about swordfish so huge that they are able to stop a ship at sea, of venomous serpents, and of bats which possess "the snout and teeth of a fox."[811] But not everything about India is weird and unbelievable to Maffei. He also enjoys giving a somewhat imaginative description of Ceylon as an earthly paradise, the beautiful pleasure gardens of the Nāyars in Malabar, and the jewels, rich dress, and costly ceremonies prized by the upper classes everywhere.

In the last decade of the sixteenth century, there is a revival of general interest in India which the newly published biographies and letters of Xavier helped to promote in Europe. Most important to the new wave of optimism, however, was the encouraging news from India itself. The three Jesuit missions to Akbar of 1580–83, 1591, and 1595–1605 stirred hopes in Europe that the Christian conquest of the Mughul empire, the greatest kingdom in India, had finally come to be within the realm of reality. Simultaneously it should be remembered, Christian fortunes were also improving in China where the Jesuit penetration was being slowly advanced by Ricci, Valignano, and others. Though a few setbacks had been experienced by the Christians in Japan, these reverses were still outshone in Europe in the last decade of the century by the triumphal tour of the Japanese embassy of 1584–86. In the Philippines, too, progress was marked. Though the united Spanish and Portuguese empire had suffered maritime defeats at the hands of the Dutch and English Protestants, the fortunes of Philip II seemed to be improving in the non-European world, and in Asia particularly, largely through the efforts of the religious Orders. The grand work which Xavier had begun a half century before seemed to be bearing fruits in India and China, the two great Asian civilizations which the Christian Europeans had hitherto found so much difficulty in penetrating.

Information about Akbar's realm, or the land of the great "Mogor," slowly appeared in published form in Europe. A short account of the first Jesuit mission was published in Paris in 1582 based upon the letters of Father Rudolf Aquaviva and others.[812] Notice of this mission was also included in the official

---

[809] For example, see *ibid.*, II, 111–23.
[810] *Ibid.*, I, 211.   [811] *Ibid.*, pp. 78–79.
[812] *Nouveaux advis de l'estat du Christianisme ès pays et royaulmes des Indes Orientales et Jappon*, (Paris, 1582), pp. 1–4.

Litterae annuae (pp. 111–12) for 1582. Nothing further is heard in Europe about Akbar until news of the second mission of 1591 reached there. In the following year extracts from the letters of the Provincial in Goa about "Mogor" were published in Italian at Rome by the Jesuit, Father Spitelli.[813] And his compendium quickly appeared in Latin translation at Antwerp (1593) and in French at Lyon (1594). It was not, however, until three years later that a little book appeared which gave substantial data on northern India and the court of Akbar.

Giovanni Battista Peruschi (1525–98), an Italian Jesuit who apparently had never visited Asia, prepared and published a summary of what was known in 1597 about Akbar's realm. His study consisting of two parts is entitled *Informatione del regno et stato del Gran Re di Mogor, della sua persona, qualita, & costumi, & congretture della sua conversione alla nostra santa fede. . . .*[814] The first section is based mainly upon a *Relaçam . . .*[815] (Account of Akbar) prepared by Father Monserrate at Goa in 1582 shortly after his return from the first mission to Akbar's court. Monserrate had received instructions before leaving Goa in 1579 that he should keep a diary of his experiences in the Mughul empire. For the next two-and-a-half years he faithfully recorded his experiences every evening. Upon his return to Goa a summary of his diary was prepared for dispatch to Europe.[816] While Peruschi faithfully gives the substance of the *Relaçam*, he reorganized it, presented it in his own language, and modified it with materials taken from letters dealing with the second mission of 1591.[817] Following his narrative, Peruschi reproduces in his second part the texts of four letters[818] written in 1595 by the members of the third mission as forwarded to Europe by the Provincial at Goa. French translations of Peruschi quickly appeared at Besançon (1597) and Paris (1598), and in 1598 at Mainz German and Latin versions came off the press.

Several other works in Italian and French reproduced parts of Peruschi's

---

[813] *Ragguaglio d'alcune missioni dell'Indie Orientali e Occidentali cavato da alcuni avvisi scritti gli anni 1590 et 1591.* Extracts from the Latin version in English translation may be found in the *Journal of the Asiatic Society of Bengal*, LXV (1896), 62–63.

[814] G. B. Peruschi, *Informatione del regno et stato del Gran Re di Mogor, della sua persona, qualita, & costumi, & congretture della sua conversione alla nostra santa fede . . .* (Rome, 1597). In the same year Peruschi had a revised version published at Brescia and added to it a map of India and the Far East. The imprimatur to the Brescia edition indicates that the Jesuit General, Claude Acquaviva, himself checked Peruschi's summary and published letters against the original materials possessed by the Society. Further references are to the revised Brescia edition of 1597.

[815] *Relaçam do Equebar Rei dos Mogores* existed in three manuscripts until the nineteenth century, but today the only one which is known is in the possession of the Society. An English translation of this lone manuscript was published by H. Hosten, S. J., in the *Journal of the Asiatic Society of Bengal*, VIII (1912), 185–221.

[816] Maclagan, *op. cit.* (n. 618), pp. 149–50.

[817] He cites (p. 5) just two sources: letters from "Mogor" dated 1582 and 1592 (?). One of the letters most generally quoted on the second embassy, and one of those probably used by Peruschi, is that of Pedro Martinez (November 1590 or 1591). For details of publication see Streit, *op. cit.* (n. 647), p. 282. Text is in Eglauer (ed.), *op. cit.* (n. 786), III, 112–16.

[818] These four letters are also available in German translation in Eglauer (ed.), *op. cit.* (n. 786), III, 136–68.

narrative of Mughul India before the end of the sixteenth century.[819] In 1597, the *Litterae annuae* (pp. 567–73), also summarized the progress being made by the Jesuits in northern India. Three letters from the third mission penned in Lahore were published in 1598 in a collection prepared by the Portuguese Jesuit, Amador Rebello (d. 1622).[820] One of these, written by Jerome Xavier, is similar to one reproduced in Peruschi, while a second of 1596 seems not to have been published elsewhere in the sixteenth century.[821] Rebello also provides a lengthy letter on the condition of the Indian mission from the Provincial of Goa, Francisco Cabral, to the General, written on December 16, 1596, which seems never to have been printed by another collector.[822]

Castanheda was the first European writer to comment at length on the advent of the Mughuls in northern India, and his story ends abruptly in 1540.[823] Thereafter, Europe appears to have been left in the dark about the subsequent activities of the Mughuls until the appearance of Peruschi's book in 1597. The Italian Jesuit, apparently unaware of Castanheda's earlier work, provides a systematic description of Hindustan under Akbar, exclusively from the Jesuit sources. It should by no means be assumed, however, that Peruschi or his sources are primarily concerned with religious matters. Rather the Jesuits seek quite consciously to describe methodically what they have been able to learn through native informants (including Akbar himself) and from their own experiences about the geography, organization, administration, and economy of Akbar's extended realm as it appeared around 1582, or about twenty years after the beginning of Akbar's personal rule. Naturally, they also show a profound interest in the personality and beliefs of Akbar, particularly since their missionary endeavor was aimed primarily at his conversion.

"Mahometto Zelaldim Echebar" (Akbar) in Peruschi's italianized form of his name, is the eighth descendant of Tamerlane and a native of "Chaquata" (Chaghata) which "lies between Tartary and Persia to the north, while India is more to the east of it."[824] The common language of Chaghata is Turkish but different from that spoken in Turkey; the court language is Persian which is not pronounced like the Persian of Persia. Chaghata borders on its Tartary side with the Uzbeks whose first ruler was Jenghis Khan. The Uzbek ruler in power, Abdullah Khan, is a descendant of Jenghis Khan and he governs the region from

[819] For example, *Appresso discipolo* (Verona, 1597) and F. B. Th., *Advis moderne de l'estat et grand royaume de Mogor . . . Jouxte la copie imprimée à Rome depuis un mois, par Loys Zanneti* (Paris, 1598).

[820] Amador Rebello, *Compendio de algunas cartas que este anno de 97, vierão dos Padres da Companhia de Iesu, que residim na India, & Corto do Grão Mogor, & nos Reynos da China et Japão, no Brasil, em que se contem varias cousas* (Lisbon, 1598). This large collection of letters which Streit (*op. cit.* [n. 649], p. 295) lists but neglects to analyze has not been used by the standard authorities on the Mughul mission. My references are to the copy preserved in the National Library at Madrid.

[821] Xavier's letter dated 1596 (in Rebello, *op. cit.* [n. 820], pp. 70–71) is not listed either in Streit or in the more recent list of Xavier letters compiled in A. Camps, *Jerome Xavier and the Muslims of the Mogul Empire* (Schöneck-Beckenried, 1957), p. 40.

[822] Streit, *op. cit.* (n. 647), p. 291.

[823] See above, pp. 420–25.

[824] Peruschi, *op. cit.* (n. 814), pp. 5–6.

Samarkand and Bokhara. This family of rulers, to whom Akbar is related, was originally heathen but had recently accepted Islam.

The kingdom of "Mogor," according to Peruschi, is bounded on the west by Hither India (region of the Indus) and on the northwest by Persia; on the east by Further India (region of the Ganges and eastward) which borders on China; across the mountains to the north is the great kingdom of Tartary;[825] on the southwest is the kingdom of Calicut and the sea; and on the southeast lies the Bay of Bengal. "Mogor," or the territory which Akbar rules, is not just one kingdom but many kingdoms joined together. Its principal territories which are situated between the Indus and the Ganges are Hindustan, Agra, the very ancient state of Māndū (Malwa), Lahore, Cambay, and Bengal.[826] Its chief cities are Cambay, Delhi, Lahore, Multan, Māndū, Patna, Jaunpur, and Ahmadābād. Some of these cities are as large as Lisbon, and Māndū with its great and beautiful edifices, invites comparison with ancient Rome.

The Mughul empire although powerful and vast (its area is 600 by 400 leagues),[827] is clearly not to be feared as a maritime rival. Akbar, even after conquering Gujarat in 1573, had only the southwestern ports of Surat, Broach, Kambhāyat, and Gogra for his use.[828] Hindustan is watered by eleven rivers, only some of which connect the hinterland with the harbors under Akbar's control. The Tāpti passes through Surat, the Narbada serves Broach, and the Chambal flows into the Jumna which passes into the Ganges which, in turn, empties into the Bay of Bengal. Five other rivers, the Sutlej, Biah, Ravi, Chanab, and Bihat (or Jhelam) are all identified correctly as affluents of the Indus.[829]

To the northeast, in the mountains called "Kumaon" (Himalayas) by the natives, there live a heathen people called "Botthantis" (Tibetans).[830] These people are white, have no Moors in their land, and are independent of Akbar's political control. They have no king of their own, but are ruled by sorcerers. Their livelihood is derived from the manufacture of felt, which they bring to India and sell at the markets of Negariott (Kangra) and Kalamur. Since they are snowbound the rest of the year, they come down from the mountains only from June to September. Their garments are made from felt and are worn until they rot and fall off. They never wash their hands because they believe it is improper to defile so pure and beautiful an element as water. While they live in clans, a man has but one wife and does not remarry if she dies. They fight on foot with bows, arrows, and swords. Even though their dishes and bowls are made from human skulls,[831] they are not cannibals and are charitably inclined towards outsiders. Monserrate's report on the Tibetans, as summarized by

[825] *Ibid.*, p. 6.   [826] *Ibid.*, pp. 7–8.

[827] *Ibid.*, p. 14. Or 2,400 by 1,600 miles.

[828] *Ibid.*, p. 13.

[829] For details on these identifications see Hosten, *loc. cit.* (n. 815), pp. 206–07.

[830] For identification see *ibid.*, pp. 219–20, n. 4; and also Peruschi, *op. cit.* (n. 814), pp. 10–12.

[831] For a picture of a Tibetan cup made from a skull see Sir Charles Bell, *Tibet, Past and Present* (Oxford, 1924), facing p. 36.

Peruschi, is to my knowledge the first substantial information on this mountain people to be printed in Europe.[832]

Details about Akbar's appearance, personality, and interests run like a thread throughout Peruschi's narrative. He is described as being of medium height, broad-shouldered, and about forty years of age (which is correct, since he was born in 1542).

His complexion is dark, his eyes are small . . . ; his nostrils are broad and on the left one he has a small wart; he carries his head somewhat inclined to the right; with the exception of his moustache which he keeps short and trimmed, he shaves his beard completely. . . .[833]

He lets his hair grow long, wears a turban, and adorns his head with pearls and precious stones. His clothes are costly and elegant and he wears slippers of his own design. He always keeps a dagger in his girdle and either wears a sword or has one near at hand. While Akbar is described as being prudent, wise, simple, brave, and kind, he is also disposed to be grave and melancholy and is endowed with a slow but violent temper. Although he is unable to read or write, he is intellectually curious and constantly keeps men of letters in his company. While perpetually busy with affairs of state, he delights in hunting wild animals, playing polo on horseback, witnessing fights of beast against beast and man against man, and participating in dances and gymnastics. Watching jesters and trained animals are also among his favorite pastimes, and he especially likes to make pigeons fly and dance in the air.[834]

The capital, Fatehpur Sīkrī, built by Akbar six leagues from Agra, has great and sumptuous palaces in which he maintains a huge court and large numbers of servants. Prominent in court affairs are his three sons and two daughters. The eldest son is "Scieco" [835] (Salīm), the middle son is called "Pahari" (nickname of Murād), and the youngest is "Dân or Danial" (Dāmyāl). Twenty gentile kings, as important as the Zamorin, serve in Akbar's retinue; some, his vassals by conquest, are forced to reside at the court, while others are there voluntarily.[836] Many other rulers pay tribute to him even though they do not reside at court. In choosing his own officials Akbar makes use of men of talent without regard to their origins. The *kotwāl* of the court, who is similar to a chief bailiff, "was originally a fencing master," while Akbar's secretary was once a poor Mullah. Commoners elevated to high office are required to wear ensignia of their former craft or trade, possibly to keep before them a reminder of their lowly origins and of their indebtedness to the ruler. Though Akbar takes counsel with his advisers, he generally makes decisions by himself.

---

[832] For references by earlier European writers to Tibet see Yule and Burnell, *op. cit.* (n. 10), pp. 698–99. For the relationship of this information on Tibet to the search for Cathay and to the later Jesuit mission in Tibet see Maclagan, *op. cit.* (n. 618), pp. 335–38.

[833] Peruschi, *op. cit.* (n. 814), p. 7.

[834] For a description of the art of pigeon-flying, see Hosten, *loc. cit.* (n. 815), p. 196, n. 3.

[835] "Scieco" is also called "Sciecogiò" (Peruschi, *op. cit.* [n. 814], p. 7), the suffix "gio" being an honorific similar to "Don" which means "spirit." *Ji* or *jiu*, as it is still pronounced in northern India, means "spirit" and it is used as an honorific. See Hosten, *loc. cit.*, pp. 202–03, n. 6.

[836] Peruschi, *op. cit.* (n. 814), p. 9.

In transacting business, Akbar appears twice each day in two great squares. One of these squares is open to all people of distinction; admission to the other square is limited to his military leaders, the literati (including the Jesuits), and foreigners. The ruler settles most of this public business just by standing and talking to the people concerned. Petitioners are presented to the king by a group who might be termed masters of ceremony. When the king speaks, scribes write down his orders, presumably to keep the records straight. In more private meetings, Akbar either sits on a cushion in Moorish fashion or in a Western-type chair.[837] He administers his finances with the greatest care, but Monserrate (and hence Peruschi) avoids discussion of how this is done because it is too lengthy a matter.[838]

Much more detail is included on the administration of justice. "The King, his justices, and his magistrates govern by reason and without differences among them; they adjudicate all kinds of controversies and questions and give their decisions verbally rather than in writing."[839] In addition to ordinary magistrates, the king appoints appelate justices and bailiffs who run the court system. The king himself, when present, administers both civil and criminal justice for high and low alike. The death penalty may never be carried out, if he is available, without his permission. Those found guilty of major crimes are beheaded, impaled on sharp stakes, or trampled to death by elephants. Rape and adultery are classified as crimes worthy of impalement or beheading. Convicted robbers have their hands cut off, and those guilty of minor offenses are whipped with the lash.[840]

The Jesuits, like Castanheda earlier, are greatly interested in the composition, organization, and effectiveness of the Mughul military forces. Monserrate, the tutor of Sultan Murād, received permission to accompany his pupil on Akbar's Kabul campaign of 1581, and so was in an excellent position to study the military system of the Mughuls as well as this particular campaign.[841] Akbar's army is a mélange of different peoples (Mughuls, Persians, Turkimales, Gujaratis, Pathans, Hindustanis, Moors, and gentiles), but the king seems to have greatest confidence in his gentile troops.[842] In times of internal order and stability, Akbar has many captains who can muster from ten to fourteen thousand horses and many elephants, as well as lesser officers who can put from six to eight thousand horses and some elephants into the field. Akbar himself maintains fifty thousand elephants which are stationed at various strategic locations in his empire.[843] In addition, he has a personal army of forty thousand cavalry

[837] *Ibid.*, pp. 24–25.

[838] Hosten, *loc. cit.* (n. 815), p. 200.

[839] Peruschi, *op. cit.* (n. 814), pp. 23–24.

[840] *Ibid.*, pp. 22–23.

[841] On Monserrate's writings as a source for the Kabul campaign see Maclagan, *op. cit.* (n. 618), p. 35.

[842] Peruschi, *op. cit.* (n. 814), p. 18.

[843] This information is not in Monserrate's report (see Hosten, *loc. cit.* [n. 815], p. 210, n. 2). Peruschi (*op. cit.* [n. 814], p. 16) probably incorporated this data from the letter of Pedro Martinez (1590–91). See Eglauer (ed.), *op. cit.* (n. 786), III, 115.

and an infinite number of foot soldiers. Workmen are constantly kept busy manufacturing arms for these vast forces, and Akbar is reputed to have artillery of fine quality.

Peruschi itemizes some of the conquests of Akbar's Mughul predecessors, and recounts how early in his reign he defeated the Pathans (Afghans) and made himself master of Bengal.[844] But Akbar's control of Bengal and Cambay is seen as far from secure, for in 1582 he faces major revolts in both areas. The attack of 1581 on the Portuguese outpost of Damão is attributed to the willful and unsanctioned action of one of these recalcitrants of Cambay, Qutb-ud-dīn Khan, the Sarkar of Broach.[845] The campaign against Akbar's brother in Kabul is said by Peruschi to have begun in February, 1582, but this date is clearly incorrect and is probably a misprint for 1581.[846] It is clear that the Jesuits, while respecting the might of Akbar's arms, were very much aware of the fact that he was constantly threatened with uprisings, particularly on the distant fringes of his empire.

Possibly this state of unrest can be attributed, though Peruschi does not say so explicitly, to Akbar's method of administering conquered territories. "The king is lord of all and nobody owns anything of his own except that which is bestowed upon him."[847] Lands conquered are parceled out to selected lords and captains who receive an annual salary and who are obliged to maintain elephants, camels, and horses all of which are sent to the royal palace each year for the king to inspect. The royal vassals, who can be removed or shifted about at the king's pleasure, place the towns and villages of their territories under the command of select subordinates who administer them. When a captain dies, his estate passes to the king. From this source, as well as from his control over trade, Akbar receives great revenues.

Peruschi closes his account of the realm of "Mogor" with a historical discussion of Akbar's meeting with the Portuguese and the development of his interest in Christianity. It was Antonio Cabral's embassy of March, 1573, to Surat, when Akbar was besieging the city, that first brought the Portuguese directly in touch with the Mughul ruler. Evidently Cabral made a favorable impression upon Akbar by his courteous and correct behavior. The ruler's interest in Christianity was aroused by his hearing news of the activities of the two Jesuits who had begun working in Bengal in 1576, by the visit of Pedro Tavares, the Portuguese captain of Bengal, to Fatehpur Sīkrī in 1577, and by the visit of Julian Pereira at his court beginning in 1578. It was probably at Pereira's suggestion that Akbar sent his letter of invitation of December, 1578, to the Jesuits at Goa. Though Akbar clearly favored Christianity over Islam, the Jesuits are forced to admit that when they left him he was still in a quandary about his beliefs. They also indicate in a number of places that his Moorish

---

[844] Peruschi, *op. cit.* (n. 814), p. 14.
[845] *Ibid.*, p. 15.
[846] See Hosten, *loc. cit.* (n. 815), p. 210, n. 4.
[847] Peruschi, *op. cit.* (n. 814), p. 19.

subjects were rebellious over his hostility to Islam, and so the Jesuits seem inclined to attribute their failure to political causes rather than to Akbar's personal unwillingness to consider Christianity the only true religion. Still the Jesuits admit that he is "dubious about all types of faith and holds that there is no divinely sanctioned faith, since he finds in all forms something to offend his reason and intelligence."[848] Even with this evaluation before them, the Jesuits and their Portuguese supporters apparently continued to hope for a change of heart since they refused to ignore the second and third invitations to send missionaries to his court.

The first three letters from the third mission to appear in print in Europe deal primarily with the experiences and observations of the Jesuits while in Cambay.[849] Delayed there for more than twenty days waiting for a caravan to take them to Lahore, the headquarters of Akbar for approximately sixteen years, the missionaries, especially Manuel Pinheiro, made good use of their time to gather data on the northwestern part of India.[850] All three letters are dated 1595 and are from the pen of Pinheiro; the first was written from Cambay and the other two from Lahore. In recent histories of Gujarat these letters have been used to supplement the otherwise meager sources available on this period.[851]

The Jesuits shipped out from Goa on December 3, 1594, stopped over in Damão, and arrived in Cambay just before Christmas. Here they commemorated the Feast of the Nativity with the one hundred Portuguese residing there. Well received by the governor and some leading citizens of Cambay, Pinheiro and his colleagues set about observing the conditions of life in the city to determine how receptive its inhabitants might be to the introduction of Christianity. They quickly concluded that the majority group were heathens inclined to piety, devotion, and charity even though their beliefs were clearly in error. Such optimistic conclusions were probably unwarranted inasmuch as the Jesuits were possibly inclined to confuse curiosity and tolerance with genuine interest.[852] And, even before leaving Cambay, Pinheiro directed a letter to Nicolas Pimenta, the Provincial in Goa, to let him know that a plentiful harvest might be reaped in Gujarat.

In this letter and more especially in the two which followed from Lahore, Pinheiro describes the city of Cambay. The "first city in Gujarat is not dissimilar to Evora in Portugal"[853] and it is within the jurisdiction of Akbar. Cambay is praised for its fine streets and buildings, and Pinheiro observes that the streets are closed off at night with tight gates similar to the city gates of Europe. Water is in short supply in Cambay even though the city has great tanks in which water is stored during the winter (the rainy season). These reservoirs, like

[848] *Ibid.*, p. 32.

[849] *Ibid.*, pp. 41–54, 60–71; Rebello, *op. cit.* (n. 820), pp. 49–55, gives an extract from the Pinheiro letter. Also reproduced in Eglauer (ed.), *op. cit.* (n. 786), III, 136–48, 153–68.

[850] But see above, pp. 395–96, for the secular accounts.

[851] For example, see Commissariat, *op. cit.* (n. 400), II, 267–73.

[852] *Ibid.*, II, 270.

[853] Peruschi, *op. cit.* (n. 814), p. 60.

many of the great houses of Cambay, are costly and beautiful structures. Pinheiro also tells of a visit to a public hospital which was built to take care of sick and crippled birds of all kinds. Somewhat aghast by this discovery, the Jesuit ironically remarks: "So they have hospitals for birds but not for humans who are generally left uncared for to die."[854]

Cambay is a center at which faithful Hindus gather, sometimes forty thousand of them, to undertake pilgrimages to the Ganges in Bengal.[855] It is their belief that bathing in its water is sanctifying and that the fortunate individuals who drink of it at the approach of death are certain of salvation. Pinheiro met a rich heathen devotee named "Gadacham" who had once journeyed to the Ganges, weighed his mother three times in the river, once with silver, then with precious stones, and then with gold, and finally distributed all of this wealth as alms to the poor. When in Lahore, Pinheiro met a prince from Bengal who assured him that sometimes three to four hundred thousand pilgrims would congregate along the banks of the Ganges.[856]

The Jesuits were escorted about Cambay by a native called "Babausa" who acted as their interpreter. "Babausa" was very congenial to Christian teachings himself and the Jesuits visited with him in his home which was constructed along Portuguese lines. It was probably through "Babausa" that the Jesuits met and talked with several of the city's notables whom they sounded out about their beliefs and their attitudes towards Christianity. This man also assured the Jesuits that the heathen doctrines were frivolous fabrications and that Cambay was awaiting Christianity.

"Babausa" also introduced the Jesuits to a group of religious men whom Pinheiro refers to as "Verteas."[857] There can be little question on the basis of context that this term, whatever its etymology, refers to the Jains, and especially their monks (*yatis*), of Gujarat.[858] The Jesuits visited a community of about fifty *yatis* who were dressed in white, an indication that they belonged to the sect known as *Svetāmbaras* (meaning, clad in white).[859] These Jain monks wear nothing on their heads and they pluck out the hairs of their chins and heads leaving only a tuft of hair on the crown. They live in poverty and accept in

---

[854] *Ibid.*, p. 52.

[855] *Ibid.*, pp. 61–62.

[856] *Ibid.*, p. 62.

[857] On the etymology and meaning of this word see T. Zachariae, "Vertea, eine Bezeichnung der Jains," *Wiener Zeitschrift für die Kunde des Morgenlandes*, XXIV (1910), 341. He derives it from Sanskrit, *Vratin*; Hindi, *Barti*; Gujarati, *Varti*. These words mean "saint" or "devotee." Dalgado (*op. cit.* [n. 44], II, 413) derives it from *Vrātya*, a Sanskrit term applied to Hindus who are expelled from their castes for not observing the *Saniskaras*, especially the rite of investiture with the sacred thread. For an identification of the *Vrātyas* with the Jains see J. Prasad Jain, *Jainism, the Oldest Living Religion* (Benares, 1951), p. 17.

[858] For a summary of what other Portuguese writers have to say about the "Verteas" see W. Caland and A. A. Fokker, "Due oude Portugeesche verhandelingen over het Hindoeisme," *Verhandelingen der koninklijke Akademie van Wetenschappen* (Afdeeling Letterkunde, nieuwe reeks), XVI (1916), 49–50.

[859] For a recent description of this rather unorthodox and lax monastic group see H. von Glasenapp, *Der Jainismus, eine indische Erlösungsreligion* (Berlin, 1925), p. 341.

alms only what is necessary for their daily sustenance. They possess no wives. They drink only hot water, because water has a soul that will be killed if it is drunk without being heated. Since it is a great crime to kill souls, they also carry cotton brooms with which they sweep the ground before walking or sitting on it to keep from taking the life and killing the soul of some small living creature. In their midst are boys of eight and nine, dedicated at this tender age to the religious life, who look like angels and are more European than Indian in color. All of them wear a cloth four fingers in width across their mouths which is hung over their ears by slits in the cloth. This face covering is designed to keep bugs from accidentally entering their mouths and being killed.

Their supreme prelate is supposed to have one hundred thousand believers under his obedience, and every year a new prelate is elected. Jain beliefs are written down in books in the Gujarati language. From these it can be gathered that they believe that the world was created many hundreds of thousands of years ago an 1 that during this time God sent to the earth twenty-three apostles. More than two thousand years ago, when their third era began, a twenty-fourth apostle was sent who, it seems, gave them their doctrines.[860]

Shortly after the Jesuits arrived in Cambay, Sultan Murād, Akbar's second son who was then the Viceroy of Gujarat, appeared in the city with a large army. He was on his way to make war in the Deccan against the kingdom of Ahmadnagar, and was about to join forces near Surat with another of Akbar's armies under Khanan Khan. The prince had with him a body of 4,000 to 5,000 horses (he was said to have sent 20,000 ahead), 400 elephants, 700 camels, 400 to 500 dromedaries, 4,000 oxen, and 15 large, 4 medium, and a number of smaller pieces of artillery.[861] Leaving his army outside the city, Murād stayed with his retinue in the "castle" of Cambay. As a boy, the prince had studied with Father Monserrate at Akbar's court. So, on learning of the presence of the Jesuits in Cambay, he summoned them to an audience at the citadel on Christmas eve, 1594. He received the fathers affectionately and told them that he was bound for Surat on his way to attack the Deccan. Before leaving Cambay, he bled the city with impositions through which he obtained a large sum of gold.

After Murād had traveled about one league (4 miles) away from Cambay toward Surat, he again called the Jesuits into his presence early on the morning of the Feast of Circumcision (January 1, 1595). Here he held an early durbar in his camp at which the Jesuits made their reverence to him and then retired to join his attendants "who were standing as silent as statues with their eyes fixed on him."[862] The formal assemblage being over, Murād retired into a tent

---

[860] Pinheiro's letter from Lahore (dated from internal evidence as of January 9, 1595) containing this discussion of "Vertea" practices and teachings was published in the sixteenth century in Peruschi *op. cit.* (n. 814), pp. 52–54 and in Rebello, *op. cit.* (n. 820), pp. 53–55. Pinheiro's understanding of Jain traditions is essentially correct as far as it goes. He accurately reports the Jain tradition that the twenty-fourth apostle (or teacher), Mahavira, died around 500 B.C. (for discussion see Majumdar *et al.*, *op. cit.* [n. 6], pp. 85–86) or about 2,100 years before Pinheiro's date of writing.

[861] Pinheiro's letter from Cambay of 1595 in Peruschi, *op. cit.* (n. 814), pp. 46–47.

[862] Rebello, *op. cit.* (n. 820), p. 47.

pavilion which enclosed a spacious courtyard. The sultan's tent stood in the middle of this square and was open on all sides and contained a small couch on which Murād reclined. He held a long conversation with the Jesuits and asked them many things about various lands, and whether Portugal had snow and wild animals for the hunt. At the end of the interview, Murād presented the Jesuits with a sum of money for their journey to Akbar, and to the Armenian who accompanied them he gave three carts with six bullocks and three fine horses. The prince then mounted a very large elephant and ascended from it to a still larger one that looked like a tower, and then continued on his journey. The fathers returned to Cambay to prepare for their trip with the impression that Murād was no friend of the Muslims, that he was primarily devoted to hunting and traveling, and was too much under the influence of youthful advisers who had already corrupted him.[863]

Around the middle of January, 1595, the Jesuits left Cambay, where Pinheiro had felt as at home as in Portugal, for the long trek by caravan to Lahore. They could not go through Sind as originally planned, and so were forced to take the longer route by way of Ahmadābād, Pathan, and Rājputāna. In Ahmadābād they had to remain longer than anticipated, apparently to wait for more of the caravan to assemble. Again Pinheiro used his time well by making observations in the sacred city of the Jains and capital of Gujarat with its great temples, tombs, and historical associations. Though Pinheiro had seen many Yogis performing penances, he was particularly impressed by a penitent of Ahmadābād. This Yogi had set himself up in the great square between the Bhadia towers and the Three Gates. The people who flocked to see him practice his austerities caused more commotion than was customarily to be seen on the quay of Lisbon when ships arrived there from India.[864] When Sultan Murād invited him to an audience, the Yogi had the temerity to respond that the prince should visit him. Once Murād heard this reply, he had the Yogi seized, soundly whipped, and driven out of the city. Pinheiro was impressed also in Ahmadābād by the care lavished upon the sacred cows. On one occasion he reports having seen the devout bring fresh grass for, stand watch over, and keep the flies off a dying cow. While the Jesuit was obviously disdainful and intolerant of such heathen practices, he was clearly appreciative of the architectural beauties of the city. He comments at length on some tombs outside the city which it appears from internal evidence were the tombs at Sirkej built in the middle of the fifteenth century. Pinheiro reports that he never saw anything more beautiful than these tombs and concludes that they are "a work of barbarians which is not at all barbarous."[865] In the capital of Gujarat, Pinheiro also met many Moors of both sexes who had come from deep in the interior of India and were pilgrims on their way to Mecca. He reports that since the Prophet

---

[863] Peruschi, *op. cit.* (n. 814), p. 47; Commissariat, *op. cit.* (n. 400), pp. 271–72.

[864] Peruschi, *op. cit.* (n. 814), p. 61.

[865] *Ibid.*, p. 63. Cf. the plan of the Sirkej tombs and mosque in J. Fergusson, *History of Indian and Eastern Architecture* (New York, 1899), II, 146.

ordained that no unmarried woman might make the journey to Mecca, the Muslims of India contract convenience marriages which are dissolved when the pilgrims return home.[866]

The caravan in which the Jesuits were traveling left Ahmadābād on March 23 and arrived on the evening of March 24, the day before Easter, in Pathan. Three days later, after having celebrated Easter mass and listening to confessions, the Jesuits left Pathan and began the arduous journey to Lahore where they finally arrived on May 5. Most of this part of the journey was through deserts and regions where the heat was stifling, water difficult to obtain, and foodstuffs in short supply. In the course of it they went through numerous large cities which were devastated, especially the mosques therein.[867] Since there were no rivers, water was drawn from wells so deep that it had to be raised by bullocks. When they did come across water in the open it was as salty as sea water, "a fact," writes Pinheiro, "which I would not have believed had I not experienced it myself."[868] At no time was there sufficient water for their huge caravan which included 400 camels, 80 to 100 ox-carts, 100 horse-carts, and a multitude of poor people on foot.[869] Every morning the captain of the caravan ordered the kettle drums to be beaten as the signal to break camp. On the route a scout was sent out ahead of the caravan to show the way. The entire journey from Goa to Lahore took the Jesuits five months and two days.

On the morning (May 6) after their arrival in Lahore, Akbar greeted them, spoke two or three words to them in Portuguese, and asked about the health of the king of Portugal (Philip II). Then, after this public meeting, the Jesuits were given a special audience before Akbar, his twenty-five year old son, Prince Salīm, and some of his chief retainers. The Mughul ruler then had a portrait of the Virgin brought in and he held it in his own arms to show it to the Jesuits. After the fathers had knelt in reverence before the portrait, Akbar showed them that he was also a collector of European books. Aside from two Bibles, Akbar's collection included a number of works by St. Thomas Aquinas and other eminent churchmen as well as the *Commentaries* of Albuquerque and the Constitutions of the Society of Jesus.[870] The king graciously offered to lend the books to the missionaries, and also suggested that they apply themselves to the study of Persian so that he might speak to them without an interpreter. At a second private interview on the evening of the same day, Akbar asked them questions about the king of Portugal and about the various kingdoms of Europe. He ordered that a house be provided for them near to his own palace, and urged them to look around for a suitable place. At midnight, after receiving a second admonition to learn Persian, the travel-weary Jesuits went to their quarters.[871]

A few days later, Akbar, acting through Prince Salīm, established the Jesuits

---

[866] Peruschi, *op. cit.* (n. 814), p. 64.
[867] *Ibid.*, p. 65.   [868] *Ibid.*
[869] Letter of Xavier of 1595 from Lahore in Rebello, *op. cit.* (n. 820), p. 56.
[870] List of books given in Peruschi, *op. cit.* (n. 814), pp. 65–66. For further discussion of them see Maclagan, *op. cit.* (n. 618), pp. 191–92.
[871] Rebello, *op. cit.* (n. 820), p. 58.

in certain houses on the royal grounds in which he had once lived himself. These houses were located close to the Ravi River and beneath the windows of the king's fortress. "This river," writes Xavier, "is called 'beautiful' and deserves its name; it has sweet water and is almost the same size as the Tagus."[872] The Ravi may be crossed by a bridge of boats and many vessels sail on it constantly carrying an infinity of supplies. On the opposite side of the river, a tent city stands where the merchants from other countries bring their goods to sell. In the middle of the river there is a place like an island where a great crowd of people wait every morning to see Akbar show himself at one of the windows of the fortress. After bowing to him, the crowd amuses itself by watching animals fight. "A fight between elephants," remarks Xavier, "is something to see. . . ."[873] Fifty men who carry torches guard the bank of the river by day and the same number patrol it at night, evidently to keep intruders from entering the royal grounds from the riverside.

At their residence beside the river the fathers built a temporary chapel large enough to accommodate the Armenian Christians residing in Lahore. While all others were forbidden admission to the royal grounds, these Christians were permitted to visit the Jesuits and attend chapel there. By September, Akbar had already given the Jesuits oral permission to build a church. When they asked for this promise in writing, he answered tartly that he was a living document and that they should go ahead with their plans.[874] Prince Salīm acted as an advocate of the Jesuits in their dealings with his father and showed real personal interest in their religious activities. As a token of his regard for their well-being, he sent them a box of snow on a summer's day when it was stifling hot.[875]

While Akbar was personally congenial to the Jesuits and curious about their faith, they quickly discerned, as had their predecessors, that his personal conversion was not to be expected. After being in Lahore just a short while, Xavier wrote:

We are very confused . . . when we try to find out the real intentions of the King—and we do not understand him. On the one hand he makes much over our religion as well as over the images of Christ and Our Lady and at the same time abominates Mafumede [Mohammed] and all his works; yet, on the other hand, he follows the ways of the Gentiles, adoring the sun in the morning and praying at night, and also at noon and midnight. The Gentiles have much influence over him, and . . . he has himself revered as a saint. It seems that his heart cannot find peace in any religion. He seems pleased with the praises given to him as a saint, and some Gentiles call him a god. It seems that Our Lord sent him to these lands to wipe out the religion of Mafumede from the hearts of men. . . .[876]

---

[872] *Ibid.*, p. 59. Pinheiro (in Peruschi, *op. cit.* [n. 814], p. 66) says that the houses were fifteen feet from a river which is the size of a lake. For further information on their residence see the extract from unpublished Xavier letters of 1596 in H. Hosten, "Mirza Zu-L-Quarnain," Pt. II of "Jesuit Letters and Allied Papers on Mogor, Tibet, Bengal and Burma," *Memoirs of the Asiatic Society of Bengal*, V (1916), 174.

[873] Rebello, *op. cit.* (n. 820), p. 59.

[874] Peruschi, *op. cit.* (n. 814), p. 69.   [875] Rebello, *op. cit.* (n. 820), p. 61.

[876] *Ibid.*, pp. 68–69. The Muslim historians of Akbar's reign never mention the Jesuits. For discussion of the Muslim histories see Vincent A. Smith, *Akbar, the Great Mogul* (Delhi, 1958), pp. 337–44.

In Lahore the Jesuits claim that mosques were torn down or converted into stables and granaries. The public call to prayer and the Koran itself were proscribed. And Akbar, in his determination to root out the baleful influence of the infidels, is reported as going out of his way to offend the Muslims by eating publicly during their fast periods and by bringing pigs into the royal courtyard. On the other hand, Akbar apparently puzzles and troubles the Jesuits by the serious attention he pays to the "Verteas" (Jains) at his court.[877]

Akbar's vassals and the great "presents" which they make to Akbar in the summer of 1595 seem to intrigue Pinheiro. He observes that there are five or six crowned kings and twenty-six royal princes residing at the court. He describes at length the ceremony of investiture to which a petty ruler is subjected upon officially becoming one of Akbar's vassals and he itemizes the tribute paid to the Mughul.[878] Sultan Murād and the King of Bengal also brought expensive presents consisting mainly of elephants to Lahore in this summer. Especially numerous were the gifts which Akbar received on the festival of "Noresa"[879] which he had ordered to be celebrated. "Hardly a day passes," Pinheiro sighs, "on which he does not receive gifts."[880]

The four Jesuits spent most of their first year in their residence by the Ravi studying the Persian language.[881] At first they encountered some difficulty because they had no one to translate the Persian into Portuguese for them. Occasionally Akbar, when he sailed on the river, would embark or disembark almost at their door, and so the Jesuits always went out to welcome and speak with him. The Jesuits also opened a school at their riverside residence which was attended by the sons of some of Akbar's leading vassals and land administrators. Since the Jesuits were not happy with the site initially allocated to them for a church, Akbar finally ordered Malik Ali, one of his bailiffs, to find a satisfactory site within the crowded city of Lahore and to speed the work of construction. Shortly thereafter, Xavier reports: "The foundations have been laid, but the materials are coming a little slowly—but what a wonder that Moors are slowly building a church for Christians in the middle of their chief city."[882] The church was finally completed and formally dedicated on September 7, 1597, in the presence of the governor of Lahore.[883]

In March, 1596, from their riverside residence, the Jesuits were treated to the sight on the opposite shore of a great congregation of Yogis. The Christians were told that the Yogis gathered annually at this time and place. Huddled

[877] Peruschi, *op. cit.* (n. 814), p. 70. On the Jain spokesmen at Akbar's court at this time see Commissariat, *op. cit.* (n. 400), II, 238–39.

[878] Peruschi, *op. cit.* (n. 814), pp. 67–68.

[879] Possibly the festival of Narasimha, commemorating one of the incarnations of Vishnu. See Caland and Fokker, *loc. cit.* (n. 858), p. 80.

[880] Peruschi, *op. cit.* (n. 814), p. 67.

[881] Xavier's letter of 1596 in Rebello, *op. cit.* (n. 820), p. 69. Their teacher, according to Smith (*op. cit.* [n. 876], p. 210) was Abu-ul-Fazl, a friend to Akbar and the author of a Persian history of Akbar's reign which was written in about 1595.

[882] Rebello, *op. cit.* (n. 820), p. 72.

[883] L. Guzman, *Historia de las missiones . . .* (Alcalá, 1601), I, 268.

together in groups of ten and twenty, the Yogis filled the plain on the opposite shore as they begged Akbar for alms. The ruler, crowds from the city, and the Jesuits crossed the river to see and talk with them. After two or three days, the Yogis scattered and left as quickly as they had come. Xavier reports that they revere "Babam Adā," [884] or Father Adam, as the creator and the only god. They venerate and worship his picture and hope by blowing buffalo horns that they will somehow blow out their sins. [885]

The best general summary of the Jesuit activities in India and the East Indies is contained in Volume I (pp. 1–273) of L. Guzman's *Historia de las missiones . . .* (Alcalá, 1601). [886] At no time does he cite his authorities directly. Study of his work, however, brings out clearly that he relied only slightly upon secular histories. The materials collected for Xavier's biography, conversations with informants, and the Jesuit letters, constitute his main sources. Guzman presents in narrative form a straightforward statement of what Europe in his day knew of the mission in India on the basis of published and, to a lesser degree, unpublished materials. One of his sources most easily identified (see Guzman, pp. 240–54) is Monserrate's *Relaçam . . . of the Mughul empire.* It appears, however, from textual comparison that the version of the *Relaçam* used by Guzman was shorter and slightly different from the one used by Peruschi, or that he had amended it from other materials. [887] It may be, since much of the material on Akbar is similar to the material in Peruschi's and Rebello's collections, that he had the Portuguese, if not the Italian, work on his bookshelf. This surmise is somewhat reinforced by the fact that his account of the condition of the Jesuit colleges in India seems to be derived from the annual report of 1596 prepared by Francisco Cabral, the Provincial, an extract from which is included in Rebello (pp. 4–48). But Guzman, because his account goes beyond these works both in terms of time and detail, obviously relied on other sources, most of which were probably unpublished when he wrote.

Guzman, unlike Maffei, [888] is concerned primarily with the progress of the Jesuit mission in the East and so the two authors supplement each other. The geographical description with which Guzman's first book begins is designed to provide a setting for Xavier's activities in India and the further East. He then recounts at some length the obstacles to the progress of the faith in India: native idolatry, the Moors, the hostility of the Nāyars and other high-caste groups in Malabar, and the control which the Brahmans and Yogis exercise over everyone, from kings to common people. [889] Incidental to this account he

---

[884] See Dalgado, *op. cit.* (n. 44), I, 73–74, under the listing *Baba*, meaning "father." The "Adā" is possibly a misrendering of *Aum*, which is a mystical representation in Yoga teachings of the "Divine Being." For a discussion of the sacred word *Aum* see Abbe J. A. Dubois, *Hindu Manners, Customs and Ceremonies*, trans. H. K. Beauchamp (3d ed.; Oxford, 1906), p. 533.

[885] Rebello, *op. cit.* (n. 820), p. 71.

[886] For general discussion see above, p. 328.

[887] Cf. Hosten, *op. cit.* (n. 815), pp. 187–88, who contends absolutely that Guzman did not use Peruschi's version.

[888] See above, pp. 324–26.

[889] Guzman, *op. cit.* (n. 883), I, 5–7.

naturally is forced to give at least some information about the social and religious beliefs of the Indians. This is followed by a brief description of Goa, and then he launches directly into the career of Xavier from his student days in Paris until his funeral in Malacca.[890]

The second book commences with a survey of the religious situation in Goa after the death of Xavier. Then follows a description of nearby Salsette, its sixty-six villages, and its recalcitrant hostility to the Portuguese and the Jesuits. From the Goa area he shifts his attention to the Fishery Coast and gives somewhat more space to the island of Manaar than is to be found in previous publications.[891] Especially interesting is the systematic presentation which follows of the progress and setbacks of the mission at Quilon, in Travancore, and at Cochin and Calicut. He does not disguise the fact that the Jesuits' position in these territories was closely related to the vagaries of Portugal's political relations with the native rulers. Guzman is somewhat less critical of the Portuguese in his appraisal of the northern settlements of Bassein, Damão, and Diu; he has a tendency to blame Jesuit difficulties in these places upon the Moors and the machinations of the rulers of Cambay. He follows the review of the mission stations with a thorough discussion of the work of St. Thomas in India and the relics of Mylapore, and concludes with a brief account of the Christian followers of St. Thomas in the south.

It is only when Guzman comes to deal with the empire of Vijayanagar, as it was in the late sixteenth century, that he goes beyond what had previously been published in Europe.[892] He discusses the power and extent of Vijayanagar under Venkāta II (reigned *ca.* 1586–1622) and mentions the uprisings of the *Nayakas* of Madura, Tanjore, and Jinjī against him. He describes briefly the city of Chandragiri, Venkāta's capital, as being located in the mountains, possessing a strong fortress, and boasting beautiful and rich palaces. He gives excellent detail on the visits of the Jesuits to Venkāta's court from their residences at the Portuguese outposts of St. Thomas and Goa, and of their receiving permission to build a church at Vellore. He concludes this discussion by describing a religious procession which the Jesuits saw in the city of Tiruvalur.[893] And this information, Guzman affirms, is derived from the letters of 1599, the latest received from the Jesuits in Vijayanagar.[894] He also records a few details on the mission of 1598 to Bengal of Fathers Francisco Fernandes and Domingo de Sousa,[895] another event which had previously not been known in Europe.

Guzman devotes more than thirty pages (240–71) of his third book to the three Jesuit missions to Akbar. While he adds little that is new regarding the first mission, he emphasizes, perhaps more than his sources justify, that the failure

---

[890] *Ibid.,* pp. 11–78.
[891] *Ibid.,* pp. 112–14.
[892] *Ibid.,* pp. 158–69.
[893] Cf. account in Saletore, *op. cit.* (n. 234), II, 390–92.
[894] *Op. cit.,* p. 169.
[895] *Ibid.,* pp. 169–71. For a summary apparently based on the same source (Nicolas Pimenta's letters) see Campos, *op. cit.* (n. 551), pp. 101.

of the Jesuits to convert Akbar was due to the baleful influence of the Moors and to political conditions within the empire.[896] In connection with the third mission he gives later data than his predecessors on events in the Mughul empire. He lists punishments which God placed upon Akbar for his refusal to become a convert, including the destruction by fire of his palace in Lahore on Easter Day, 1597. Shortly thereafter, in 1597, Akbar and Prince Salīm took Xavier and Brother Benedict with them to their summer retreat in Kashmir to await the rebuilding of the palace. Kashmir, surrounded in large part by extremely high mountains, is described as one of the freshest lands in India, being watered by beautiful rivers which make it into a garden spot. Close by the principal city, Srinigar, is a mountain topped by a stone mosque which houses the throne of "Salomon."[897] According to local legend, "Salomon" from his throne drove the demons from the land and so permitted it to be fertile and thriving. In antiquity this land was inhabited by gentiles, but in the 1300's it was invaded by the Moors, possibly a reference to Timur, and since then the majority of the people accept Islam.[898] After a six months absence from Lahore, Akbar's party returned to the capital to find that Pinheiro, who had stayed behind to superintend its construction, had already completed and dedicated the Jesuit church. Towards the end of 1598, Akbar left Lahore accompanied by Xavier to assume personal conduct over his campaign against the stubborn rulers of the Deccan.[899]

In 1598, while in Lahore, Xavier met an old Muslim merchant who claimed to have lived and worked in "Xetay" (Cathay) for thirty years. This man assured his questioners that Cathay is a great land with fifteen hundred populous cities, that its people are "white," and that a majority of them profess Christianity. The king of Cathay lives in the city of "Cambalu" (Cambaluc) and his court can be reached overland by traveling through Kashmir and Tibet.[900] In the following year, while in the company of Akbar, Xavier wrote further on Cathay from Agra, and recommended that an emissary should be sent there by way of Lahore and Kabul.[901] In the meantime Matteo Ricci had been suggesting in his letters from China that the Cathay of the Middle Ages and China were one and the same place. It was in these circumstances that the Society decided to try to ascertain its identity, to reclaim the supposedly Christian population of the Asian interior for the Roman church, and to find a land-route as a substitute for the long and dangerous sea voyage to China. In 1601, both the Pope and Philip III gave their permission for the dispatch of the Cathay mission by way of India, and Benedict de Goes was entrusted with it.[902]

---

[896] Guzman, *op. cit.* (n. 883), I, 249–51, 253–54.

[897] What "Salomon" refers to, I do not know. There is a hill on the north side of the city topped with a mosque. See E. Thornton, *op. cit.* (n. 13), p. 913.

[898] Guzman, *op. cit.* (n. 883), I, 267–68. [899] *Ibid.*, p. 269.

[900] *Ibid.*, pp. 271–72, summarizes Xavier's letter of 1598 from Lahore.

[901] *Ibid.*, p. 273, summarizes Xavier's letter of 1599 from Agra.

[902] C. Wessels, *Early Jesuit Travellers in Central Asia* (The Hague, 1924), pp. 11–13. Also see below, p. 823.

3

THE ITALIAN, ENGLISH, AND DUTCH COMMENTATORS

The number of non-Iberians who actually journeyed to India increased in the latter half of the century as the Portuguese monopoly on trade gradually broke apart and as the Jesuits and the other Orders were forced constantly to go further afield in their search for capable missionaries. While Philip II sought after 1581 to maintain an Iberian monopoly in the overseas world, the rivalry between the Spanish and the Portuguese, as well as between the various religious orders favored by them, helped to open the door to Asia to the representatives of other European nationalities: Italians, Netherlanders, Germans, Frenchmen, and Englishmen. Near the end of the century even a Polish gentleman, Christophe Pawlowski, had journeyed to Goa and had sent back to his homeland an account of his adventure written in his native language.[903] Finally, the decline of Iberian power in northern Europe and on the sea made it possible for the English and the Dutch to crack the maritime monopoly of the Iberians and to proceed directly to the East in their own vessels.

The Italians were particularly prominent as participants both in the spice trade and in the Society of Jesus.[904] The Florentine merchants, agents of the Gualterotti and Frescobaldi interests, were associated with the Portuguese, and several of them had been sent as factors to India early in the century. The Venetians, who were as a rule strictly excluded from Portuguese Asia, had occupied themselves primarily in the early years of the century with spying in Lisbon and with encouraging the Turks to resist the Portuguese in the Indian Ocean. In the latter half of the century, as the Portuguese hold on the spice trade in Europe and their control over the sea lanes of Asia became weaker, and as Akbar established political control over northern India and central Asia, the Venetians from their trading stations in the Levant became constantly bolder in their efforts to revive the land route to India and to penetrate directly the marts of India and the East Indies.[905]

903 Pawlowski's lengthy letter from Goa of November 20, 1596, appears in *Rocznik orjentalistyczny*, III (1925), 1–56; also see Stefan Stasiak, *Les Indes portugais à la fin du XVIe siècle, d'après la relation du voyage fait à Goa en 1596 par Christophe Pawlowski, gentilhomme polonais* (Lvov, 1926).

904 For a summary of the Italian participation see Angelo de Gubernatis, *Storia dei viaggiatori italiani nelle Indie Orientali* (Leghorn, 1875), chap. i; Tomaso Sillani, *L'Italia e l'Oriente medio ed estremo* (Rome, 1935), *passim*; Pietro Amat di San Filippo, *Bibliografia dei viaggiatori italiani ordinate cronologicamente* (Rome, 1874).

905 Most of those Venetians who published accounts or who were active in trade are discussed in Placido Zurla, *Di Marco Polo e degli altri viaggiatori veneziani piu illustri* (Venice, 1818); summaries and comments on Fedrici are in II, 252–58 followed by a similar treatment of Balbi in II, 258–65. When the notarial archives of Venice have been more closely examined it might be discovered that many other Venetian merchants were involved in similar enterprises. For a survey, based on the notarial archives, of the part played by Michael Stropeni and the Altan brothers in the effort to revive overland relations between Venice and India in the 1580's see Ugo Tucci, "Mercanti veneziani in India alla fine del secolo XVI," *Studi in onore di Armando Sapori* (Milan, 1957), II, 1091–1111.

In 1563, at a time when the English and Dutch were looking for a north-eastern route to Asia and when Akbar was just establishing his personal sway over the Mughul empire, a Venetian merchant, Cesare de Fedrici, boarded a vessel bound for Cyprus. Very desirous of seeing the East, according to his own testimony, Fedrici went on to Syria and then overland to Aleppo and Ormuz. For the next eighteen years, he traveled and traded in the East, finally returning to Venice in 1581. In the course of his voyage he evidently kept a diary or notebook which was then hammered into a narrative by the Venetian publisher, Andrea Muschio. Six years after his return, Muschio published the *Viaggio di M. Cesare de Fedrici, nell' India Orientale, et oltra l'India* ... (Venice, 1587). The following year it was translated into English by Thomas Hickock, a merchant who spent his time at sea on the way back from the Mediterranean to England rendering it "into our vulgar tongue." [906] Hickock's translation was republished verbatim by Hakluyt in 1599, and, as we shall see, Fedrici's work was callously plagiarized by at least two other sixteenth-century writers.

Fedrici's *Viaggio*, which resembles in form and content the *Book* of Duarte Barbosa and the *Suma oriental* of Tomé Pires, was separately published in full during the sixteenth century, as they were not. But the Venetian's account, unlike those of his two Portuguese precursors, was not incorporated into the Ramusio collection until the appearance of the 1606 version of Volume III. Unfortunately, however, Fedrici was less careful about dates and organization than the earlier writers, including among them his compatriot Marco Polo. It is practically impossible from simply reading his account to determine exactly where he was on a given date, or how long he spent in each place about which he comments. [907] His book is nevertheless valuable for the simple and clear descriptions which he gives of the trade routes, products, and customs of the East. It also adds substantially to our narrative because he reports about a period (1563–81) for which the Portuguese and Jesuit

---

[906] My quotation is from the preface "to the Courteous Reader" in *The Voyage and Travaile: of M. Caesar Frederick, Merchant of Venice, into the East India and beyond the Indies. Wherein are conteined Very Pleasant and Rare Matters, with the Customs and Rites of These Countries. Also Herein Are Discovered the Marchandises and Commodities of Those Countreyes, as well the Aboundance of Goulde and Silver, as well Spices, Drugges, Pearles, and other Jeweles.* "Written at Sea in the Hercules of London Comming from Turkie, the 25 of March 1588. For the Profitable Instruction of Merchants and all Other Travellers for their Better Direction and Knowledge of These Countreyes. Out of Italian by T. Hickock. At London, Printed by Richard Jones and Edward White, 18 Junij, 1588." A copy of this rare work is in the Bodleian Library. Hickock acknowledges that he is not a scholar and that in his translation he has "simplie followed the Authors sence in that phraze of speech that we commonly use." E. Teza, "Il viaggio di Cesare dei Fedrici e la versione inglese dell'Hickocke," *Atti del reale istituto veneto di scienze, lettere, ed arti,* Vol. LXVIII (Ser. 8, Vol. XI, 1908–9), pp. 327–37, has compared the English translation with the original and admits that Hickock's rendition "is faithful" (p. 331) even though it contains a number of mistranslations, misprints, and omissions which he itemizes. Since Hickock's version is essentially correct in the matters which concern us and inasmuch as the Hakluyt version is much easier to consult, the following notes will refer to Richard Hakluyt, *The Principal Navigations, Voyages, Traffiques, and Discoveries of the English Nation* ("Extra Series of the Publications of the Hakluyt Society," Vol. V [Glasgow, 1903–5]).

[907] An effort has been made to work out the details of his itinerary in Jarl Charpentier, "Cesare di Fedrici and Gasparo Balbi," *Indian Antiquary,* LIII (1924), 51–54.

materials on India printed during the sixteenth century supply only scanty documentation. The travels of Fedrici took him from Venice to Malacca and back again. Without attempting to follow his Indian peregrinations in detail, it is essential to extract a few of the highlights from his observations to show the nature of his contribution to Europe's stock of information.

Like Barbosa's, Fedrici's account of India begins with Cambay.[908] The city of Diu is pictured (*ca.* 1564) as a great center of trade where merchandise from Cambay is loaded into the large vessels destined for the Persian Gulf and the Red Sea. While the owners of the freight-carrying vessels are both Christians and Moors, the followers of Islam are forced to obtain trading permits from the Portuguese authorities. The large vessels docked at Diu draw too much water to sail directly to Cambay through the Gulf of Cambay with its shoals and great tidal waves (*maccareo*).[909] Small barks of shallow draft enter and leave the Gulf of Cambay every fortnight at the time of the full moon when the waters of the Gulf are deepest and least dangerous. At Cambay it is the practice of the foreign merchants to market their wares and buy native products through gentile brokers. The broker acts as the exclusive seller and buyer for the foreign trader. He takes complete responsibility for the merchandise brought in: he makes storage arrangements for it and pays all port charges and taxes on it. The broker also provides housing for the foreign merchant and his companions. Fedrici took advantage of his own stay in Cambay to visit Ahmadābād (which he aptly compares to Cairo) and to learn something about the decline of the native dynasty of Gujarat and the gradual assumption of power by the Mughuls.

After short stopovers at Damão, Bassein, and Tana, Fedrici arrived in Chaul. The walled Portuguese city of Chaul, which commands the mouth of the harbor, he differentiates from the nearby Moorish city of Chaul governed by the Nizamu 'l-Mulk, the king of Ahmadnagar whose capital city is seven or eight days' journey into the interior from Chaul.[910] While describing the trade of Chaul, Fedrici digresses at length on the great value of the palm tree and itemizes its multiple uses. By 1566, the Venetian was in Goa where he was to visit again in 1570 and probably on one or two other occasions.[911] Ordinarily, he asserts, five or six large vessels from Portugal arrive at Goa between September 6 and 10 to disembark their cargoes. After remaining forty to fifty days at Goa, one of the vessels is sometimes loaded with goods for Portugal, but most of the return cargo of spices is reportedly taken aboard at Cochin. Ships from Ormuz, providing that they carry twenty or more horses to the port of Goa, pay no charges or duties on their entire cargo; but if trading vessels come to the

[908] Fedrici in Hakluyt, *op. cit.* (n. 906), V, 374–77.

[909] Etymology of this term is uncertain, but it is repeatedly used by European writers of the sixteenth century to refer to the tidal waves in the Gulf of Cambay and the Sittang estuary of Pegu. See Yule and Burnell, *op. cit.* (n. 10), pp. 402–3, and Dalgado, *op. cit.*, pp. 3–5.

[910] Fedrici in Hakluyt, *op. cit.* (n. 906), V, 378–80.

[911] *Ibid.*, pp. 380–82. See also Charpentier, *loc. cit.* (n. 907), pp. 52–54. On his return in 1570, Fedrici was caught in the siege of Goa by Adil Khan of Bijapur. It lasted for fourteen months.

capital of Portuguese India without horses they pay 8 per cent duty on everything imported. An export tax is levied on each horse sent from Goa into the interior.

In 1567, Fedrici accompanied two horse traders from Goa to the city of Vijayanagar.[912] Since he arrived there just two years after the disastrous battle of Talikota, the Venetian comments at some length on the battle and the sack of the city by the four Deccan rulers—a discourse which is one of the fullest left to posterity by a contemporary observer.[913] He also gives detail on the political condition of the Vijayanagar court prior to the battle, and of how its internal divisions contributed to the defeat of the Hindu state by the Muslim princes. Though the Deccan forces plundered the city for six months, the Muslim conquerors were unable to maintain political control over a city so far removed from their own centers of strength. Following the withdrawal of the conquerors, the Regent, "Temiragio" (Tirumala), returned to the depopulated city and began to restore its buildings and to re-establish trading relations with Goa. The Venetian remained in Vijayanagar for seven months, even though he could have concluded his business in one month, because of the disorders and raids which made travel back to Goa too dangerous to attempt. Because the house in which he lived was located near to the gate through which widows passed on their way to be burnt, we have from Fedrici's pen one of the fullest and most authoritative accounts of the Hindu practice of *sati* prepared in the sixteenth century.[914] Though he did not actually visit the diamond mines of the region, the Venetian learned about them from informants.[915]

Evidently it was towards the end of Fedrici's stay in Vijayanagar that Tirumala gave up in his effort to rebuild the city and transferred his court to Penugonda,[916] a hill fortress eight days away from the ravaged capital. Nonetheless, in Fedrici's eyes, semi-deserted Vijayanagar was still the greatest royal capital of all those he had seen in his travels and he describes its physical appearance and trade.[917] The account of his trials and tribulations on the return trip reflect clearly the disordered condition of life in the territories which were still nominally tributaries of Vijayanagar. En route to Ancolâ on the west coast, the Venetian found that each of the governors along the way was issuing his own coinage and refusing to accept any other. In his journey from Ancolâ back to Goa, the Venetian continued to suffer from the depredations of the numerous bandits who made travel unsafe in what was technically the coastal territory of Vijayanagar.

From Goa, Fedrici resumed his sea journey by embarking for Cochin. On the voyage southward he stopped at four of the intermediate Portuguese ports

---

[912] Fedrici in Hakluyt, *op. cit.* (n. 906), V, 382–84.
[913] See Saletore, *op. cit.* (n. 234), I, 133.
[914] Fedrici in Hakluyt, *op. cit.* (n. 906), V, 384–86.
[915] *Ibid.*, pp. 386–87.
[916] Cf. Saletore, *op. cit.* (n. 234), I, 139–40.
[917] Fedrici in Hakluyt, *op. cit.* (n. 906), V, 387–89.

and he comments on their trade and political condition.[918] His arrival at Cochin, where he visited for extended periods on at least two occasions, gives him an opportunity to talk about the pepper trade. He categorically affirms that the pepper sold to the Portuguese is inferior to that which the Moors buy for sale in Mecca. The deliveries to the Portuguese are "green and full of filthe"[919] because they pay only the low fixed price agreed upon in their treaty with Cochin, a policy inaugurated by Vasco da Gama.

Like Chaul, Cochin is divided into two riverine cities, the one nearer to the sea belonging to the Portuguese and the other which is upriver towards the "Kingdom of Pepper" being the capital of the native king. Western Christians who marry in Cochin (and thereby become permanent residents with direct personal interest in the welfare of the city) receive good posts and extraordinary privileges. These married Westerners, for example, are exempted like natives from paying duties on China silk and Bengal sugar, the two principal imports of Cochin. On all other commodities, the privileged Westerners pay but 4 per cent tax while the unmarried Westerners pay the normal 8 per cent on all imports, and this situation continues to be unchanged in Fedrici's time despite efforts on the part of the Portuguese to upset it. While the Venetian comments on the marital and inheritance practices of the Nāyars, he shows an unusual degree of interest in the way in which the members of this caste puncture their ear lobes and gradually stretch the openings into "great holes."[920]

In proceeding south of Cochin, Fedrici once again has an opportunity to show his keenness as an observer as well as his business acumen. He provides an excellent description of pearl fishing and ascertains that there are four major grades of commercial pearls: the round variety sold in Portugal, those sent to Bengal which are not round, and two inferior and cheaper types named for Kanara and Cambay respectively.[921] He also discusses the difficulties of navigation in the strait which runs between the islands (commonly called Adam's Bridge) separating the Gulf of Manaar and Palk Strait, and notes that large vessels headed for the East Indies normally go around Ceylon because they cannot pass through the narrows at Adam's Bridge.[922] About Ceylon, which he judges to be a "great deale bigger than Cyprus,"[923] Fedrici has nothing to add to the earlier accounts except his remarks on prevailing political conditions. The king (Dharmapāla) is described as a Christian convert who rules under the guidance of Portugal and whose sway has been threatened by the rebellious actions of "Madoni" (Maaya Dunnai) and his sons.[924]

Of particular interest is the Venetian's account of conditions along the east coast of India. Negapatam, which is rich in nothing "save a good quantitie of

[918] *Ibid.*, pp. 390–95.

[919] *Ibid.*, p. 392. Cf. above, p. 144 for European charges that the Portuguese pepper was inferior and adulterated.

[920] Fedrici in Hakluyt, *op. cit.* (n. 906), V, 394.

[921] *Ibid.*, pp. 395–97.   [922] *Ibid.*, pp. 397–98.

[923] *Ibid.*, p. 398.

[924] *Ibid.*, p. 399.

Rice"[925] and textiles, has declined as a port because of the uncertain political conditions produced by the defeat of Vijayanagar in 1565. The Portuguese city of St. Thomas, also within the jurisdiction of Vijayanagar, is still a great entrepôt in the trade between India and the East Indies despite its poor harbor and unstable political condition. Arriving in Orissa after a hectic voyage from Malacca, the Venetian judges it to be a "fair kingdome and trustie, through the which a man might have gone with gold in hand without any danger at all"[926] if only the Hindu ruler with his seat at "Catech" (Cuttack)[927] had not been deposed by the Pathans sixteen years before. Prior to the conquest of the Hindu state of Orissa, trade at its ports was flourishing and practically free of duty. Once the Pathans came to power they imposed a 20 per cent tax on trade. The Pathans were shortly thereafter replaced by the Mughuls in Bengal and as a result their power was likewise broken in Orissa.[928]

Like most itinerant merchants of the East, Fedrici eventually visited the emporiums at the mouths of the Ganges. From Orissa he was rowed along the shore and up the Ganges in large flat-bottomed boats which made their progress upriver with the incoming tide. Seagoing vessels, he indicates, are able to go upriver only to "Buttor" (Betor, near modern Howrah) where they unload and load at a temporary mart built of straw which is constructed and burned annually at the arrival and departure of the trading ships.[929] Fedrici remained at Sātgāon for four months and, like the other merchants, went up and down the Ganges to the numerous marts along its banks. He too observed on his river voyages how the Hindus daily entrust their dead to the sacred waters of the Ganges. In 1569 the Venetian visited Chittagōng, "the great port of Bengala,"[930] where the Portuguese were having trouble with the local authorities. It was also at this time that he landed by chance on the island of "Sondiva" (Sandwīp, northwest of Chittagōng), which he describes while commenting particularly on the abundance and low cost of food and the friendly reception received from the local authorities despite the hostility which the Bengalis then felt for the Portuguese at Chittagōng.[931]

While Fedrici was working his way back to the Levant and thence Europe in 1579, the Venetian jeweler, Gasparo Balbi, set out for India. For the next nine years, Balbi followed almost the same route to the East and back again which Fedrici had used. Two years after his return to Venice in 1588, the printer

[925] *Ibid.*, p. 400.

[926] *Ibid.*, pp. 401–2.

[927] Derived from Sanskrit word for camp, *kataka*. Probably a reference to the most imposing of the royal camps or headquarters, called Varanasi Kataka. See Chakravarti, *loc. cit.* (n. 548) XII (1916), 30.

[928] Fitch in Hakluyt, *op. cit.* (n. 906), V, 410. The Mughuls did not annex Orissa to their empire until 1592 but the northern part was invaded by the Pathans in 1568–69 and two years later they overran the south. See Chakravarti, *loc. cit.* (n. 548), pp. 30–35.

[929] For comment on this assertion see Campos, *op. cit.* (n. 551), pp. 49–50.

[930] Fedrici in Hakluyt, *op. cit.* (n. 906), V, 438. For the dating of this visit see Charpentier, *loc. cit.* (n. 907), p. 53.

[931] Fedrici in Hakluyt, *op. cit.* (n. 906), V, 437–38.

Camillo Borgominieri published Balbi's *Viaggio dell'Indie Orientali* ... *Nel quale si contiene quanto egli in detto viaggio ha veduto por lo spatio di 9. Anni consumati in esse dal 1579, fino al 1588* ... (Venice, 1590). Dedicated to his noble Venetian relative, Teodoro Balbi,[932] this work is said to have been reissued in 1600 but I have not been able to find a copy of a second edition.[933] In 1600 the entire text appeared in Latin translation in De Bry's collection and ten illustrations were added depicting hook-swinging and various other ceremonies and events.[934] The part of Balbi's account relating to St. Thomas, Negapatam, and Pegu was eventually summarized in English and published by Purchas.[935]

Balbi's work, much more than Fedrici's, is a commercial handbook reminiscent of the fourteenth-century "La prática della mercatura" compiled by Pegolotti.[936] As a diarist and compiler of data, Balbi is far more accurate and painstaking than Fedrici. He is very careful to record the dates on which he visited particular places and at each stopover he carefully notes the coins, weights, and measures then in use. To the end of his diary he also appends a summary account of the trade routes customarily followed in the India commerce and a table of the monsoons.[937] With respect to India, he interlards his *Viaggio* with a few general observations on geography, manners, and customs. In a number of instances he has clearly taken whole descriptive passages from Fedrici's book and has unblushingly inserted them into his own composition.[938] Most of these plagiarized passages relating to India are those which describe cities, customs, and natural vegetation such as the palm and cinnamon trees. In the latter part of the *Viaggio*, where he deals with Pegu, Balbi's work is almost entirely original—a fact which his contemporaries probably realized when they selected only the Pegu section for publication in English. As a general description of India, Balbi's work in itself is therefore of very little value except on matters relating to trade. This is not to say that the book is utterly worthless for India. Balbi comments independently, for instance, on the cave temples of Elephanta and credits their construction to Alexander the Great.[939] But his distinctly in-

---

[932] On the Balbi family see Gubernatis, *op. cit.* (n. 904), p. 24, n. 1.

[933] See Charpentier, *loc. cit.* (n. 907), p. 51.

[934] J. T. and J. H. De Bry (eds.), *India Orientalis* (Frankfurt am Main, 1600), Pt. VII, pp. 43–126. Since the first edition is extremely rare, I consulted this translation.

[935] See the reprint of the 1625 edition of Purchas in Samuel Purchas (ed.), *Hakluytus Posthumus, or Purchas His Pilgrimages* ... ("Extra Series of the Hakluyt Society Publications" [20 vols.; Glasgow, 1905–7]), X, 143–64. See below, pp. 549–50.

[936] See above, pp. 45–46.

[937] For comments on Balbi's merit as an observer and recorder see Zurla, *op. cit.* (n. 905), II, 258. For his possible influence on cartography see Olga Pinto, "Ancora il viaggiatore veneziano Gasparo Balbi a proposito della ristampa italiana di una Carta dell'Asia di W. J. Blaev," *Atti della Accademia nazionale dei Lincei* ("Classe di scienze morali, storiche e filologiche," Series VIII, Vol. III [Rome 1948]), pp. 465–71.

[938] Charpentier (*loc. cit.* [n. 907], pp. 57–61) has made a textual comparison of Balbi's book with the version of Fedrici which appeared in Ramusio (1606). From this comparison he is able to cite extracts which Balbi, quite in accord with the custom followed by many writers of his day, unhesitatingly plundered from Fedrici's account to extend and improve his own.

[939] Balbi in De Bry, *op. cit.* (n. 934), Pt. VII, p. 78.

dividualistic observations occur only at rare intervals, even though he lived in Goa for eighteen months. As an aside of interest, he tells of meeting the Japanese legates to Europe when they were in Goa in 1587 on their way home.[940]

In contrast to the private enterprise of the Venetian merchants, Fedrici and Balbi, stands the career in India of the Florentine Humanist and merchant, Filippo Sassetti (lived from 1540 to 1588). While the Venetians hoped to revive the direct overland trade with India, Sassetti, like other Tuscans of his day and earlier, worked harmoniously within the Portuguese system and went to India by rounding the Cape of Good Hope. As the great-grandson of Francesco Sassetti, who had been manager of the far-flung enterprises of the Medicis in the fifteenth century,[941] Filippo was descended from a notable family with numerous connections in the business capitals of Europe. And, like most aristocratic families of Tuscany, the Sassettis possessed, even after they ran into financial trouble, a vital and profound interest in affairs of the mind. So, it is not surprising to find young Filippo studying for six years (1568–74) at the University of Pisa and of being for some years thereafter an active participant in the learned societies of Florence. It was not until 1578, when Sassetti was already thirty-eight years old, that the decline of the family fortune and the growth of his immediate household combined to force the young intellectual to turn his hand to commerce, a way of life for which he personally had little taste.[942]

For four years (1578–81), Sassetti acted as a commercial agent of the Capponi interests in Spain and Portugal. While occupied with business affairs, Sassetti still found time to correspond with his academic and business associates in Florence.[943] When the Capponis decided to close down their enterprises in the Iberian peninsula, Sassetti took employment with Rovellasca, head of the syndicate which had purchased the spice monopoly.[944] He was sent out to India almost at once as factor for the Rovellasca interests. In November, 1583, he arrived in Cochin where he worked in the pepper trade as a supervisor for Rovellasca as he sought to recoup his family's fortune. He traveled both by land and water to the western Indian cities of Onor and Mangalor, and in

---

[940] *Ibid.*, p. 122; also see below, p. 487.

[941] Florence E. de Roover, "Francesco Sassetti and the Downfall of the Medici Banking House," *Bulletin of the Business Historical Society*, XVII (1943), 65–80.

[942] For the Sassetti family see Filippo Luigi Polidori, *Archivio storico italiano*, Vol. IV, Pt. 2 (1853), pp. xviii–xxi (preface); for a general account of Filippo's career see Mario Rossi, *Un letterato e mercante fiorentino del secolo XVI: Filippo Sassetti* (Castello, 1899).

[943] The standard edition which contains 111 of his letters is Ettore Marcucci (ed.), *Lettere edite e inedite di Filippo Sassetti* (Florence, 1855). A subsequent and cheaper edition came out at Milan in 1874 with a preface and a commentary by Eugenio Camirini. An edition of letters specially selected for the public, including a number from India, is Gino Raya (ed.), *Filippo Sassetti. Lettere scelte* (Milan, 1932). Sassetti's letters from India have been published separately in Arrigo Benedetti (ed.), *Filippo Sassetti. Lettere indiane* (2d ed.; Turin, 1961); the best study of his circle of correspondents is to be found in Giuseppe Caraci, *Introduzione al Sassetti epistolografo (indagini sulla cultura geografica del secondo cinquecento)* (Rome, 1960).

[944] See above, pp. 135–36. For details on his own employment and of Rovellasca's part in the spice trade see letter to Francesco Valori (April, 1582) in Marcucci (ed.), *op. cit.* (n. 943), pp. 204–10.

1586 he accompanied the Portuguese embassy to Calicut to treat with the Zamorin. Unfortunately, Sassetti died at Goa in 1588 before he could realize his hope for a leisurely round-the-world return trip to Florence.[945]

During the six years of his tenure in India, Sassetti dispatched at least thirty-five letters to Florence which are full of his observations on the subcontinent.[946] A number of his other letters sent from India have been lost.[947] From perusal of his extant letters (from India and his earlier ones written from Portugal), it can readily be ascertained that Sassetti had read widely about Asia in the classical authors, in the accounts contained in the collection of Ramusio, and in the works of Barros, Orta, Cristobal de Acosta, and Maffei (in his first work published in 1571). While still in Portugal he interviewed pilots who had made the trip east. Even before leaving Lisbon, he was sent a sum of money and commissioned by Francis I, Grand Duke of Tuscany, to buy samples of exotic plants and wares, and to ship them back to Florence.[948] He was also asked by Baccio Valori, an intellectual of Florence close to the Grand Duke, to find out what he could about the alphabets of the oriental languages, especially the "hieroglyphics" of the Chinese.[949] From the extant letters it is apparent that in India Sassetti continued to study and read; he collected a wide variety of data, both by direct observation and by interviewing his fellow countrymen and natives; and he systematized and interpreted the data so collected. It also appears that Sassetti expected his friends, including Francis I, to circulate his letters among the literati of his native city. Unfortunately, however, none of his illuminating and learned letters appears to have been printed during the sixteenth century.

Though we will not examine Sassetti's letters in detail (as they were not published in our period), it should be noticed that he, and Garcia da Orta, are the only lay Humanists from Europe who, to our knowledge, observed and wrote in India during the sixteenth century. A man of Sassetti's training and interests naturally saw and commented intelligently on many matters which either escaped or seemed irrelevant to observers concerned with trade, administration, or religion. Large sections of his letters are concerned with his meteorological observations, including detailed and acute comments on typhoons,[950] seasonal

---

[945] His letter, outlining a projected voyage from Goa via the East Indies and America back to Europe, is included in Polidori, *op. cit.* (n. 942), pp. lxxviii–lxxix. For his travels on the west coast of India, see *ibid.*, pp. lxxiii–lxxvii.

[946] One hundred and fourteen of his letters are still extant. Besides appearing in the standard edition (Marcucci [ed.], *op. cit.* [n. 943], pp. 245–425), six of his most important letters from the East have been republished by Gubernatis (*op. cit.* [n. 904], pp. 187–227) along with commentaries based on them. For further analysis see Caraci, *op. cit.* (n. 943), pp. 83–110.

[947] On the lost letters see Caraci, *op. cit.* (n. 943), pp. 135–43.

[948] This was the Grand Duke who, along with his wife, entertained the Japanese ambassadors so royally on their visit to Tuscany in 1585 (see below, pp. 694–95) and who sought earlier to buy into the spice trade (see above, p. 133).

[949] See letters to Valori, of March, 1583, from Lisbon (Marcucci [ed.], *op. cit.* [n. 943], pp. 239–40), and of January 17, 1588, from Cochin (*ibid.*, p. 408).

[950] Raya (ed.), *op. cit.* (n. 943), pp. 64–65.

changes, and climate.[951] While he comments on ways of life and social organizations, especially of the Brahmans, he frankly admits that he can say little about such matters because he has not himself lived according to native customs.[952] He wrote a letter, which is virtually a scientific paper, for the academicians of Florence on aspects of Indian folklore.[953] On matters of trade and on those trading cities of India with which he had more than a passing familiarity, he wrote directly to the Grand Duke. About natural history and botany he wrote to the Accademia degli Alterati in some detail. Evidently he learned something of Indian medical lore by conversing with a Hindu physician. This learned and agreeable scholar introduced Sassetti to certain Sanskrit texts on pharmaceuticals, and evidently helped him to translate passages from one of them, a document which modern scholarship holds to be the *Rāganighaṇṭu* (a textbook of chemistry).[954] From this and other evidence to be found in his letters it is clear that Sassetti, from around 1585 until his death three years later, was making an effort to learn Sanskrit.

In 1583, the year when Sassetti arrived in India, a trading expedition set sail for the Levant from London headed by John Newbery, an English merchant. Newbery, who had previously worked in the Levant, had earlier traveled overland to Ormuz on the Persian Gulf. Like the Venetians, the English of this period were not yet able to challenge effectively the Iberian control of the maritime passage around the Cape of Good Hope, and as a result they had sought on a number of occasions to reach Asia by other routes. The Newbery expedition of 1583 over the land route of the Levant to Ormuz and thence to India was but one of the many English efforts to circumvent the Portuguese monopoly. Like its predecessors, it produced no tangible results in terms of trade; it did, however, make possible the publication of the first description of India and the East Indies by an Englishman.

Newbery was accompanied in 1583 on his overland trip to India by Ralph Fitch (d. 1611)[955] and two others. Among the papers which they carried, the adventurers had two letters of introduction from Queen Elizabeth prepared in February, 1583; one was addressed to Akbar and the other to the emperor of China.[956] Four days after their arrival in Ormuz, the Englishmen were accused by Michael Stropeni,[957] the Venetian merchant, of being spies for Dom António, the pretender to the Portuguese throne, who was then residing in London.[958]

---

[951] Gubernatis, *op. cit.* (n. 904), pp. 194–200. See also Polidori, *op. cit.* (n. 942), pp. xciii–xcvi, n. 4, in which a nineteenth-century Italian scientist writes a complimentary estimate of the observations made by Sassetti during the sea voyage to India.

[952] Gubernatis, *op. cit.* (n. 904), p. 189. On the Brahmans see Raya (ed.), *op. cit.* (n. 943), pp. 89–103.

[953] Raya (ed.), *op. cit.* (n. 943), pp. 142–52.

[954] Gubernatis, *op. cit.* (n. 904), pp. 329–30.

[955] For his biography see J. Horton Ryley, *Ralph Fitch, England's Pioneer to India and Burma* (London, 1899). For details on the last years of his life after his return from India see William Foster, *Early Travels in India, 1583–1619* (London, 1921), pp. 7–8.

[956] Text in Hakluyt, *op. cit.* (n. 906), II, 245.

[957] See above, p. 468n.

[958] Letter from Newbery to Leonard Poore dated Goa, January 20, 1584. See Hakluyt, *op. cit.* (n. 906), II, 248–50.

The Portuguese captain in charge of the garrison at Ormuz acted upon Stropeni's denunciation quite readily, since the Portuguese were already outraged at Drake's audacity in sailing through their waters and firing on their ships. Once in custody, the Englishmen were sent to prison in Goa. The Jesuit Thomas Stevens and one of his colleagues in Goa acted as intermediaries with the authorities, and their activities were ably seconded by the Dutch trader Jan van Linschoten,[959] who was then attached to the staff of the archbishop. Before the end of a month, after professing to be honest merchants and good Catholics, the Englishmen were freed and given permission to set up a trading station. Shortly after their release both Newbery and Fitch wrote letters in which they tell of their first brush with the law and their rising hopes for a lucrative trade in Goa. These prospects soon dimmed, however, and it was leaked to them that the viceroy intended sending them back to Portugal with the next fleet. In response to this news, Newbery and Fitch slipped out of Goa, and, like so many other fugitives from the Portuguese, took refuge in the territory of Bijapur.

It was after their escape in April, 1584, that the Englishmen began to see something of the interior of India. The two fugitives went first to the city of Bijapur and then to Golconda, the residence of the Kutb Shāhī kings. Then they entered the Mughul empire near Burhānpur and went on to the imperial cities of Agra and Fatehpur Sīkrī, where they evidently visited the court of Akbar. It is not known whether or not they presented Queen Elizabeth's letter to Akbar, but they did decide at this point to part company. Newbery hoped to return to Europe by the land route and to come back to Bengal by sea within two years to pick up Fitch. In the meanwhile Fitch was to spend his time scouting prospects for trade in northeastern India. When Newbery failed to turn up at the agreed time (apparently he died before getting back to Europe), Fitch in 1586 extended his travels eastward to Burma and Malacca. He finally began his arduous and dangerous trip back to Europe by way of Goa, Ormuz, and Syria, arriving in London in April, 1591, after an absence of more than eight years.

The England to which Fitch returned (after being given up by his family and friends as dead) was at war with Spain. Those, like Hakluyt, who were interested in overseas enterprise, were now calling upon the government to defy openly the Spanish control of the Cape route and to sail directly to India in English vessels. Thomas Cavendish had returned in 1588 from his circumnavigation of the world. James Lancaster proved by his voyage to Penang and the Nicobars in 1591, the year of Fitch's return, that English vessels could safely defy the monopolists without pretending to be en route to America. Fitch himself, who was regarded as another Marco Polo in England, was called upon to give his advice on Eastern matters to those interested in developing trade with the Indies. It was probably his publisher, Hakluyt, who pressed him to write

959 Cf. account in Linschoten's *Itinerario* as republished in English in *ibid.*, pp. 265–68, of their imprisonment and flight from Goa. See below, p. 487.

the narrative of his "wonderful travailes." The narrative made its world debut in *The Principal Navigations* (1599)[960] along with related materials, such as Newbery's letters.

Fitch, unlike Balbi, apparently did not keep a diary of his travels and so was forced to rely upon his memory when writing up his voyage. We conclude this because dates and exact references are conspicuous by their absence, and because the narrative of his eight long years of wandering is disappointingly brief. His lack of ready data may also help to explain why he incorporated almost word for word into his own composition Fedrici's descriptions of those places where they had both visited. Though Fitch could possibly have consulted Balbi's *Viaggio* (1590) as well, no convincing evidence exists to show that he referred to it.[961] Fitch's account, even though he depends heavily upon Fedrici for what he has to say about Portuguese India, is nonetheless original and valuable for his comments on interior places where Fedrici did not visit. Hakluyt, who published both Fitch and Fedrici in his collection, appears to rank the Englishman's account, along with those of Castanheda and Fedrici, as an important source of information on the East.[962]

Upon escaping from Goa in April, 1584, Newbery and Fitch made their way on foot to Belgaum and then went on to Bijapur. Apparently interested in learning about diamonds and other precious stones, Fitch reports that they next went to Golconda "the king whereof is called *Cutup de lashach*."[963] The city of Golconda, which today stands in ruins about five miles west of Hydera-bad, is in Fitch's eyes "a veery faire towne, pleasant, with faire houses of bricke and timber."[964] Though Fitch complains about it being hot in Golconda, he found also that the city was amply supplied with water and local fresh fruit, and well serviced with foreign products through the port of Masulipatam.[965] From Golconda, Fitch and Newbery made their way northward to the Mughul empire and Fitch notices en route a "fine countrey" which he calls "Servidore" (possibly Bīdar, an independent state).[966] From here they journeyed to Balapur in Berar and then to Surhanpur which is described as being within Akbar's territories.[967] In connection with his account of Burhānpur and its surroundings,

[960] For easier consultation the references to Fitch which follow will refer to the version published in Hakluyt, *op. cit.* (n. 906), V, 465–505.

[961] See Foster, *op. cit.* (n. 955), p. 8.

[962] See the notes prepared in 1600 and attributed to Hakluyt's pen in which are listed the Portuguese, Spanish, Italian, English, and Dutch authorities on Asiatic matters. Reproduced in E. G. R. Taylor, *The Original Writings and Correspondence of the Two Richard Hakluyts* (London, 1935), Vol. II, doc. 78, pp. 467–68.

[963] Fitch in Hakluyt, *op. cit.* (n. 906), V, 472. This is clearly a reference to one of the Muslim kings of the Kutb Shāhī dynasty, possibly to Ibrahim (reigned 1550–1611).

[964] *Ibid.*

[965] The English established their first factory on the Coromandel coast at this place in 1611. See Shah Manzoor Alam, "Masulipatam, a Metropolitan Port in the Seventeenth Century A.D.," *Indian Geographical Journal*, XXXIV (1959), 33–42.

[966] See Foster, *op. cit.* (n. 955), p. 16, n. 2.

[967] The Deccan kingdom of Khāndesh with its capital of Burhānpur was technically in vassalage to Akbar when Fitch was there. It was not actually annexed to the Mughul state until 1600.

Fitch comments on child marriages at some length, one of his few independent excursions into social questions.[968] On the way to Akbar's court, the two companions went through Māndū, Ujjain, and Sironj and crossed many rivers "which by reason of the raine were so swollen that wee waded and swamme oftentimes for our lives."[969]

On their arrival in Agra, the Englishmen learned that Akbar's court was now located at Fatehpur Sīkrī, a new city "greater than Agra, but the houses and streetes be not so faire."[970] Both cities Fitch considers to be much larger than London, and he marvels how the road between them (23 miles long) "all the way is a market . . . as full as though a man were still in a towne."[971] Akbar's court is housed in a "dericcan" (dārikhāna, Persian, meaning palace) and he keeps great numbers of animals in both imperial cities. None but the harem eunuch is permitted to enter the royal palace. The Mughul ruler dresses in a muslin tunic that is made like a shirt and on his head he wears "a little coloth . . . coloured oftentimes with red or yealow."[972] The capital of the Mughul empire is a great mart to which merchants come from Persia and Portuguese India. Fitch at this point inserts into his narration a short description of a vehicle common to market towns, the two-wheeled carts pulled by bullocks which carry two to three people and are "used here as our coches be in England."[973]

Leaving his companion and striking out alone after visiting Akbar's court, Fitch accompanied for five months a large fleet of merchant-boats downriver to Bengal. On his trip down the Jumna, Fitch observes many "strange customs" for he saw Hindus bathe, worship, and purify themselves in and beside the river. At "Prage" (Prayāga, now Allahābād), he tells us, the Jumna enters the Ganges which "commeth out of the northwest, and runneth east into the Gulfe of Bengala."[974] As he progresses through the Gangetic plain, Fitch notices and remarks on the numerous wild animals, fish, and birds, the naked beggars and ascetics, the islands, and the fruitfulness of the land. Benares is a great city peopled exclusively by Hindus "who be the greatest idolaters that ever I saw."[975] About the strange religious practices of the pilgrims who go to Benares to worship at its shrines and temples and to bathe in the sacred waters of the Ganges, Fitch becomes unusually detailed and interesting. The Ganges between Benares and Patna is "so broad that in time of raine you cannot see from one side to the other,"[976] and the surrounding countryside is fruitful but full of thieves. Patna, which is correctly described as having once been

---

[968] Hakluyt, *op. cit.* (n. 906), V, 473.
[969] *Ibid.*
[970] *Ibid.*, p. 474.
[971] *Ibid.*
[972] *Ibid.*
[973] *Ibid.*
[974] *Ibid.*, p. 476.
[975] *Ibid.*, p. 477.
[976] *Ibid.*, p. 480.

the seat of an independent king, is now within the Mughul empire. Though it "is a very long and a great towne," with wide streets, Patna's houses are very simple buildings made of dirt and covered with straw. The local governor, "Tipperdas" (Tripura Dās), is held in high esteem in this town where Fitch found a great exchange of cotton, cotton textiles, opium, and sugar. He concludes the remarks on his five-month-long river trip by talking about Tāndā, the town which had replaced Gaur as the capital of Bengal a decade or so before Fitch visited there.

From Tāndā, Fitch proceeded northwest as he penetrated to Kuch Bihar, an assembly place for trading caravans, possibly to inquire about commerce with China by way of Tibet.[977] This area he sees as peopled entirely by Hindus, and he remarks on their extended ear lobes, and the use they make of almonds as small coins.[978] The territory of Kuch Bihar is protected by a fence of sharpened canes or bamboos; in times of war the land is flooded to prevent the enemy from entering it.[979] Upon leaving Kuch Bihar, Fitch went back to the Gangetic plain and, by way of Gaur, he then went downriver to the Portuguese settlements. In his discussion of the Portuguese settlements and of the kingdom of Orissa he again returns to his earlier practice of following Fedrici's narrative. But he also gives a few comments of his own on Tippera and on the activities of the "Mugs" of western Arakan. Then, almost as an afterthought, Fitch introduces a description of the trading activities carried on in Bhutan where merchants reportedly come from China, Muscovy, Bengal, and Tibet. This fascinating summary appears to be accurate, even though Fitch probably did not visit Bhutan himself but pieced his story together from what he had learned during his stay in Kuch Bihar.[980]

From Chittāgong, the Porto Grande of the Portuguese, Fitch concluded his mercantile explorations of India by investigating parts of eastern Bengal.[981] He first stopped at "Bacola" (possibly a town on the west bank of the Titulia River) and then went on to Srīpur at the confluence of the Meghira and Padma rivers. Although Srīpur (near modern Rajabari) has long since been washed away by the shifting of the Padma, Fitch notes that it was a center of resistance in his day for those Bengalis still fighting the Mughuls. Its ruler, Chand Rai, evidently helped the enemies of Akbar to find sanctuary in the numerous islands around Srīpur from the mounted Mughuls who pursued them. Sonārgāon, the capital

---

[977] *Ibid.*, p. 481. It is conceivable that Fitch, like the Jesuits who visited Akbar's realm, heard about such a route. See above, p. 467. For a summary of the Muslim sources, see H. Blochmann, "Koch Bihar, Koch Hajo and A'sam in the 16th and 17th centuries . . . ," *Journal of the Asiatic Society of Bengal*, XLI (1872), 49–54.

[978] On the use of almonds as coins in India see A. B. Burnell and P. A. Tiele (eds.), *The Voyage of John Huyghen van Linschoten to the East Indies . . .* ("Old Series of the Hakluyt Society," Vol. LXX [London, 1885]), I, 246, n. 6.

[979] Fitch in Hakluyt, *op. cit.* (n. 906), V, 481–82.

[980] *Ibid.*, pp. 483–84. See R. Boileau Pemberton, *Report on Bootan* (Calcutta, 1839), pp. 147–48, who quotes Fitch's account and asserts that the trade activity and the mode of dress are almost exactly what they are in his day. Also see the identifications in Foster, *op. cit.* (n. 955), p. 27.

[981] Fitch in Hakluyt, *op. cit.* (n. 906), V, 484–85.

of eastern Bengal from 1351 to 1608, was clearly not under Akbar's rule when Fitch visited there in 1586. Isa Khan, leader of the Afghans who dominated eastern Bengal, is named as "chiefe of all the other kings, and is a great friend to all Christians." [982] Evidently, the Christians were interested in Sonārgāon, located just fifteen miles east of Dacca, for its famous muslins, "the best and finest cloth made of cotton that is in all India." [983] It was from this great commercial region that Fitch started out in November, 1586, having apparently decided that Newbery would not return, for his peregrinations in Pegu and in the further East.

While Fitch traveled through the interior of northern India, Jan van Linschoten remained in the Portuguese service in Goa. The Dutchman's *Itinerario* naturally centers on Goa and he provides therein what is probably the best geographical description of the island city, the neighboring islands and peninsulas, and the relationships of one to the other and to the mainland to appear in print before 1600. Many of the details in this description may have been derived from the Portuguese map of Goa which he had in his possession, but he adds many observations to his narrative of the sort which maps ordinarily do not portray. For example, he affirms that Bardez and Salsette "are by the Kings of Portingale let out to farme, and the rents thereof are imployed to the payment of the Archbishop, Cloysters, Priests, Viceroy, and other of the Kings Officers, yearely stipends...." [984] And, at another point, Linschoten asserts that freedom of conscience exists in Goa even though the public celebration of heretical and pagan rites is repressed. [985]

From this general description, Linschoten moves on to talk at some length about the relationships between the Portuguese and Luso-Indians (*mestiços*), including therein a few snide comments on miscegenation. He also digresses from his main concern to discuss the auctions (*lei-lâos*) which are held daily in Goa and the other Portuguese centers and which "resemble the meeting upon the burse in Andwarpe." [986] Ordinarily, the Portuguese of Goa who are not engaged in commerce are supported by the labors of their slaves, by lending and exchanging currencies, and by rents which they collect on palm groves, pastures, and fields. In short, aside from a few craftsmen, "the Portingales and Mesticos in India never worke...." [987] The Portuguese in Goa belong to one of two groups: free citizens, defined as those who are married and residents of the city; and the bachelors, who are categorized as soldiers, whether they actually are or not. Both classes include *fidalgos* of many ranks. Though the bachelor-soldiers are not necessarily attached to a command, they are all registered and are expected to volunteer for military service whenever the need arises; they are paid according to the rank under which they are registered. Linschoten

[982] *Ibid.*
[983] *Ibid.*, p. 485.
[984] Burnell and Tiele (eds.), *op. cit.* (n. 978), I, 177.
[985] *Ibid.*, pp. 181–82.
[986] *Ibid.*, pp. 184–85.
[987] *Ibid.*, p. 187.

then goes on to detail recruitment procedures and to talk about the certificates required to authorize the return of individual soldiers to Portugal.

The proud and overweening manners of the Portuguese of Goa have been captured by Linschoten in a number of classical word portraits. For example, he reports how they walk "very slowly forwards, with a great pride and vaineglorious maiestie." One slave holds a shade over his master's head and another walks behind carrying his sword so that it may not trouble him as he walks, or "hinder . . . [his] gravities." [988] Marriages and christenings are celebrated in lavish style by the free citizens of the city in the presence of friends and relatives as well as the dignitaries of church and state. The unmarried men ("soldiers") also "goe verie gravely along the streets with their slaves," [989] but they are forced to live in dormitories which house from ten to twelve, to dine in common on simple foods, and to share their wardrobes with one another. The majority of the bachelors, when not at war, are either supported by the amorous wives of the community or by the profits derived from engaging in commerce. Most of them, Linschoten asserts, have little concern for "the common profit or the service of the King, but only their particular profits. . . ." [990]

The native wives of the Portuguese, the Luso-Indians, and the Indian Christians likewise receive a lengthy and critical appraisal. Even though they are ordinarily kept indoors and are jealously guarded by their husbands, these women revel in finery and conspire at infidelity. Many husbands are fed *datura*, a powerful narcotic derived from the thorn apple, by their wives to put them into a drugged sleep while the ladies pursue their amours. Should the husband become suspicious of their adultery, these vile women will not hesitate to poison or kill them. Many women are also killed by their husbands who manage through connivance with their friends to escape punishment and to obtain permission to remarry. Conjugal fidelity, according to Linschoten's account, is conspicuous in Goa by its absence.

A new viceroy is sent to Goa every three years, and a few have their appointments renewed. [991] From his residence in Goa, where the viceroy has a council, tribunal, chancellery, and courts, he rules all of Portuguese India according to the laws of the motherland. Justice is in the hands of the viceroy, but civil cases may be appealed to Portugal for adjudication. Criminal cases are handled exclusively by the viceroy unless the accused is a titled person and hence outside of his jurisdiction. *Fidalgos* are normally sent back as prisoners to Portugal to be put on trial. Ordinarily the viceroy makes but few public appearances, but when he does it is in a regal procession. On the walls of the entrance hall in the viceregal palace are painted pictures of all the ships which ever set out for India, and on the walls of the council chamber hang the portraits of all the viceroys. In the last year of their tenure, the viceroys visit the settlements to the north and south of Goa "more to fill their purses . . . than to further the commonwealth." [992]

---

[988] *Ibid.*, pp. 193–94. [989] *Ibid.*, p. 199. [990] *Ibid.*, p. 203.
[991] *Ibid.*, pp. 217–22. [992] *Ibid.*, p. 219.

From the crown the viceroy is given complete control over the treasury of India. Ordinarily, a new viceroy receives rich presents from the native rulers allied with the Portuguese. For a period these gifts were handed over to the Jesuits, but around 1570 the viceroys began to keep them for themselves much to the disappointment of the Jesuits. Whenever a viceroy leaves India, he takes all his possessions with him, including the last piece of furniture from the palace at Bardez. The greed and covetousness of the viceroys is attributed to the short tenure of three years; the new incumbent, according to local analysis, must spend his first year furnishing his residence and learning his way around; the second year he begins to look out for his own profit "for the which cause he came into India"; and the last year he spends in setting his affairs in order to hand over the office in good shape to his successor so "that he may returne into Portingall with the goods which he had scraped together."[993] The lesser officials, it is alleged, proceed in much the same fashion.

Aside from the Portuguese, Linschoten discourses at some length on the customs of the heathens, Moors, Jews, and Armenian Christians who do business in the capital. While he adds little that is new in his discussion of beliefs, Linschoten makes a number of acute observations on the habits of everyday life and on the purification customs of the Hindus. Furthermore, he describes at some length the natives' shops of Goa and the various streets in which the merchants dwell and sell their goods.[994] He comments in some detail on the barbers who have no shops of their own but visit their customers' homes to cut their hair, to give manicures, pedicures, and massages, and to perform other personal services. The native physicians of Goa are consulted by the highest Portuguese dignitaries who "put more trust in them, than in their own countrimen. . . ."[995] This discussion he concludes by observing that the Indians must follow in the trades of their fathers, marry within their own occupational groups, and respect the inheritance custom which ordains that the possessions of the father are passed on only to his sons.[996]

After discussing the climate, seasons, diseases, currencies, weights, and measures of Goa, Linschoten passes on to more detailed descriptions of the practices followed by the natives, both residents and transients, in the Portuguese capital. The Brahmans, he concludes, "are the highest in rank and most esteemed nation amonge the Indian heathens."[997] They are the chief advisers of the native rulers and they occupy the highest administrative posts. At the same time they are the religious leaders and the single most authoritative group in India. In Goa and other seaports many Brahmans sell spices and drugs and are so sharp-witted and learned that they easily "make other simple Indians believe what they will."[998] Linschoten adds nothing to earlier appraisals of Brahman beliefs; he accounts for the practice of *sati* by telling the story which Fedrici recounted at an earlier date, of how the inconstant women of India often poisoned their

993 *Ibid.*, p. 222.   994 *Ibid.*, pp. 228–30.
995 *Ibid.*, p. 230.   996 *Ibid.*, p. 231.
997 *Ibid.*, p. 247.   998 *Ibid.*, p. 248.

husbands and of how *sati* was introduced to make them protect rather than take their husbands' lives.[999]

Many natives of Cambay, whom he divides into Gujaratis and Banyās, are reported to live in Goa and other India seaports. Linschoten portrays the Banyās as being sharper in their business practices than any other traders in India, including the Portuguese. Though he does not identify them as Jains, he recounts practices of the Banyās which are usually followed by the Jains. The Gujaratis are clearly much more concerned about the taking of life, ritual purification, and pollution through eating than are the other Indians known to Linschoten. They and their women are light in color and their features and figures are similar to those of the Europeans. A Gujarati dresses in a thin, white gown which covers him from the neck down, and on his feet he wears shoes of red leather with sharp toes that turn up, and on his head he wears a white turban. He is also clean-shaven, except for a mustache, and on his forehead he wears a mark "as a superstitious ceremonie of their law."[1000]

The Kanarese and Deccanese, many of whom are in Goa as purchasers of foreign merchandise, come from "Ballagate" (Balghat)[1001] the country to the east of Goa and the source of the capital's foodstuffs in time of peace. Aside from being merchants, many of the Deccanese are craftsmen and barbers and as a group they are almost as numerous as the Portuguese, Luso-Indians, and Indian Christians combined. In dress they resemble the Gujaratis, except that they wear hempen sandals instead of pointed, leather shoes. They wear their hair and beards long and cover their heads with a turban. Apparently, Linschoten felt that they, more than other Indians, were devoted to the cow, for he details how they treat them "as if they were reasonable creatures."[1002] He also describes the wedding ceremonies of the Deccanese and concludes that their practices are generally the same as those of the other Hindus. In the Goa area they act as tax collectors for the Portuguese authorities and gather the revenues from Bardez and Salsette. They are so well versed in Portuguese and canon law that they are able to present their own cases and petitions without aid of attorney. In order to place them under oath, they are required to stand within a circle of ashes, put a few ashes on their bare heads and, while placing one hand on the head and the other on the breast, swear in their own language and by their own gods that they will tell the truth.[1003]

Of even greater interest is Linschoten's account of life among the lower castes of Goa. He mentions the "maynattos" (*Mainattu*) as a people who "does nothing els but wash cloathes."[1004] He notices the "Patamares" (*Patemari*) who

---

[999] *Ibid.*, pp. 250–51; also see above, p. 471.

[1000] *Ibid.*, pp. 255–56.

[1001] The "country above the passes" or the highlands of the Deccan. See Yule and Burnell, *op. cit.* (n. 10), p. 38.

[1002] Burnell and Tiele (eds.), *op. cit.* (n. 978), I, 257.

[1003] *Ibid.*, p. 259.

[1004] *Ibid.*, p. 260. The Portuguese from Barbosa onward call them *mainatos*. See Dalgado, *op. cit.* (n. 44), II, 12–13.

serve as messengers by carrying letters overland.[1005] Linschoten shows most concern, however, for the "Corumbijns" (*Kutumbi*), an agricultural caste of Kanara whom he observed on a visit to the mainland behind Goa. While these people hold the same beliefs as the Deccanese, they are "the most contemptible, and the miserablest of India." [1006] They labor at fishing, tilling the rice paddies, and tending the palm groves which line the banks of the rivers and the seashore. In color they are dark brown and many of them are baptized Christians. Their tiny houses of straw have such low doors that they must be entered on hands and knees and are furnished only with sleeping mats and a few cooking utensils. The women deliver their own children and Linschoten writes in wonder about how quickly the new mother is up and about. Though these poor agriculturists live in exceedingly primitive circumstances, he asserts that they swim and dive well and live to a ripe old age "without any headach, or toothach, or loosing any of their teeth." [1007] Still, most of them are so thin, weak, and cowardly that the Portuguese treat them like animals without fear of reprisal.

Arabs, Ethiopians, and Kaffirs from Mozambique also walk the streets of Goa. While the Arabs are strictly Muslim in their faith, the Ethiopians are divided between those who accept the Prophet and those who are Christians of Prester John. Many of the Ethiopians, both men and women, are slaves and they are "sold like other Oriental Nations." [1008] The free Arabs and Ethiopians serve as sailors on the ships which sail from Goa eastward; they have no trouble getting berths as common seamen because even untrained Portuguese sailors set themselves up as officers for the voyages to the Far East. Linschoten gives considerable detail on the outfitting of the ships for Eastern voyages and notices that they never carry casks of water but have aboard only a square wooden cistern in the keel of the ship. The Kaffirs, some of whom are Muslims, are "as black as pitch," [1009] inclined to walk about in nature's raiment, to thrust bones through their cheeks for beauty's sake, and to sear their faces and bodies with irons. The Jesuits take no pains to missionize in the lands of the Kaffirs "for they see no greate profite to be reaped there, as they doe in India and the Ilands of Japan . . . where they find great quantities of riches, with the sap whereof they increase much and fill their beehyves, to satisfy their insatiable desires." [1010]

Linschoten, while discussing the enslavement of the Kaffirs, interpolates into his account a review of the slave trade in general. He explains that the political and cultural fragmentation of Mozambique produces a condition of almost perpetual warfare among its many petty rulers. The prisoners taken in these

---

[1005] This term is used in this sense primarily by the writers of the sixteenth century; later writers use it as the name for a lateen-rigged ship common to the west coast of India. See Dalgado, *op. cit.* (n. 44), II, 186–88.

[1006] Burnell and Tiele (eds.), *op. cit.* (n. 978), I, 260.

[1007] *Ibid.*, p. 262.

[1008] *Ibid.*, p. 265.

[1009] *Ibid.*, p. 271.

[1010] *Ibid.*, p. 272.

numerous wars are kept as slaves and marketed to the Portuguese when their ships put into the ports of Mozambique for water or other necessities. But the Kaffirs and other Africans are not the only people sold on the block in Goa. Linschoten observes that while he was in Goa a famine hit the mainland of India and as a result many of the natives brought their children to the Portuguese capital to sell in exchange for food. While he is not the first European writer to report on the sale of persons in India,[1011] he is the most graphic. He asserts: "I have seene Boyes of eight or ten yeares given in exchange for five or sixe measures of rice . . . and some came with their wives and children to offer themselves to bee slaves so that they might have meate and drinke to nourish their bodies."[1012] The Portuguese who trade at many eastern places distant from one another "make a living by buying and selling [slaves] as they doe with other wares"[1013] and presumably market them wherever the price is best.

During his residence in Goa, Linschoten met numerous fellow Europeans and other foreign dignitaries. His report of the imprisonment of Newbery and Fitch, and the efforts which were made to obtain their release, probably is the best source available on the event.[1014] He was also in Goa at the time of the arrival of the emissaries from Japan and he was still there when they returned from Europe.[1015] On their arrival from Japan in 1583 the Japanese youths were dressed as Jesuits; on their return from Europe in 1587 "they were all three apparelled in cloth of Golde and Silver, after the Italian manner. . . ."[1016] In June, 1584, legates arrived in Goa from Persia, Cambay, Calicut, and Cochin. Among other things a treaty was concluded by the representative of the Zamorin for the establishment of a Portuguese fort at Panan near Calicut, and after mentioning this agreement Linschoten digresses at length on the problem of piracy along the Malabar Coast.[1017] He further recounts how difficult the Portuguese found it in 1584 to force the erection of a custom house at Cochin against native resistance. He reports on the departure from Goa in April, 1585, of Bernard Burcherts, his associate in the archbishop's retinue, and summarizes from letters relayed to him the route which Burcherts followed overland from Ormuz to Tripoli in Syria and to his native city of Hamburg.[1018] News apparently arrived rather regularly in Goa during 1585 as travelers and mail came there over both the land and the sea routes. In May, 1586, Turkish galleons built in Egypt began to prey on Portuguese vessels in the Red Sea and so a fleet was outfitted in Goa to chase them down.[1019] Around the same time the

---

[1011] Above, p. 409.

[1012] Burnell and Tiele (eds.), *op. cit.* (n. 978), I, 276.

[1013] *Ibid.*, p. 277.   [1014] *Ibid.*, II, 158–66.

[1015] For details see below, pp. 691–701. Linschoten, who refers to a "book in Spanish," apparently depends for his summary of their visit to Europe and their reception in Japan upon the compilation entitled *Breve relacion del recibimiento que en Espana i en toda Italia se hiço a tres embajadores* (Seville, 1586).

[1016] Burnell and Tiele (eds.), *op. cit.* (n. 978), II, 168.

[1017] *Ibid.*, pp. 169–73.

[1018] *Ibid.*, p. 175.

[1019] *Ibid.*, pp. 183–87.

queen of Ormuz came to Goa to be baptized after she had married a Portuguese man.[1020] In 1587, he notes that fleets were being prepared in Goa to relieve the sieges of the Portuguese forts at Colombo and Malacca.[1021]

In addition to his observations made in Goa, Linschoten is able on the basis of personal experience to comment generally on the places and peoples of Malabar. His discussion of the Nāyars and of the matrilineal system of inheritance adds nothing to the earlier accounts and is inferior to a number of them. Particularly interesting are his references to the Sephardic Jews resident in Cochin who are rich merchants and are ". . . the king of Cochins neerest counsellers."[1022] The Cochin Jews have their own synagogue and Linschoten knew them well enough to be permitted to see and touch the Torah. His acquaintance with the Moors of Cochin is not nearly so close and he blames them for the difficulties encountered by the Christian missionaries in their efforts to convert the Indians. His descriptions of the native temples at Elephanta and elsewhere likewise add little to what earlier writers had reported. More revealing is his account of the Portuguese theft in 1554 of the tooth of Buddha (an ape's tooth) from Ceylon, the consternation which it caused among a number of pious south Indian rulers, the heartless burning of the relic in Goa, and the subsequent "discovery" of a new tooth which was enshrined at Vijayanagar as if it were the original which had miraculously escaped the flames.[1023]

Linschoten's descriptions of the flora, fauna, and jewels of India are fascinating. He discourses on a wide variety of topics such as the elephant, the rhinoceros, the mango, and the palm tree and its uses. While he clearly depends upon the natural histories based on Orta, he interpolates many original remarks, observations, and experiences. For example, he tells about the boldness of the black crows who do not hesitate to enter houses to snatch food off the table.[1024] He records that in 1581 an elephant and a rhinoceros were presented to King Philip II in Lisbon and the two animals were then driven to Madrid.[1025] Philip was also sent a painting of a monstrous fish caught in a river of Goa while Linschoten was there. Gigantic seashells from Malacca were sent by the Jesuits to Lisbon to decorate the facade of their church.[1026] The ship on which Linschoten voyaged to India was entirely equipped with ropes and cables made in India of coir.[1027] After describing the manufacture and use of *olas* (palm leaf sheets used as paper), he remarks: "Of this paper with Indian writing upon it, you may see some at Dr. Paludanus' house, which I gave him for a present."[1028]

[1020] *Ibid.*, p. 187.

[1021] *Ibid.*, pp. 196–200.

[1022] *Ibid.*, I, 286.

[1023] *Ibid.*, pp. 292–94.

[1024] *Ibid.*, p. 302.

[1025] *Ibid.*, II, 10. Cf. reference in Mendoza (below, p. 569n) to the reception of the rhinoceros in Madrid.

[1026] *Ibid.*, p. 16.

[1027] *Ibid.*, p. 46.

[1028] *Ibid.*, p. 50. Paludanus' collection of exotic oddities was the pride of the town of Enkhuizen and often viewed by foreign visitors (*ibid.*, I, xxix).

Rhubarb, he tells us, comes exclusively from the interior of China. Rhubarb which is brought overland across Asia to Venice is better than the rhubarb which is shipped to Portugal and which deteriorates on the long sea voyage.[1029] Emperor Charles V, he comments, tried "roots of China"[1030] with good results as a cure for the gout. Mother-of-pearl ornaments and utensils manufactured in China and Bengal are imported into Portugal in large quantities.[1031] Emeralds, which are rarely found in the East, are imported from America and traded by the Venetians for the rubies of Burma.[1032] Such unconnected and incidental references are scattered like nuggets throughout his text and many of them are important enough to make a thorough mining of his book worth the effort.

Linschoten's work had a direct effect upon the Dutch and English merchants of his own day. This is plainly evident from even a cursory survey of the materials relating to their enterprises. Linschoten's routier of the East (*Reys-geschrift*), published in 1595, was actually made use of on board the ships which comprised the first Dutch armada that went directly to the East Indies (1595–97).[1033] Meanwhile, the Dutch, including Linschoten, continued persistently to believe in the existence of a northeastern passage to the Far East, though the English had long before abandoned hope of finding it. Linschoten himself sailed with and kept records of the two exploratory voyages of 1594 and 1595. These voyages, and a third one of 1596, finally convinced the stubborn Dutch that a northeastern passage was not possible.[1034] More than ever the Dutch thereafter pinned their hopes on the success of the southern expedition, only to find on its return in 1597 that little trading had been done because of strife among the Dutch commanders themselves.[1035] Still, the first fleet had got safely to Java and back again and had thereby shown that the Iberian monopoly was not effectively guarded. Almost immediately small fleets were outfitted in the ports of the Netherlands to sail directly for the East Indies. These private enterprises were finally combined under the guidance of Jan van Olden-barnevelt into the Dutch East India Company (1602). The English quickly learned from the Dutch experience and accelerated their plans for direct and systematic voyages. In 1598, William Phillip, the translator of Linschoten,

[1029] *Ibid.*, II, 102.

[1030] *Ibid.*, p. 110; this is the *radix chinae*, the tuber of various species of *smilaceae*.

[1031] *Ibid.*, pp. 135–36.

[1032] *Ibid.*, p. 141.

[1033] J. C. Mollema (ed.). *De eerste Schipvaart der Hollanders naar Oost-Indië, 1595–97* (The Hague, 1935), pp. 30–32.

[1034] The journals of these ill-fated voyages were published by Gerrit de Veer in his *Waerachtige Beschrijvinghe van drie Seylagien, ter werelt noyt soo vreemt ghehoort, drie Jaeren achter Malcanderen deur de Hollandtsche ende Zeelandtsche Schepen by noorden, Noorweghen, Moscovia, ende Tartaria, na de coninck-rijcken van Catthay ende China, so mede vande opdveninghe vande Weygats, Nova Sembla, en van't Landt op de 80 grade dat men acht Groenlandt te zijn ...* (Amsterdam, 1598). Though unsuccessful, these voyages apparently were still of lively interest to contemporaries because De Veer's work reappeared by 1600 in at least one reprinting and in Latin, French, German, and Italian translations. In 1609 it was translated into English by William Phillip.

[1035] See the newsletter from Amsterdam dated August 8, 1597, in W. Noel Sainsbury (ed.), *Calendar of State Papers, Colonial Series; East Indies, China and Japan* (London, 1862), pp. 98–99, item 253.

published in London another translation of a Dutch work entitled *The Description of a Voyage Made by Certaine Ships of Holland into the East Indies, with
Their Adventures and Successe . . . Who Set Forth on the Second of Aprill, 1595, and
Returned on the 14 of August, 1597.*[1036] In a memorandum of 1600 by Foulke
Grevil to Sir Robert Cecil, a brief rundown is given of the economic and
political conditions prevailing in the Portuguese trading centers of the East
which is drawn "specially out of the voyages of John Huighen [Linschoten]."[1037]

The merchant commentators reviewed in this chapter had their experiences
in India during the period between 1564 and 1591. Fedrici, the first of this
group to travel in India, was absent from Venice for eighteen years and he
spent a far longer time in the East than any of the rest. The four other writers
(Balbi, Sassetti, Fitch, and Linschoten) were all in India during the decade of the
1580's and we know from them and other sources that there were also many
other non-Iberians in Portuguese India at the time. Two of the commentators
(Sassetti and Linschoten) worked within the Portuguese trading system in
India, and so are particularly authoritative on matters relating to the west
coast and its place in the overseas empire. The other three (Fedrici, Balbi, and
Fitch) are best described as commercial interlopers or private merchants who
gathered their materials haphazardly and with a view to advancing the ambitions
of their homelands in breaking into the spice monopoly. Fedrici's book and
Sassetti's letters appear to be the product of their independent efforts. Balbi and
Fitch clearly borrowed from Fedrici; and Linschoten relied upon a number of
already published sources. All of their writings (except Sassetti's) appeared in
book form within a brief span of twelve years (1587–99) and all of their books,
except Fitch's, were translated into other languages and included in travel
collections by 1600. But what is perhaps most important is the fact that these
materials deal with a period in Indian history on which published Jesuit and
Iberian sources were few and slight, the missionaries being more concerned with
China, Japan, and the Mughul empire, and the Portuguese with the survival of
their nation and empire in the last two decades of the sixteenth century.

The sixteenth-century European sources on India—Portuguese secular materials, Jesuit letterbooks and histories, and the narrative of the non-Iberian travelers—complement and supplement one another in many ways. Chronologically,
they blanket every decade of the century. When the Portuguese chronicles end
around 1540, the story is taken up by the Jesuit sources. When the Jesuit sources
taper off in the 1560's, the story is taken up by Fedrici who first arrived in
India in 1564. As the Jesuit letters become more official and less informative

[1036] The original work is entitled *Vehael vande Reyse by de Hollandtsche Schepen gedaen naer Oost
Indien.* It was published at Middelburg in 1597. It contains much material on the strife between
Houtman and Van Beuningen, and it is attributed to the pen of Barent Langenes. See G. P. Rouffaer
and J. W. Ijzerman (eds.), *De eerste Schipvaart der Nederlanders naar Oost-Indië onder Cornelis de
Houtman, 1595–1597* (3 vols.; The Hague, 1915–18), II, xxvii. A copy of the English version of
1598 is in the Library of Congress.

[1037] *Ibid.*, pp. 104–5, item 266.

after 1581, the unofficial writings of the commercial interlopers and Linschoten provide additional detail and give a new dimension to what was known about India in the last two decades of the century. The great weakness of the sources to 1580 is the complete dominance of the Portuguese and Jesuit official historiography. Philip II, while no more tolerant of dissent than were earlier rulers of Portugal, was forced under pressure from his own *conquistadores* and missionaries to allow modifications in the monopolistic practices of the Portuguese and Jesuits. While the monopolists resisted change as best they could, criticism of their policies in India and elsewhere were frequently heard in Madrid. Even the Jesuit letterbooks and histories take on a more polemical tone near the close of the century.

The sources, taken together, also blanket the physical scene, supplementing one another neatly. The Portuguese secular writings are best on the west coast and the trading centers of Gujarat and Bengal; at the end of the century, when there are practically no Portuguese materials being published, the narratives of the commercial travelers and Linschoten continue to maintain this emphasis while generally concentrating the fire of their criticism on Goa. The Jesuits, perhaps advisedly, have very little to say in their published writings about political and social conditions in the Portuguese-controlled towns and territories. Except for horse-traders and mercenary soldiers, very few lay Portuguese penetrated into the interior of India.

Whenever the Portuguese chroniclers deal with affairs in the interior of the subcontinent, they seem to rely on the reports of merchants, soldiers, and native informants. As a result, their accounts stress routes, entrepôts, products, and military activities, and almost completely ignore the social practices, religions, and languages of interior regions. The Jesuit writings, by contrast, dwell at considerable length on everyday events along the remote Fishery Coast, within the Serra of the St. Thomas Christians, and at the imperial headquarters of Akbar. While the Jesuits were more assiduous about learning Indian languages than any other group, they are very little impressed by native scholarship or high culture. Orta and Sassetti, the two leading secular Humanists to spend time in India, appear to show more genuine interest in and sympathy for the presuppositions of Indian civilization than the missionaries. The Jesuits of this era, like the merchants and administrators, are little disposed to understand Indian values and beliefs. Their comments on social practices, astute as they sometimes are, are clearly hostile; social practices are viewed as impediments to trade and Christianity.

In the reconstruction of Indian history during the sixteenth century too little attention has so far been given to the great chronicles of Castanheda and Barros, and to the Jesuit letterbooks and histories. Some specialists in Indian history, as for example Commissariat on Gujarat or Campos on Bengal, have utilized advantageously the works of the travelers of the early sixteenth century. The writings of the commercial interlopers and Linschoten at the end of the century have also been mined by students of Indian history. But in the general histories of India, as for example that of Majumdar, the Portuguese appear primarily as intruders rather than contributors and the records which they left to posterity are generally slighted or ignored. Such omissions are to be deplored, because the Portuguese and Jesuit writings are dotted with valuable and concrete data for a period of Indian history when other sources are extremely thin or non-existent. The Portuguese and Jesuit writers, conscious of the need to give statistics, though not always too precise about them, include figures in their books and letters on the populations of Indian cities and regions, the revenues of particular rulers, and the composition and size of Indian armies. Some of these statistics do not appear in other sources, and even if they do, the European figures should certainly be collated with them. Castanheda's account of Humayun's wars in Gujarat and Bengal has so far been overlooked in most historical studies of the early Mughuls. The descriptions of caste, matrilineal, familial and inheritance practices, *sati*, sexual customs, and slavery have been used, and could be even more diligently exploited, by cultural anthropologists interested in adding historical dimensions to their studies.

To Europeans of the sixteenth century much of this material on India must have seemed highly exotic and questionable. Nevertheless, as shown earlier, the Portuguese accounts were translated beginning in 1550 into other European languages, most of them thereafter being available in whole or in part in Ramusio's collection. The Jesuit and merchant writings of the latter half of the century also enjoyed general distribution in Europe. That information on India was positively sought by scholars outside of the Iberian Peninsula is attested by the efforts that Ramusio, Paulus Jovius, the Fuggers, and the English made to acquire copies of Portuguese and Jesuit works.